An Economic Interpretation of the Constitution of the United States

Charles A. Beard

Dover Publications, Inc.
Mineola, New York

Bibliographical Note

This Dover edition, first published in 2004, is an unabridged republication of the work originally published in 1913 by The Macmillan Company, New York.

Library of Congress Cataloging-in-Publication Data

Beard, Charles Austin, 1874-1948.
　An economic interpretation of the Constitution of the United States / Charles A. Beard.
　　p. cm.
　Originally published: New York : Macmillan Co., 1913.
　Includes index.
　ISBN-13: 978-0-486-43365-3 (pbk.)
　ISBN-10: 0-486-43365-X (pbk.)
　　1. Economic liberties (U.S. Constitution) 2. Constitutional law—Economic aspects—United States. 3. United States. Constitution—Economic aspects. I. Title.

KF4753.B43 2004
330.973'04—dc22

　　　　　　　　　　　　　　　　　　　　　　　　　　　　　　2004041429

Manufactured in the United States by RR Donnelley
43365X08　　2015
www.doverpublications.com

PREFACE

THE following pages are frankly fragmentary. They are designed to suggest new lines of historical research rather than to treat the subject in an exhaustive fashion. This apology is not intended as an anticipation of the criticism of reviewers, but as a confession of fact. No one can appreciate more fully than I do how much of the work here outlined remains to be done. The records of the Treasury Department at Washington, now used for the first time in connection with a study of the formation of the Constitution, furnish a field for many years' research, to say nothing of the other records, printed and unprinted, which throw light upon the economic conditions of the United States between 1783-1787.

If it be asked why such a fragmentary study is printed now, rather than held for the final word, my explanation is brief. I am unable to give more than an occasional period to uninterrupted studies, and I cannot expect, therefore, to complete within a reasonable time the survey which I have made here. Accordingly, I print it in the hope that a few of this generation of historical scholars may be encouraged to turn away from barren "political" history to a study of the real economic forces which condition great movements in politics.

Students already familiar with the field here surveyed will discover that I have made full use of the suggestive work already done by Professor Turner, Drs. Libby, Ambler, and Schaper.

I am indebted to Mr. Merwin of the Treasury Department for his great courtesy in making available the old records under his jurisdiction; to Mr. Bishop, of the Library of Congress, for facilitating the examination of thousands of pamphlets as well as for other favors; and to Mr. Fitzpatrick, of the Manuscript Division, for keeping his good humor while bringing out hundreds of manuscripts which seemed to yield results wholly out of proportion to the labor entailed.

I am under deep obligation to two friends, nameless here, without whose generous sympathy and encouragement, this volume could not have been written.

CHARLES A. BEARD.

WASHINGTON, D.C.,
February, 1918.

CONTENTS

AN ECONOMIC INTERPRETATION OF THE CONSTITUTION OF THE UNITED STATES

CHAPTER I

HISTORICAL INTERPRETATION IN THE UNITED STATES

BROADLY speaking, three schools of interpretation have dominated American historical research and generalization. The first of these, which may be justly associated with the name of Bancroft, explains the larger achievements in our national life by reference to the peculiar moral endowments of a people acting under divine guidance; or perhaps it would be more correct to say, it sees in the course of our development the working out of a higher will than that of man. There is to be observed in the history of the struggle for the Constitution, to use Bancroft's words, "the movement of the divine power which gives unity to the universe, and order and connection to events." [1]

Notwithstanding such statements, scattered through Bancroft's pages, it is impossible to describe in a single phrase the ideal that controlled his principles of historical construction, because he was so often swayed by his deference to the susceptibilities of the social class from which he sprang and by the exigencies of the public life in which he played a by no means inconspicuous part. Even telling

[1] *The History of the Constitution of the United States* (1882 ed.), Vol. II, p. 284.

1

the whole truth did not lie upon his conscience, for, speaking on the question of the number of Americans who were descendants from transported felons and indented servants, he said that "Having a hand full, he opened his little finger."[1]

Nevertheless, Bancroft constantly recurs in his writings to that "higher power" which is operating in human affairs, although he avoids citing specific events which may be attributed to it. It appears to him to be the whole course of history, rather than any event or set of events, which justifies his theory. "However great," he says, "may be the number of those who persuade themselves that there is in man nothing superior to himself, history interposes with evidence that tyranny and wrong lead inevitably to decay; that freedom and right, however hard may be the struggle, always prove resistless. Through this assurance ancient nations learn to renew their youth; the rising generation is incited to take a generous part in the grand drama of time; and old age, staying itself upon sweet Hope as its companion and cherisher, not bating a jot of courage, nor seeing cause to argue against the hand or the will of a higher power, stands waiting in the tranquil conviction that the path of humanity is still fresh with the dews of morning, that the Redeemer of the nations liveth."[2]

The second school of historical interpretation, which in the order of time followed that of Bancroft, may be called the Teutonic, because it ascribes the wonderful achievements of the English-speaking peoples to the peculiar political genius of the Germanic race. Without distinctly repudiating the doctrine of the "higher power" in history, it finds the secret to the "free" institutional development of the Anglo-Saxon world in innate racial qualities.

[1] American Historical Review, Vol. II, p. 13.
[2] Bancroft, *op. cit.*, Vol. I, p. 6.

The thesis of this school is, in brief, as follows. The Teutonic peoples were originally endowed with singular political talents and aptitudes; Teutonic tribes invaded England and destroyed the last vestiges of the older Roman and British culture; they then set an example to the world in the development of "free" government. Descendants of this specially gifted race settled America and fashioned their institutions after old English models. The full fruition of their political genius was reached in the creation of the Federal Constitution.

For more than a generation the Teutonic theory of our institutions deeply influenced historical research in the United States; but it was exhausted in the study of local government rather than of great epochs; and it produced no monument of erudition comparable to Stubbs' *Constitutional History of England*. Whatever may be said of this school, which has its historical explanation and justification,[1] it served one exceedingly useful purpose: it was scrupulously careful in the documentation of its preconceptions and thus cultivated a more critical spirit than that which characterized the older historians.[2]

The third school of historical research is not to be characterized by any phrase. It is marked rather by an absence of hypotheses. Its representatives, seeing the many pitfalls which beset the way of earlier writers, have resolutely turned aside from "interpretation" in the larger sense, and concerned themselves with critical editions of the documents and with the "impartial" presentation of related facts.

---

[1] It has been left to a Russian to explain to Englishmen the origin of Teutonism in historical writing. See the introduction to Vinogradoff, *Villainage in England*. W. J. Ashley, in his preface to the translation of Fustel de Coulanges, *Origin of Property in Land*, throws some light on the problem, but does not attempt a systematic study.

[2] Note the painstaking documentation for the first chapters in Stubbs' great work.

This tendency in American scholarship has been fruitful in its results, for it has produced more care in the use of historical sources and has given us many excellent and accurate surveys of outward events which are indispensable to the student who would inquire more deeply into underlying causes.[1]

Such historical writing, however, bears somewhat the same relation to scientific history which systematic botany bears to ecology; that is, it classifies and orders phenomena, but does not explain their proximate or remote causes and relations. The predominance of such a historical ideal in the United States and elsewhere is not altogether inexplicable; for interpretative schools seem always to originate in social antagonisms.[2] The monarchy, in its rise and development, was never correctly understood as long as it was regarded by all as a mystery which must not be waded into, as James I put it, by ordinary mortals. Without the old régime there would have been no Turgot and Voltaire; Metternich and Joseph de Maistre came after the Revolution.

But the origin of different schools of interpretation in controversies and the prevalence of many mere preconceptions bolstered with a show of learning should not lead us to reject without examination any new hypothesis, such as

[1] What Morley has said of Macaulay is true of many eminent American historical writers: "A popular author must, in a thoroughgoing way, take the accepted maxims for granted. He must suppress any whimsical fancy for applying the Socratic elenchus; or any other engine of criticism, scepticism, or verification to those sentiments or current precepts or morals which may in truth be very equivocal and may be much neglected in practice, but which the public opinion of his time requires to be treated in theory and in literature as if they had been cherished and held *semper, ubique, et ab omnibus*." *Miscellanies*, Vol. I, p. 272.

[2] For instance, intimate connections can be shown between the vogue of Darwinism and the competitive ideals of the mid-Victorian middle-class in England. Darwin got one of his leading ideas, the struggle for existence, from Malthus, who originated it as a club to destroy the social reformers, Godwin, Condorcet, and others, and then gave it a serious scientific guise as an afterthought.

the theory of economic determinism, on the general assumption of Pascal "that the will, the imagination, the disorders of the body, the thousand concealed infirmities of the intelligence conspire to reduce our discovery of justice and truth to a process of haphazard, in which we more often miss than hit the mark." Such a doctrine of pessimism would make of equal value for the student who would understand, for instance, such an important matter as the origin of the state, Mr. Edward Jenk's severely scientific *History of Politics* and Dr. Nathaniel Johnston's *The Excellency of Monarchical Government, especially the English Monarchy, wherein is largely treated of the Several Benefits of Kingly Government and the Inconvenience of Commonwealths. . . . Likewise the Duty of Subjects and the Mischief of Faction, Sedition, and Rebellion*, published in 1686.

It is not without significance, however, that almost the only work in economic interpretation which has been done in the United States seems to have been inspired at the University of Wisconsin by Professor Turner, now of Harvard. Under the direction of this original scholar and thinker, the influence of the material circumstances of the frontier on American politics was first clearly pointed out. Under his direction also the most important single contribution to the interpretation of the movement for the federal Constitution was made: O. G. Libby's *Geographical Distribution of the Vote of the Thirteen States on the Federal Constitution.*

In a preface to this work, Professor Turner remarks that the study was designed to contribute "to an understanding of the relations between the political history of the United States, and the physiographic, social, and economic conditions underlying this history. . . . It is believed that many phases of our political history have been obscured by the attention paid to state boundaries and to the sectional lines of North and South. At the same time the economic interpretation of our history has been neglected. In the study of the persistence of the struggle for state particularism in American constitutional history, it was inevitable that writers should make prominent the state as a political factor. But, from the point of view of the rise and growth of sectionalism and nationalism, it is much more important to note the existence of great social and economic areas, independent of state lines, which have acted as units in political history, and which have changed their political attitude as they changed their economic organization and divided into new groups."[1]

Although the hypothesis that economic elements are the chief factors in the development of political institutions has thus been used in one or two serious works, and has been more or less discussed as a philosophic theory,[2] it has not been applied to the study of American history at large — certainly not with that infinite detailed analysis which it requires. Nor has it received at the hands of professed historians that attention which its significance warrants. On the contrary, there has been a tendency to treat it with scant courtesy and to dismiss it with a sharpness bordering on contempt.[3] Such summary judgment is, of course, wholly unwarranted and premature; for as Dr. William Cunningham remarks, the validity of no hypothesis can be

[1] See also the valuable and suggestive writings on American history by Professor W. E. Dodd, of Chicago University; W. A. Schaper, "Sectionalism in South Carolina," *American Historical Association Report* (1900), Vol. I; A. Bentley, *The Process of Government*; C. H. Ambler, *Sectionalism in Virginia*. There are three works by socialist writers that deserve study: Simons, *Social Forces in American History*; Gustavus Myers, *History of Great American Fortunes* and *History of the Supreme Court*.

[2] See Seligman, *The Economic Interpretation of History.*

[3] Vincent, in his treatise on *Historical Research* (1911), dismisses the economic theory without critical examination.

determined until it has been worked to its utmost limits. It is easier to write a bulky volume from statutes, congressional debates,[1] memoirs, and diplomatic notes than it is to ascertain the geographical distribution and political significance of any important group of economic factors. The theory of economic determinism has not been tried out in American history, and until it is tried out, it cannot be found wanting.

Sadly as the economic factors have been ignored in historical studies, the neglect has been all the more pronounced in the field of private and public law. The reason for this is apparent. The aim of instruction in these subjects is intensely practical; there are few research professorships in law; and the "case" system of teaching discourages attempts at generalization and surveys.[2] Not even the elementary work has been done. There has been no generous effort to describe the merely superficial aspects of the development of private law in the United States. There has been no concerted attempt to bring together and make available to students the raw materials of such a history. Most of the current views on the history of our law are derived from occasional disquisitions of judges which are all too frequently shot through with curious errors of fact and conception.

Nor has England advanced far beyond us in the critical interpretation of legal evolution — its explanation in terms of, or in relation to, the shifting economic processes and

---

[1] The *Congressional Record* requires more care in use than any other great source of information on American politics.

[2] Attention should be drawn, however, to the good work which is being done in the translation of several European legal studies, the "Modern Legal Philosophy Series," under the editorial direction of the Association of American Law Schools. Perhaps the most hopeful sign of the times is the growth of interest in comparative jurisprudence. See Borchard, "Jurisprudence in Germany," Columbia Law Review, April, 1912.

methods in which the law is tangled. It is true that English scholars have produced admirable histories of the law in its outward aspects, such as the monumental work of Pollock and Maitland; and they have made marvellous collections of raw materials, like the publications of the Selden Society. But apart from scattered and brilliant suggestions thrown off occasionally by Maitland[1] in passing, no interpretation has been ventured, and no effort has been made to connect legal phases with economic changes.

In the absence of a critical analysis of legal evolution, all sorts of vague abstractions dominate most of the thinking that is done in the field of law. The characteristic view of the subject taken by American commentators and lawyers immersed in practical affairs is perhaps summed up as finely by Carter as by any writer. "In free, popular states," he says, "the law springs from and is made by the people; and as the process of building it up consists in applying, from time to time, to human actions the popular ideal or standard of justice, justice is only interest consulted in the work. . . . The law of England and America has been a pure development proceeding from a constant endeavor to apply to the civil conduct of men the ever advancing standard of justice."[2]   In other words, law is made out of some abstract stuff known as "justice." What set the standard in the beginning and why does it advance?

[1] For examples of Maitland's suggestiveness, see the English Historical Review, Vol. IX, p. 439, for a side light on the effect of money economy on the manor and consequently on feudal law. See also the closing pages of his *Constitutional History of England*, where he makes constitutional law in large part the history of the law of real property. "If we are to learn anything about the constitution, it is necessary first and foremost that we should learn a good deal about the land law. We can make no progress whatever in the history of parliament without speaking of tenure; indeed our whole constitutional law seems at times to be but an appendix to the law of real property" (p. 538). Maitland's entire marvellous chapter on "The Definition of Constitutional Law" deserves the most careful study and reflection. He was entirely emancipated from bondage to systematists (p. 539).

[2] J. C. Carter, *The Proposed Codification of Our Common Law* (1884), pp. 6–8.

The devotion to deductions from "principles" exemplified in particular cases, which is such a distinguishing sign of American legal thinking, has the same effect upon correct analysis which the adherence to abstract terms had upon the advancement of learning — as pointed out by Bacon. The absence of any consideration of the social and economic elements determining the thought of the thinkers themselves is all the more marked when contrasted with the penetration shown by European savants like Jhering, Menger, and Stammler. Indeed, almost the only indication of a possible economic interpretation to be found in current American jurisprudence is implicit in the writings of a few scholars, like Professor Roscoe Pound and Professor Goodnow,[1] and in occasional opinions rendered by Mr. Justice Holmes of the Supreme Court of the United States.[2]

What has here been said about our private law may be more than repeated about our constitutional history and law. This subject, though it has long held an honorable position in the American scheme of learning, has not yet received the analytical study which its intrinsic importance merits. In the past, it has often been taught in the law schools by retired judges who treated it as a branch of natural and moral philosophy or by practical lawyers

---

[1] Of the newer literature on law, see the following articles by Professor Roscoe Pound: "Do we need a Philosophy of Law?" Columbia Law Review, Vol. V, p. 339; "Need of a Sociological Jurisprudence," Green Bag, Vol. XIX, p. 607; "Mechanical Jurisprudence," Columbia Law Review, Vol. VIII, p. 605; "Law in Books and Law in Action," American Law Review, Vol. XLIV, p. 12; Professor Munroe Smith, "Jurisprudence" (in the Columbia University Lectures in Arts and Sciences); Goodnow, *Social Reform and the Constitution.*

[2] Consider, for example, the following remarks by this eminent Justice in his dissenting opinion in the New York Bakery case: "This case is decided upon an economic theory which a large part of the country does not entertain. . . . The Fourteenth Amendment does not enact Mr. Herbert Spencer's *Social Statics.* . . . General propositions do not decide concrete cases. The decision will depend on a judgment or intuition more subtle than any articulate major premise." 198 U. S. 75.

who took care for the instant need of things. Our great commentaries, Kent, Story, Miller, are never penetrating; they are generally confined to statements of fact; and designed to inculcate the spirit of reverence rather than of understanding. And of constitutional histories, strictly speaking, we have none, except the surveys of superficial aspects by Curtis and Bancroft.

In fact, the juristic theory of the origin and nature of the Constitution is marked by the same lack of analysis of determining forces which characterized older historical writing in general. It may be stated in the following manner: The Constitution proceeds from the whole people; the people are the original source of all political authority exercised under it; it is founded on broad general principles of liberty and government entertained, for some reason, by the whole people and having no reference to the interest or advantage of any particular group or class. "By calm meditation and friendly councils," says Bancroft, "they [the people] had prepared a Constitution which, in the union of freedom with strength and order, excelled every one known before. . . . In the happy morning of their existence as one of the powers of the world, they had chosen justice for their guide; and while they proceeded on their way with a well-founded confidence and joy, all the friends of mankind invoked success on their endeavor as the only hope for renovating the life of the civilized world."[1]

With less exaltation, Chief Justice Marshall states the theory, in his opinion in the case of McCulloch v. Maryland: "The government proceeds directly from the people; is 'ordained and established' in the name of the people; and is declared to be ordained 'in order to form a more perfect union, to establish justice, insure domestic tranquillity, and

[1] *Op. cit.*, Vol. II, p. 367.

secure the blessings of liberty' to themselves and to their posterity. The assent of the states, in their sovereign capacity, is implied in calling a convention, and thus submitting that instrument to the people. But the people were at perfect liberty to accept or reject it; and their act was final. . . . The government of the Union, then (whatever may be the influence of this fact on the case) is emphatically and truly a government of the people. In form and in substance it emanates from them. Its powers are granted by them, and are to be exercised directly on them, and for their benefit. . . . It is the government of all; its powers are delegated by all; it represents all, and acts for all " [1]

 In the juristic view, the Constitution is not only the work of the whole people, but it also bears in it no traces of the party conflict from which it emerged. Take, for example, any of the traditional legal definitions of the Constitution; Miller's will suffice: "A constitution, in the American sense of the word, is any instrument by which the fundamental powers of the government are established, limited, and defined, and by which these powers are distributed among the several departments for their more safe and useful exercise, for the benefit of the body politic. . . . It is not, however, the origin of private rights, nor the foundation of laws. It is not the cause, but the consequence of personal and political freedom. It declares those natural and fundamental rights of individuals, for the security and common enjoyment of which governments are established." [2]

Nowhere in the commentaries is there any evidence of the fact that the rules of our fundamental law are designed to protect any class in its rights, or secure the property of

---

[1] 4 Wheaton, p. 316. No doubt the learned Justice was here more concerned with discrediting the doctrine of state's rights than with establishing the popular basis of our government.

[2] S. F. Miller, *Lectures on the Constitution* (1891), p. 71.

one group against the assaults of another. "The Constitution," declares Bancroft, "establishes nothing that interferes with equality and individuality. It knows nothing of differences by descent, or opinions, of favored classes, or legalized religion, or the political power of property. It leaves the individual along-side of the individual. . . . As the sea is made up of drops, American society is composed of separate, free, and constantly moving atoms, ever in reciprocal action . . . so that the institutions and laws of the country rise out of the masses of individual thought, which, like the waters of the ocean, are rolling evermore." [1]

In turning from the vague phraseology of Bancroft to an economic interpretation of constitutional history, it is necessary to realize at the outset that law is not an abstract thing, a printed page, a volume of statutes, a statement by a judge. So far as it becomes of any consequence to the observer it must take on a real form; it must govern actions; it must determine positive relations between men; it must prescribe processes and juxtapositions. [2] A statute may be on the books for an age, but unless, under its provisions, a determinate arrangement of human relations is brought about or maintained, it exists only in the imagination. Separated from the social and economic fabric by which it is, in part, conditioned and which, in turn, it helps to condition, it has no reality.

Now, most of the law (except the elemental law of community defence) is concerned with the property relations of men, which reduced to their simple terms mean the processes by which the ownership of concrete forms of property is determined or passes from one person to another. As society becomes more settled and industrial in character,

[1] *Op. cit.*, Vol. II, p. 324.
[2] See A. Bentley, *The Process of Government.*

mere defence against violence (a very considerable portion of which originates in forcible attempts to change the ownership of property) becomes of relatively less importance; and property relations increase in complexity and subtlety.

But it may be said that constitutional law is a peculiar branch of the law; that it is not concerned primarily with property or with property relations, but with organs of government, the suffrage, administration. The superficiality of this view becomes apparent at a second glance. Inasmuch as the primary object of a government, beyond the mere repression of physical violence, is the making of the rules which determine the property relations of members of society, the dominant classes whose rights are thus to be determined must perforce obtain from the government such rules as are consonant with the larger interests necessary to the continuance of their economic processes, or they must themselves control the organs of government. In a stable despotism the former takes place; under any other system of government, where political power is shared by any portion of the population, the methods and nature of this control become the problem of prime importance — in fact, the fundamental problem in constitutional law. The social structure by which one type of legislation is secured and another prevented — that is, the constitution — is a secondary or derivative feature arising from the nature of the economic groups seeking positive action and negative restraint.

In what has just been said there is nothing new to scholars who have given any attention to European writings on jurisprudence. It is based in the first instance on the doctrine advanced by Jhering that law does not "grow," but is, in fact, "made"—adapted to precise interests which may

be objectively determined.[1] It was not original with Jhering. Long before he worked out the concept in his epoch-
making book, *Der Zweck im Recht*, Lassalle had set it forth
in his elaborate *Das System der erworbenen Rechte*,[2] and
long before Lassalle had thought it through, our own Madison
had formulated it, after the most wide-reaching researches
in history and politics.[3]

In fact, the inquiry which follows is based upon the
political science of James Madison, the father of the Constitution and later President of the Union he had done so
much to create. This political science runs through all of
his really serious writings and is formulated in its most
precise fashion in *The Federalist*[4] as follows: "The diversity in the faculties of men, from which the rights of property originate, is not less an insuperable obstacle to a

[1] In the preface to his first edition, Jhering says: "Die Schrift, von der ich
hiermit die erste Hälfte der Öffentlichkeit übergebe, ist eine Ausläuferin von
meinem Werk über den Geist des römischen Rechts. Der letzte Band desselben
. . . schloss ab mit einer Grundlegung der Theorie der Rechte im subjektiven Sinn,
in der ich eine von der herrschenden abweichende Begriffsbestimmung des Rechts
im subjektiven Sinn gab, indem ich an Stelle des Willens, auf der jene den Begriff
desselben gründete, das Interesse setze. Dem folgenden Bande war die weitere
Rechtfertigung und Verwertung dieses Gesichtspunktes vorbehalten. . . . Der
Begriff des Interesses nötigte mich, den Zweck ins Auge zu fassen, und das Recht
im subjektiven Sinn drängte mich zu dem im objektiven Sinn, und so gestaltete
sich das ursprüngliche Untersuchungsobjekt zu einem ungleich erweiterten, zu dem
des gegenwärtigen Buches: der Zweck im Recht. . . . Der Grundgedanke des
gegenwärtigen Werkes besteht darin, dass der Zweck der Schöpfer des gesamten
Rechts ist, dass es keinen Rechtssatz gibt, der nicht einem Zweck, d.i. einem prak-
tischen Motiv seinen Ursprung verdankt."

[2] Was ist es, das den innersten Grund unserer politischen und sozialen Kämpfe
bildet? Der Begriff des erworbenen Rechts ist wieder einmal streitig geworden —
und dieser Streit ist es, der das Herz der heutigen Welt durchzittert und die tief
inwendigste Grundlage der politisch-sozialen Kämpfe des Jahrhunderts bildet.
Im Juristischen, Politischen, Oekonomischen ist der Begriff des erworbenen Rechts
der treibende Springquell aller weitern Gestaltung, und wo sich das Juristische als
das Privatrechtliche völlig von dem Politischen abzulösen scheint, da ist es noch
viel politischer als das Politische selbst, dann da ist es das sociale Element. Preface
to *Das System der erworbenen Rechte* by Ferdinand Lassalle.

[3] And before Madison's century, Harrington had perceived its significance,
H. A. L. Fisher, *Republican Tradition in Europe*, p. 51.

[4] Number 10.

uniformity of interests. The protection of these faculties is the first object of government. From the protection of different and unequal faculties of acquiring property, the possession of different degrees and kinds of property immediately results; and from the influence of these on the sentiments and views of the respective proprietors, ensues a division of society into different interests and parties. . . . The most common and durable source of factions has been the various and unequal distribution of property. Those who hold and those who are without property have ever formed distinct interests in society. Those who are creditors, and those who are debtors, fall under a like discrimination. A landed interest, a manufacturing interest, a mercantile interest, a moneyed interest, with many lesser interests, grow up of necessity in civilized nations and divide them into different classes, actuated by different sentiments and views. The regulation of these various and interfering interests forms the principal task of modern legislation, and involves the spirit of party and faction in the necessary and ordinary operations of the government."

Here we have a masterly statement of the theory of economic determinism in politics.[1] Different degrees and kinds of property inevitably exist in modern society; party doctrines and "principles" originate in the sentiments and views which the possession of various kinds of property

---

[1] The theory of the economic interpretation of history as stated by Professor Seligman seems as nearly axiomatic as any proposition in social science can be: "The existence of man depends upon his ability to sustain himself; the economic life is therefore the fundamental condition of all life. Since human life, however, is the life of man in society, individual existence moves within the framework of the social structure and is modified by it. What the conditions of maintenance are to the individual, the similar relations of production and consumption are to the community. To economic causes, therefore, must be traced in the last instance those transformations in the structure of society which themselves condition the relations of social classes and the various manifestations of social life." *The Economic Interpretation of History*, p. 3.

creates in the minds of the possessors; class and group divisions based on property lie at the basis of modern government; and politics and constitutional law are inevitably a reflex of these contending interests. Those who are inclined to repudiate the hypothesis of economic determinism as a European importation must, therefore, revise their views, on learning that one of the earliest, and certainly one of the clearest, statements of it came from a profound student of politics who sat in the Convention that framed our fundamental law.

The requirements for an economic interpretation of the formation and adoption of the Constitution may be stated in a hypothetical proposition which, although it cannot be verified absolutely from ascertainable data, will at once illustrate the problem and furnish a guide to research and generalization.

It will be admitted without controversy that the Constitution was the creation of a certain number of men, and it was opposed by a certain number of men. Now, if it were possible to have an economic biography of all those connected with its framing and adoption,—perhaps about 160,000 men altogether,—the materials for scientific analysis and classification would be available. Such an economic biography would include a list of the real and personal property owned by all of these men and their families: lands and houses, with incumbrances, money at interest, slaves, capital invested in shipping and manufacturing, and in state and continental securities.

Suppose it could be shown from the classification of the men who supported and opposed the Constitution that there was no line of property division at all; that is, that men owning substantially the same amounts of the same kinds of property were equally divided on the matter of adoption or rejection — it would then become apparent that the Constitution had no ascertainable relation to economic groups or classes, but was the product of some abstract causes remote from the chief business of life — gaining a livelihood.

Suppose, on the other hand, that substantially all of the merchants, money lenders, security holders, manufacturers, shippers, capitalists, and financiers and their professional associates are to be found on one side in support of the Constitution and that substantially all or the major portion of the opposition came from the non-slaveholding farmers and the debtors — would it not be pretty conclusively demonstrated that our fundamental law was not the product of an abstraction known as "the whole people," but of a group of economic interests which must have expected beneficial results from its adoption? Obviously all the facts here desired cannot be discovered, but the data presented in the following chapters bear out the latter hypothesis, and thus a reasonable presumption in favor of the theory is created.

Of course, it may be shown (and perhaps can be shown) that the farmers and debtors who opposed the Constitution were, in fact, benefited by the general improvement which resulted from its adoption. It may likewise be shown, to take an extreme case, that the English nation derived immense advantages from the Norman Conquest and the orderly administrative processes which were introduced, as it undoubtedly did; nevertheless, it does not follow that the vague thing known as "the advancement of general welfare" or some abstraction known as "justice" was the immediate, guiding purpose of the leaders in either of these great historic changes. The point is, that the direct, impelling motive in both cases was the economic advantages which the beneficiaries expected would accrue to themselves first, from their action.   Further than this, economic interpretation cannot go.   It may be that some larger world-process is working through each series of historical events; but ultimate causes lie beyond our horizon.

CHAPTER II

A SURVEY OF ECONOMIC INTERESTS IN 1787

THE whole theory of the economic interpretation of history rests upon the concept that social progress in general is the result of contending interests in society — some favorable, others opposed, to change. On this hypothesis, we are required to discover at the very outset of the present study what classes and social groups existed in the United States just previous to the adoption of the Constitution and which of them, from the nature of their property, might have expected to benefit immediately and definitely by the overthrow of the old system and the establishment of the new. On the other hand, it must be discovered which of them might have expected more beneficial immediate results, on the whole, from the maintenance of the existing legal arrangements.

The importance of a survey of the distribution of property in 1787 for economic as well as political history is so evident that it is strange that no attempt has been made to undertake it on a large scale. Not even a beginning has been made. It is, therefore, necessary for us to rely for the present upon the general statements of historians who have written more or less at length about the period under consideration; but in the meanwhile it can do no harm to suggest, by way of a preface, the outlines of such a survey and some of the chief sources of information.

I. In the first place, there were the broad interests of real property which constituted, in 1787, a far larger proportion of all wealth than it does at the present time. The size, value, and ownership of holdings and their geographical distribution ought to be ascertained. In the absence of a general census, the preparation of such an economic survey would entail an enormous labor, and it could never be more than approximately complete. Neither the census of 1790 nor the assessment for direct taxes under the law of 1798 covers this topic. The assessment rolls of the several states for taxation, wherever available, would yield the data desired, at least in part; but a multitude of local records would have to be consulted with great scrutiny and critical care.

II. In order to ascertain the precise force of personalty in the formation and adoption of the Constitution, it would be necessary to discover not only the amount and geographical distribution [1] of money and public securities; but also the exact fields of operation in which personalty looked for immediate and prospective gains. A complete analysis of the economic forces in the Constitution-making process would require the following data:—

1. The geographic distribution of money on hand and loaned and the names of the holders. It is apparent that much of the material from which evidence on these points may be obtained has disappeared; but an intensive study of the tax returns of the states, the records of the local assessors, wills probated, mortgages recorded, and suits in courts over loans and mortgages, would no doubt produce an immense amount of illuminating information.

2. The geographic distribution and ownership of the public securities. Fortunately the unpublished and unworked records of the Treasury Department at Washington throw great light on this fundamental problem. Shortly

---

[1] The question of geographic distribution will be considered below, Chap. X.

after the federal government was established the old debt was converted into a new consolidated, or funded, debt; and holders of public securities, state and continental, brought their papers to their local loan office (one for each state) or to the Treasury to have them recorded and transformed into the stocks of the new government.

The records of this huge transaction (which was the first really great achievement of nascent capitalism in the United States), if they had been kept intact, would constitute, perhaps, the most wonderful single collection on economic history ever possessed by any country. Were they complete, they would form a veritable Domesday Book of the politics during the first years of the new government. But unfortunately they are not complete. The records of Hamilton's administration at the Treasury itself seem to have largely disappeared, and the records of the loan offices in the several states are generally fragmentary, although in one or two instances they are indeed monumental.

A complete set of these financial documents should show: (1) the owners of certificates of the old government as issued, during the Revolution and afterward, to original holders; (2) the transfers of certificates from original holders to other parties; (3) the names of those who held certificates in 1787, when the Convention was called to frame the Constitution; (4) the records of transactions in stocks between the announcement of the Convention's work and the adoption of Hamilton's funding system; (5) the names of those who brought in securities for funding into the new debt; (6) the names of those for whom the brokers, whose names appear on the loan office books, were, in fact, operating.

None of the records preserved at the Treasury Department presents all of the evidence required for the scientific study of a single state. Nearly one-third of the operations were at the Treasury and of these only a meagre fragment seems to have escaped the ravages of time. In the documents of some of the commonwealths, however, it is possible to ascertain the names of hundreds of patriots who risked their money in original certificates or received certificates for services rendered. The books of a few loan offices are so kept that it can be easily discovered who brought in securities to be funded into the new debt and also to whom these securities were originally issued.

In some states the ledgers were carefully preserved and it is possible to find out the names and addresses of the holders of securities funded at the local loan office and the amount held by each person. The ledgers of Connecticut, for example, offer a rich field for the study of the names and geographical distribution of public creditors, and the tracing of these interests through their myriad local ramifications would afford an interesting and profitable undertaking. But unfortunately multitudes of the most significant operations are forever lost; it is to be particularly deplored that the "powers of attorney" for the period are not forthcoming. Unless the Government at Washington follows the example of enlightened administrations in Europe and establishes a Hall of Records, the precious volumes which have come down to us will be worked only with great difficulty, if they do not disintegrate and disappear altogether.[1]

3. The geographic distribution of small mortgaged farms and their connection with various schemes for depreciation of the currency and impairment of the obligation of contract.

___

[1] A few years ago a negro attendant at the Treasury sold a cart-load or more of these records to a junk dealer. He was imprisoned for the offence, but this is a small consolation for scholars. The present writer was able to use some of the records only after a vacuum cleaner had been brought in to excavate the ruins.

No doubt work in local records would yield valuable results in this field.

4. Owners and operators in western lands. Speculation in western lands was one of the leading activities of capitalists in those days. As is well known, the soldiers were paid in part in land scrip and this scrip was bought up at low prices by dealers, often with political connections. Furthermore, large areas had been bought outright for a few cents an acre and were being held for a rise in value. The chief obstacle in the way of the rapid appreciation of these lands was the weakness of the national government which prevented the complete subjugation of the Indians, the destruction of old Indian claims, and the orderly settlement of the frontier. Every leading capitalist of the time thoroughly understood the relation of a new constitution to the rise in land values beyond the Alleghanies. This idea was expressed, for example, by Hugh Williamson, a member of the Convention from North Carolina and a land speculator in a letter to Madison.[1] The materials for the study of land operations exist in enormous quantities, largely in manuscript form in Washington; and a critical scrutiny of the thousands of names that appear on these records, in their political relations, would afford results beyond all measure. Here, too, is the work for a lifetime.

5. The geographic distribution of manufacturing establishments and the names of owners and investors. On this important topic a mass of printed and manuscript materials exists, but no attempt has yet been made to catalogue the thousands of names of persons with a view to establishing political connections. To produce the materials for this study, searches must be made in the local records from New Hampshire to Georgia. Wills probated, trans-

[1] See below, p. 50.

fers of property, law suits, private papers, advertisements in
newspapers, shipping records, Hamilton's correspondence
in the Manuscript Division of the Library of Congress,
unclassified Treasury Records and correspondence, and
innumerable other sources must be searched and lists of
names and operations made.

Pending the enormous and laborious researches here
enumerated, the following pages are offered merely as an
indication of the way in which the superficial aspects of
the subject may be treated.[1] In fact, they sketch the broad
outlines of the study which must be filled in and corrected
by detailed investigations.

THE DISFRANCHISED

In an examination of the structure of American society
in 1787, we first encounter four groups whose economic
status had a definite legal expression: the slaves, the indented servants, the mass of men who could not qualify
for voting under the property tests imposed by the state
constitutions and laws, and women, disfranchised and subjected to the discriminations of the common law. These
groups were, therefore, not represented in the Convention
which drafted the Constitution, except under the theory
that representation has no relation to voting.

How extensive the disfranchisement really was cannot be
determined.[2] In some states, for instance, Pennsylvania and
Georgia, propertyless mechanics in the towns could vote; but
in other states the freehold qualifications certainly excluded
a great number of the adult males.

[1] See Curtis, *The Constitutional History of the United States*, Book I, Chaps. II–
VII; Fiske, *Critical Period of American History*; McMaster, *History of the People
of the United States*, Vol. I; Channing, *History of the United States*, Vol. III.

[2] See below, Chaps. IV and IX.

In no state, apparently, had the working-class developed a consciousness of a separate interest or an organization that commanded the attention of the politicians of the time. In turning over the hundreds of pages of writings left by eighteenth-century thinkers one cannot help being impressed with the fact that the existence and special problems of a working-class, then already sufficiently numerous to form a considerable portion of society, were outside the realm of politics, except in so far as the future power of the proletariat was foreseen and feared.[1]

When the question of the suffrage was before the Convention, Madison warned his colleagues against the coming industrial masses: "Viewing the subject in its merits alone, the freeholders of the Country would be the safest depositories of Republican liberty. In future times a great majority of the people will not only be without landed, but any other sort of property. These will either combine under the influence of their common situation; in which case,[2] the rights of property and the public liberty will not be secure in their hands, or, which is more probable, they will become the tools of opulence and ambition; in which case there will be equal danger on another side."[3]

So far as social policy is concerned, however, the working-class problem had not made any impression on the statesmen of the time. Hamilton in his report on manufactures,[4] dismisses the subject with scant notice. He ob-

---

[1] Working-men in the cities were not altogether indifferent spectators. See Becker, *Political Parties in New York*. They would have doubtless voted with the major interests of the cities in favor of the Constitution as against the agrarians had they been enfranchised. In fact, this is what happened in New York. See below, Chap. IX.

[2] "If the authority be in their hands by the rule of suffrage," struck out in the Ms. See also the important note to this speech in Farrand, *Records*, Vol. II, p. 204, note 17.

[3] Farrand, *Records*, Vol. II, p. 203.

[4] December 5, 1791. *State Papers: Finance*, Vol. I, p. 126.

serves that one of the advantages of the extensive introduction of machinery will be "the employment of persons
who would otherwise be idle, and in many cases, a burthen
on the community, either from bias of temper, habit, infirmity of body, or some other cause, indisposing or disqualifying them for the toils of the country. It is worthy of
remark, that, in general, women and children are rendered
more useful, and the latter more early useful, by manufacturing establishments, than they would otherwise be. Of
the number of persons employed in the cotton manufactories
of Great Britain, it is computed that four-sevenths, nearly,
are women and children; of whom the greatest proportion
are children, many of them of a tender age." Apparently
this advantage was, in Hamilton's view, to accrue principally to the fathers of families, for he remarks: "The
husbandman himself experiences a new source of profit
and support, from the increased industry of his wife and
daughters, invited and stimulated by the demands of the
neighboring manufactories."

Passing beyond these groups which were politically nonexistent, except in so far as those who possessed the ballot
and economic power were compelled to safeguard their
rights against assaults from such quarters, we come to the
social groupings within the politically enfranchised mass.
Here we find no legal class distinctions. Social distinctions were very sharp, it is true, as every student of manners
and customs well knows; but there were no outward legal
signs of special class privileges.

GROUPS OF REAL PROPERTY HOLDERS

Nevertheless, the possessors of property were susceptible
of classification into several rather marked groups, though
of course they shade off into one another by imperceptible

gradations. Broadly speaking, there were the interests of real and personal property. Here, however, qualifications must be made. There was no such identity of interest between the large planters and the small inland farmers of the south as existed in England between the knights and yeomen. The real property holders may be classified into three general groups: the small farmers, particularly back from the sea-coast, scattered from New Hampshire to Georgia, the manorial lords, such as we find along the banks of the Hudson,[1] and the slaveholding planters of the south.

1. The first of these groups, the small farmers, constituted a remarkably homogeneous class. The inland section was founded and recruited by mechanics, the poorer whites, and European (particularly Scotch-Irish) immigrants. It had peculiar social and political views arising from the crude nature of its environment, but its active political doctrines were derived from an antagonism to the seaboard groups. One source of conflict was connected with the possession of the land itself. Much of the western country had been taken up by speculators and the settlers were either squatters or purchasers from large holders. This is illustrated by the situation in Virginia, where, as Ambler points out, "liberality in granting her unoccupied lands did not prove to be good policy. True, large numbers of settlers were early attracted to the state, where they made permanent homes, but much of the land fell into the hands of speculators. Companies were formed in Europe and America to deal in Virginia lands, which were bought up in large tracts at the trifling cost of two cents per acre. This wholesale engrossment soon consumed practically all the most desirable lands and forced the home seeker to

---

[1] Roosevelt, *Gouverneur Morris*, pp. 14 ff.

purchase from speculators or to settle as a squatter."[1]   As the settler sought to escape from the speculator by moving westward, the frontier line of speculation advanced.

In addition to being frequently in debt for their lands, the small farmers were dependent upon the towns for most of the capital to develop their resources.   They were, in other words, a large debtor class, to which must be added, of course, the urban dwellers who were in a like unfortunate condition.

That this debtor class had developed a strong consciousness of identical interests in the several states is clearly evident in local politics and legislation.[2]   Shays' Rebellion in Massachusetts, the disturbances in Rhode Island, New Hampshire, and other northern states, the activities of the paper-money advocates in state legislatures, the innumerable schemes for the relief of debtors, such as the abolition of imprisonment, paper money, laws delaying the collection of debts, propositions requiring debtors to accept land in lieu of specie at a valuation fixed by a board of arbitration, — these and many other schemes testify eloquently to the fact that the debtors were conscious of their status and actively engaged in establishing their interest in the form of legal provisions.   Their philosophy was reflected in the writings of Luther Martin, delegate to the Convention from Maryland, who disapproved of the Constitution, partly on the ground that it would put a stop to agrarian legislation.[3]

2. The second group of landed proprietors, the manorial lords of the Hudson valley region, constituted a peculiar aristocracy in itself and was the dominant class in the politics of New York during the period between the Revolu-

---

[1] Ambler, *Sectionalism in Virginia*, p. 44.

[2] Libby has shown the degree of correspondence between the rural vote on paper money measures, designed for the relief of debtors, and the vote against the ratification of the Constitution. *Op. cit.*, pp. 50 ff.

[3] See below, p. 205.

tion and the adoption of the Constitution, as it had been before the War. It was unable or unwilling to block the emission of paper money, because the burden of that operation fell on the capitalists rather than itself. It also took advantage of its predominance to shift the burden of taxation from the land to imports,[1] and this fact contributed powerfully to its opposition to the Constitution, because it implied a transference of the weight of taxation for state purposes to the soil. Its spokesmen indulged in much high talk of state's rights, in which Federalist leaders refused to see more than a hollow sham made to cover the rural gentry's economic supremacy.

3. The third group of landed proprietors were the slave-holders of the south. It seems curious at the first glance that the representatives of the southern states which sold raw materials and wanted competition in shipping were willing to join in a union that subjected them to commercial regulations devised immediately in behalf of northern interests. An examination of the records shows that they were aware of this apparent incongruity, but that there were overbalancing compensations to be secured in a strong federal government.[2]

Money-lending and the holding of public securities were not confined to the north by any means; although, perhaps, as Calhoun long afterward remarked,[3] the south was devoid

[1] The landholders were able to do this largely because New York City was the entry port for Connecticut and New Jersey. The opportunity to shift the taxes not only to the consumers, but to the consumers of neighboring states, was too tempting to be resisted.

[2] For a paragraph on nascent capitalism in South Carolina, see W. A. Schaper, "Sectionalism in South Carolina," *American Historical Association Report* (1900), Vol. I. See the letter of Blount, Davie, and Williamson to the governor of North Carolina, below, p. 169.

[3] It is not without interest to note that about the time Calhoun made this criticism of New England capitalist devices he was attempting to borrow several thousand dollars from a Massachusetts mill owner to engage in railway enterprise in the south.

of some of the artifices of commerce which characterized New England. Neither were attempts at relieving debtors by legislative enactment restricted to Massachusetts and Rhode Island. The south had many men who were rich in personalty, other than slaves, and it was this type, rather than the slaveholding planter as such, which was represented in the Convention that framed the Constitution. The majority of the southern delegates at Philadelphia in 1787 were from the towns or combined a wide range of personalty operations with their planting. On this account there was more identity of interest among Langdon of Portsmouth, Gerry of Boston, Hamilton of New York, Dayton of New Jersey, Robert Morris of Philadelphia, McHenry of Baltimore, Washington on the Potomac, Williamson of North Carolina, the Pinckneys of Charleston, and Pierce of Savannah than between these several men and their debt-burdened neighbors at the back door. Thus nationalism was created by a welding of economic interests that cut through state boundaries.

The southern planter was also as much concerned in maintaining order against slave revolts as the creditor in Massachusetts was concerned in putting down Shays' "desperate debtors." And the possibilities of such servile insurrections were by no means remote. Every slave owner must have felt more secure in 1789 when he knew that the governor of his state could call in the strong arm of the federal administration in case a domestic disturbance got beyond the local police and militia. The north might make discriminatory commercial regulations, but they could be regarded as a sort of insurance against conflagrations that might bring ruin in their train. It was obviously better to ship products under adverse legislation than to have no products to ship.

GROUPS OF PERSONAL PROPERTY INTERESTS

A second broad group of interests was that of personal property as contrasted with real property. This embraced, particularly, money loaned, state and continental securities, stocks of goods, manufacturing plants, soldiers' scrip, and shipping. The relative proportion of personalty to realty in 1787 has not been determined and it is questionable whether adequate data are available for settling such an important matter.[1]

PERSONALTY IN MONEY.—Although personalty in the form of money at interest or capital seeking investment did not constitute in 1787 anything like the same amount, relative to the value of real estate, which it does to-day, it must not be thought that it was by any means inconsiderable in any state. The tax returns of New Hampshire for 1793 report the value of all buildings and real estate as £893,327 : 16 : 10 and the amount of money on hand or at interest as £35,985 : 5 : 6. The Massachusetts tax returns of 1792 show £196,698 : 4 : 6 at interest and £95,474 : 4 : 5 on hand. The Connecticut returns for 1795 show £63,348 : 10 : 1 at interest.[2]

Money capital was suffering in two ways under the Articles of Confederation. It was handicapped in seeking profitable outlets by the absence of protection for manufactures, the lack of security in investments in western lands, and discriminations against American shipping by foreign countries. It was also being positively attacked by the makers of paper money, stay laws, pine barren acts, and other devices for depreciating the currency or delaying the collection of debts. In addition there was a widespread de-

---

[1] See, however, *State Papers: Finance*, Vol. I, pp. 414 ff.
[2] *Ibid.*, Vol. I, pp. 442 ff.

rangement of the monetary system and the coinage due to the absence of uniformity and stability in the standards.[1]

Creditors, naturally enough, resisted all of these schemes in the state legislatures, and failing to find relief there at length turned to the idea of a national government so constructed as to prevent laws impairing the obligation of contract, emitting paper money, and otherwise benefiting debtors. It is idle to inquire whether the rapacity of the creditors or the total depravity of the debtors (a matter much discussed at the time) was responsible for this deep and bitter antagonism. It is sufficient for our purposes to discover its existence and to find its institutional reflex in the Constitution. It was to the interest of the creditors to see the currency appreciate, to facilitate the process for securing possession of forfeited mortgaged property, and to hold the rigor of the law before the debtor who was untrue to his obligations. Whether the creditors were driven into class consciousness by the assaults of their debtors or attained it by the exercise of their wits is, for scientific purposes, immaterial.

PERSONALTY IN PUBLIC SECURITIES.—Even more immediately concerned in the establishment of a stable national government were the holders of state and continental securities. The government under the Articles of Confederation was not paying the interest on its debt and its paper had depreciated until it was selling at from one-sixth to one-twentieth of its par value.[2] Grave uncertainties as to the actions of legislatures kept state paper at a low price, also, even where earnest attempts were being made to meet the obligations.

The advantage of a strong national government that

---

[1] See the picturesque description of the monetary system or lack of system in Fiske, *Critical Period of American History.*

[2] See below, p. 146.

could discharge this debt at its face value is obvious; and it was fully understood at the time. The importance of this element of personalty in forcing on the revolution that overthrew the Articles of Confederation is all the more apparent when it is remembered that securities constituted a very large proportion of the intangible wealth. In Massachusetts, for example, it is set down in 1792 at a sum greater than all the money at interest and on hand in the state.[1]

The amount of the public securities of the United States and of the several states at the establishment of the new government was estimated by Hamilton, in his first report on credit, as Secretary of the Treasury.[2] The foreign debt, that is, money borrowed abroad, was fixed at $10,070,307 and arrears of interest up to December, 1789, were estimated at $1,640,071.62, making a total of $11,710,378.62. The domestic continental debt, including the registered debt, army certificates, etc., amounted to $27,383,917.74, to which was added arrears of interest to the amount of $13,030,168.20, making a total of $40,414,085.94. The amount of the state debts was unknown in 1790, but Hamilton placed it at about $25,000,000, which appears to have been rather high. The issue, later authorized to cover them, was $21,500,000 and the amount actually paid out was $18,271,786.47.[3]

The enormous total of the national debt after state and national securities were funded is shown by Hamilton's report of January 16, 1795 :—

Foreign Debt	$13,745,379.35
Funded domestic debt	60,789,914.18
Unsubscribed debt	1,561,175.14
Total unredeemed debt	$76,096,468.67

[1] *State Papers: Finance*, Vol. I, p. 451; also see below, pp. 261–2.
[2] *State Papers: Finance*, Vol. I, p. 19.
[3] W. De Knight, *History of the Currency*, p. 21.

In addition to this sum, there was an amount of $1,400,000 due to the Bank of the United States on account of the loan from that institution, but this was more than counterbalanced by the value of the stock.[1]

It is evident from this statement that a vast mass of state and continental securities was scattered throughout the country in 1787. The degree of its concentration or distribution cannot be determined until the Domesday Books of the Treasury Department have been carefully studied, and their incompleteness makes an absolute statement impossible. The value of this paper in the hands of the holders in the spring when the Convention met cannot be ascertained with mathematical precision, for prices varied from state to state. Furthermore, the prices obtained by the holders of public paper after Hamilton's funding system had gone into effect can only be roughly estimated, for it depends upon the market in which they were sold. For example, 6 per cents were bringing 17 shillings in the pound on March 5, 1791, and 22 shillings in the pound on October 3, 1792. On these dates, deferred sixes were 9/1 and 13/7, respectively, and 3 per cents were 9/1 and 13/1, respectively.[2]

If we leave out of account the foreign debt, it appears that some $60,000,000 worth of potential paper lay in the hands of American citizens in the spring of 1787. This paper was changing hands all of the time at varying prices. The common selling price in good markets before the movement for the Constitution got under way ranged from one-sixth to one-tenth its face value; and some of it sold as low as twenty to one. In fact, many holders regarded continental paper as worthless, as it might have been had the formation of the Constitution been indefinitely delayed.

[1] *State Papers: Finance*, Vol. I, p. 325.   [2] *Ibid.*, Vol, I, p. 231.

It seems safe to hazard a guess, therefore, that at least $40,000,000 gain came to the holders of securities through the adoption of the Constitution and the sound financial system which it made possible.   This leaves out of account the large fortunes won by the manipulation of stocks after the government was established and particularly after the founding of the New York Stock Exchange in 1792.[1]

It should be pointed out, however, that this was not all gain for the original holders of public paper, that is, for those who had loaned the Revolutionary government money or had rendered it services during the War.   Nevertheless, they would have lost all their continental securities under the prevailing methods of the Congress.   As Pitkin points out, "The interest of the debt was unpaid, public credit was gone, the debt itself was considered of little value, and was sold at last by many of the original holders for about one-tenth of its nominal value." [2]   From this point of view, the appreciation due to the adoption of the new government was so much clear gain, even to original holders;   and in some states more than one-half of the paper had passed into the hands of speculators at low figures.

The significance of this huge national debt and of the enormous gain made in the appreciation of securities can

---

[1] Callender, not a very reliable authority on most matters concerning Hamilton, claims that twenty-five million dollars was made by the funding of the public debt, and that about ten millions more was made out of the state debt assumption process.   He further declared that a public debt of eighty million dollars had been created of which only about thirty millions was all that was necessary.   Gallatin held also that the unnecessary debt created by the assumption act amounted to about eleven million dollars.   Callender, *A History of the United States for 1796*, pp. 224 ff.   The ethics of redeeming the debt at face value is not here considered although the present writer believes that the success of the national government could not have been secured under any other policy than that pursued by Hamilton. Callendar claims that those who held it were, in large measure, speculators and that they made huge fortunes out of the transaction.   By a stroke of the pen the federal government created capital to the amount of millions in the hands of the holders.

[2] *A Statistical View of the Commerce of the United States*, p. 31.

be understood only in comparison with other forms of wealth at that time. Unfortunately, our statistics for the period of the formation of the Constitution are meagre, but under an act of Congress passed in 1798 a valuation of lands was made for the purposes of direct taxation. The surveys were made between the years 1798 and 1804. The following table [1] exhibits the value of lands (not including houses, which amounted to more than $140,000,000 in addition) in each of the states at the close of the eighteenth century, and also the amount of money paid out by the loan offices of the respective states for the year 1795 in discharging the interest on the public debt and the payment of 2 per cent towards the reimbursement of the 6 per cent stocks held in the several commonwealths : —

	Value of Lands	Interest, etc., Disbursed [2]
New Hampshire	$19,028,108.03	$20,000.00
Massachusetts	59,445,642.64	309,500.00
Rhode Island	8,082,355.21	31,700.00
Connecticut	40,163,955.34	79,600.00
Vermont	15,165,484.02	
New York	74,885,075.69	367,600.00
New Jersey	27,287,981.89	27,350.00
Pennsylvania	72,824,852.60	86,379.19
Delaware	4,053,248.42	2,980.00
Maryland	21,634,004.57	74,000.00
Virginia	59,976,860.04	62,300.00
North Carolina	27,909,479.70	3,200.00
South Carolina	12,456,720.94	109,500.00
Georgia	10,263 506.95	6,800.00
Kentucky	20,268,325.07	
Tennessee	5,847,562.00	
Total	$479,293,263.13	$1,180,909.19

[1] Tables from Pitkin, *A Statistical View of the Commerce of the United States*, pp. 367–368, and *An Account of the Receipts and Expenditures of the United States for the Year 1795*, p. 65.

[2] No table showing the capital amount on the loan office books of the states after the funding was complete was discovered, so that the interest payment is given here.

To the total amount of payments made through the loan offices must be added the payments made at the Treasury on the securities registered there, bringing the total annual interest and capital disbursements to $2,727,959.07.

It seems safe to assume from the table that $400,000,000 would cover the total taxable value of all the lands in the thirteen states in 1787.[1] Very probably the estimate should be much lower, but letting the figures stand at this amount, it will be seen that an advance of $40,000,000 in securities would have represented one-tenth of the total taxable value of all the land in the thirteen United States at the time of the formation of the Constitution.

To put the matter in another way : The amount gained by public security holders through the adoption of the new system was roughly equivalent to the value of all the lands as listed for taxation in Connecticut. It was but little less than the value of the lands in New Hampshire, Vermont, and Rhode Island. It was about equivalent to one-half the value of the lands in New York and to two-thirds the value of the lands in Massachusetts. It amounted to at least ten dollars for every man, woman, and child in the whole United States from New Hampshire to Georgia.[2]

The significance of the figures showing the annual interest disbursement also when the debt had been funded becomes

---

[1] Undoubtedly a large appreciation had taken place between 1787 and 1800.

[2] "The public securities of the United States of America were a dead, inactive kind of property, previous to the establishment of the constitution of the new government; then they became at once the object of avarice. They before had an existence as to value, on the slender hope of having something done for them at some distant future period ; and obtained a motion only from the sagacity of the few, who happened to be right in their conjectures respecting the then future events of American financeering. Upon the adoption of the new system of government they assumed all the properties of a rising credit, and became an immense active capital for commerce." James Sullivan, *An Inquiry into the Origin and Use of Money* (1792). Duane Pamphlets, Library of Congress.

evident only by comparison. Tench Coxe, as commissioner of the revenue, estimated the amount of goods, wares, and merchandise exported from the United States between October 1, 1791, and September 30, 1792, at $21,005,568. In other words, the annual interest on the domestic debt was more than one-tenth the total value of the goods exported annually. The average imports for each of the three years ending March 4, 1792, was $19,150,000, so that the interest on the domestic debt was more than one-tenth of the value of the goods imported into the United States.[1]

One of the most potent effective forces of these public securities was the Society of the Cincinnati which was composed of the officers of the Revolutionary Army organized into local branches in the several states. Like other soldiers, the members of this order had been paid for their patriotic services partly in land warrants and depreciated paper; but unlike the privates, they were usually men of some means and were not compelled to sacrifice their holdings to speculators at outrageously low prices. The members of this Society appear in large numbers on the loan office records of the several states preserved in the Treasury Department; and many, if not all, of the state branches had funds derived from this source.

The political influence of the Society was recognized in the Convention. When the popular election of President was under consideration, Gerry objected to it. "The ignorance of the people," he said, "would put it in the power of some one set of men dispersed through the Union and acting in concert to delude them into any appointment. He observed that such a Society of men existed in the Order of the Cincinnati. They were respectable, United, and in-

---

[1] Tench Coxe, *A View of the United States of America* (1795), p. 360. Tucker, *Progress of the United States* (1843), p. 205.

fluential. They will in fact elect the chief Magistrate in every instance, if the election be referred to the people — His respect for the characters composing this Society could not blind him to the danger and impropriety of throwing such a power into their hands." [1]   In this view Colonel Mason concurred. [2]

An observant French chargé d'affaires, writing to his home secretary of state for foreign affairs in June, 1787, calls attention to the weight of the Order of the Cincinnati in the movement for a new government, but remarks that their power has been greatly exaggerated. "Les Cincinnati," he says, "c'est à dire les officiers de l'ancienne armée américaine, sont intéressés à l'établissement d'un Gouvernement solide, puisqu'ils sont tous créanciers du public, mais, considérant la foiblesse du Conseil national et l'impossibilité d'être payés par la présente administration, ils proposent de jeter tous les États dans une seule masse et de mettre à leur tête le gal. Washington avec toutes les prérogatives et les pouvoirs d'une tête couronné." He also says that they threaten a revolution by arms in case the Convention fails, but adds that this project is too extravagant to merit the least consideration. [3]

This society was, however, compactly organized. Correspondence among the members was frequent, extensive, and frank. Almost uniformly, they were in favor of a reconstruction of the national government on a stronger basis. [4] They were bitter in their denunciation of the popular

---

[1] Farrand, *Records*, Vol. II, p. 114.   [2] *Ibid.*, Vol. II, p. 119.
[3] *Ibid.*, Vol. III, p. 43.
[4] "A large majority of the officers of the army of the Revolution were in favor of the new Constitution. The Cincinnati were mostly among its warmest advocates; and as they were organized and were, many of them, of exalted private and public worth and could act in concert through all the states, their influence was foreseen and feared by its opponents." Blair, *The Virginia Convention of 1788,* Vol. I, p. 36, note 41.

movements in the states, particularly Shays' revolt in Massachusetts. War had given them a taste for strong measures, and the wretched provisions which had been made for paying them for their military services gave them an economic interest in the movement to secure a government with an adequate taxing power. Moreover, they were consolidated by the popular hostility to them on account of their "secret" and "aristocratic" character.

PERSONALTY IN MANUFACTURING AND SHIPPING.— The third group of personalty interests embraced the manufacturing population, which was not inconsiderable even at that time. A large amount of capital had been invested in the several branches of industry and a superficial study of the extensive natural resources at hand revealed the immense possibilities of capitalistic enterprise. The industrial revolution was then getting under way in England and the fame of Arkwright was being spread abroad in the land. In the survey of the economic interests of the members of the federal Convention, given below, it is shown that a few leading men were directly connected with industrial concerns, although it is not apparent that the protection of industries was their chief consideration, in spite of the fact that they did undoubtedly contemplate such a system. But outside of the Convention vehement appeals were made by pamphleteers for protection, on the score that the discriminatory measures of Great Britain were disastrous to American economic independence.

As early as April, 1785, a memorial from prominent merchants and business men of Philadelphia was laid before the legislature of the state lamenting that Congress did not have "a full and entire power over the commerce of the United States," and praying that the legislature request Congress to lay a proposal conferring such a power before the states for their ratification. The memorialists assured the legislature that there was a "disposition in the mercantile interest of Pennsylvania favorable thereto."[1] Among the signers were T. Fitzsimons and George Clymer, who were destined to sit in the constitutional Convention as representatives of the state of Pennsylvania and of the mercantile interest which they had so much at heart.

The supporters of the Constitution were so earnest and so persistent in their assertion that commerce was languishing and manufactures perishing for the lack of protection that there must have been some justification for their claims, although it is impossible to say how widespread the havoc really was. The exaggeration of danger threatened by a tariff reduction is not peculiar to our times; it was sharply marked in older days. That the consumer suffered from the lack of the protection sought in 1787 by merchants and manufacturers is not apparent. Indeed the "mechanics and manufacturers of New York" in their humble petition to Congress for relief in 1789 complain that "their countrymen have been deluded by an appearance of plenty; by the profusion of foreign articles which has deluged the country; and thus have mistaken excessive importation for a flourishing trade. To this deception they [the petitioners] impute the continuance of that immoderate prepossession in favor of foreign commodities which has been the principal cause of their distresses, and the subject of their complaint."[2]

That innumerable manufacturing, shipping, trading, and commercial interests did, however, look upon the adoption of the Constitution as the sure guarantee that

---

[1] *American Museum*, Vol. I, p. 313. Other signers were C. Pettit, J. Ross, I. Hazlehurst, M. Lewis, T. Coxe, R. Wells, J. M. Nesbit, J. Nixon, J. Wilcocks, S. Howell, and C. Biddle.

[2] *State Papers: Finance*, Vol. I, p. 9.

protection could be procured against foreign competition, is fully evidenced in the memorials laid before Congress in April, May, and June, 1789, asking for the immediate enactment of discriminatory tariff laws.[1]

The first of these petitions was from Baltimore in particular and Maryland generally, and was communicated to the House of Representatives on April 11, 1789, a few days after that body had settled down to business. The second was laid before the House a week later by a committee representing the mechanics and manufacturers of New York. On May 25, 1789, the shipwrights of Philadelphia laid their pleas before Congress; and on June 5, the tradesmen and manufacturers of Boston put in their appearance. These petitions for protection from the four great trading and shipping centres of the country, Baltimore, Philadelphia, New York, and Boston, which had been most zealous in securing the establishment of the new government, are in themselves eloquent documents for the economic interpretation of the Constitution.

The first of these, from Baltimore, bears the names of two members of the federal Convention from that state, Daniel Carroll and James McHenry, and the names of two or three hundred other citizens of that community, the analysis of whose politico-economic connections would doubtless repay the detailed scrutiny which the painful labor would entail. The petition cites the sad state of decline in which manufacturing and trading interests have been since the close of the Revolution and the ineffectual attempts of the states acting alone to remedy the evils. "The happy period having now arrived," the memorialists exultingly exclaim, "when the United States are placed in a new situation; when the adoption of the General Government gives one

[1] *American State Papers: Finance*, Vol. I, pp. 5 ff.

sovereign Legislature the sole and exclusive power of laying
duties upon imports; your petitioners rejoice at the prospect this affords them, that America, freed from the commercial shackles which have so long bound her, will see and
pursue her true interest, becoming independent in fact as
well as in name; and they confidently hope that the encouragement and protection of American manufactures will
claim the earliest attention of the supreme Legislature of
the nation."

The Maryland petitioners are conscious of no narrow
motives in asking for relief at the hands of the government:
"the number of her poor increasing for want of employment; foreign debts accumulating; houses and lands
depreciating in value; trade and manufactures languishing
and expiring" — these are the evidences of need for the
expected legislation. They, therefore, ask for duties on all
foreign articles that can be made in America, which will
give "a just and decided preference to their labors." And
lest Congress might not understand the precise character
of the relief for which they ask, they append a long list of
articles, which are, or can be, manufactured in Maryland,
and on which protection is needed — including ships, hard-
ware, clocks, boots, shoes, saddles, brushes, food-stuffs, and
raw iron, to mention only a few.

The second petition, from the mechanics and manufacturers of New York, recites how the memorialists had expected
great prosperity on the successful issue of the Revolution
and had seen their hopes blasted "by a system of commercial usurpation, originating in prejudices, and fostered
by a feeble government." They had struggled in vain
against dire adversity and "wearied by their fruitless exertions, your petitioners have long looked forward with
anxiety to the establishment of a government which would

have the power to check the growing evil, and extend a protecting hand to the interests of commerce and the arts. Such a government is now established. On the promulgation of the Constitution just now commencing its operations, your petitioners discovered in its principles the remedy which they had so long and so earnestly desired. They embraced it with ardor, and have supported it with persevering attachment." Lest Congress might not have the information necessary for the formulation of a protective tariff on correct principles, the petitioners subjoined a list of articles manufactured in the state and susceptible of protection.

The petitioners from Philadelphia, humbly seeking protection for shipping, lament that the tonnage built at that harbor has fallen to about one-third the amount constructed before the Revolution, and call attention to the fact that the British navigation act totally prevents them from building for English customers. They add that they "have waited, with anxious expectation, for the sitting of the honourable Congress under the new Constitution of the United States, firmly relying that every exertion would be used to reinstate so necessary and useful a branch of business." Like the representatives from Baltimore and New York, they append for the information of Congress a list of suggestions as to the best method of protecting American shipping interests.

Finally come the manufacturers and ship-builders of Boston. Ship-building with them has also declined since the Revolution, and the revival of manufacturing in the north depends upon adequate protection from the federal government. Accordingly they request that "heavy duties may be laid on such articles as are manufactured by our own citizens, humbly conceiving that the impost is not solely considered by Congress as an object of revenue, but, in its operation, intended to exclude such importations, and, ultimately, establish these several branches of manufacture among ourselves." Rope-makers, hatters, pewterers, soap-boilers, and tallow-chandlers, wool card-makers, ship-carvers, sailmakers, cabinet-makers, coachmakers, tailors, cordwainers, glue and starch makers, brass-founders, and coppersmiths are among the memorialists.

In the processions which celebrated the adoption of the Constitution in Boston, Philadelphia, Baltimore, Charleston, and New York, the several local manufacturing concerns were extensively represented by floats and bannermen, which shows that they were not unaware of the gain that had been made in their favor by the establishment of the new system. But it must not be supposed that the consolidation of interests in support of the Constitution was purely local in character. On the contrary it was nation-wide.

Immediately after the Revolution the local groups were being welded into a national interest by correspondence committees. Before the formation of the Constitution, Boston merchants were sending out appeals to other merchants in the several states to join in a national movement for protection; and before the new government went into effect, they were active in stirring up united action among the merchants and manufacturers of the whole country. In 1788, a committee of the association of Boston merchants and manufacturers sent out a circular to "their brethren in the several seaports of the union," asking for coöperation in this grave juncture.[1] To this Boston appeal are appended the names of John Gray, Gibbins Sharp, Benjamin Austin, Jr.,

[1] Carey, *American Museum*, Vol. IV, p. 348. See also Winsor, *Memorial History of Boston*, Vol. IV, p. 77.

Larson Belcher, William Hawes, and Joshua Witherle — all of whom signed the petition addressed to Congress the following year asking for protection.[1]

During the struggle over the reconstruction, the advocates of a constitution made use of the argument that the consumption of foreign luxuries, manufactured stuffs, was one of the chief causes of the economic distress which was said to prevail; and declared that national legislation was the only source of relief from this heavy importation. A writer in the *American Museum* for February, 1787, complains that "the articles of rum and tea alone, which are drank in this country, would pay all its taxes. But when we add sugar, coffee, gauzes, silks, feathers, and the whole list of baubles and trinkets, what an enormous expense! No wonder you want paper currency. My countrymen are all grown very tasty. Feathers and jordans must all be imported. Certainly, gentlemen, the *devil* is among you. A Hampshireman, who drinks forty shillings worth of rum in a year and never thinks of the expense, will raise a mob to reduce the governor's salary."[2]

The Connecticut Courant, of November 12, 1787, in an argument for ratification declares: "In the harbour of New York there are now 60 ships of which 55 are British. The produce of South Carolina was shipped in 170 ships, of which 150 were British. . . . Surely there is not any American who regards the interest of his country but must

---

[1] For illustrative evidence that the protection of manufactures and shipping was being widely agitated previous to the adoption of the Constitution, and that an extensive consciousness of identity of interest was being developed among the individuals concerned, see the articles in *The American Museum*, Vol. I, on American Manufactures; Winsor, *Memorial History of Boston*, Vol. IV, Chap. III. See memorials in *The American Museum*, from Philadelphia mercantile interests (April 6, 1785), Vol. I, p. 313; from Boston merchants, *ibid.*, Vol. I, p. 320. For the merchants' movement in New York, see the Magazine of American History, April, 1893, pp. 324 ff.

[2] Vol. I, p. 117.

see the immediate necessity of an efficient federal government; without it the Northern states will soon be depopu-
lated and dwindle into poverty, while the Southern ones
will become silk worms to toil and labour for Europe."

It is worthy of remark, however, that the gloomy view
of economic conditions persistently propagated by the advocates of a new national system was not entertained by all
writers of eminence and authority. One of the members
of the Convention, Franklin, early in 1787, before the
calling of that assembly, declared that the country was, on
the whole, so prosperous that there was every reason for
profound thanksgiving.[1] He mentioned, it is true, that
there were some who complained of hard times, slack trade,
and scarcity of money, but he was quick to add that there
never was an age nor a country in which there were not
some people so circumstanced as to find it hard to make a
living and that "it is always in the power of a small number
to make a great clamour." But taking the several classes
in the community as a whole, prosperity, contended Franklin, was widespread and obvious. Never was the farmer
paid better prices for his products, "as the published prices
current abundantly testify. The lands he possesses are
continually rising in value." In no part of Europe are the
laboring poor so well paid, fed, or clothed. The fishing
trade, he thinks, is in a rather bad way, and mercantile
branches are overcrowded; but he is not distressed by the
extensive importation of English goods, because this is nothing
new, and America has prospered in spite of it.

It may very well be that Franklin's view of the general
social conditions just previous to the formation of the
Constitution is essentially correct and that the defects in
the Articles of Confederation were not the serious menace

[1] M. Carey, *The American Museum,* for January, 1787, Vol. I, pp. 5 ff.

to the social fabric which the loud complaints of advocates
of change implied. It may be that "the critical period"
was not such a critical period after all; but a phantom of
the imagination produced by some undoubted evils which
could have been remedied without a political revolution.
It does not seem to have occurred to those historians, who
have repeated without examination Fiske's picturesque
phrase that it is a serious matter to indict a whole system,
an entire epoch, and a whole people. It does not appear
that any one has really inquired just what precise facts
must be established to prove that "the bonds of the social
order were dissolving." Certainly, the inflamed declara-
tions of the Shaysites are not to be taken as representing
accurately the state of the people, and just as certainly the
alarmist letters and pamphlets of interested persons on the
other side are not to be accepted without discount. When
it is remembered that most of our history has been written
by Federalists, it will become apparent that great care should
be taken in accepting, without reserve, the gloomy pictures
of the social conditions prevailing under the Articles of
Confederation. In fact, a very learned, though controversial, historian, Henry B. Dawson, in an article published
more than forty years ago makes out quite a plausible case
(documented by minute research) for the statement that
the "chaos" of which historians are wont to speak when
dealing with the history of the years 1783–87, was a creation
of their fancies.[1]

However this may be, and whether or not Franklin's
view is correct,[2] it cannot be denied that the interests seeking
protection were extensive and diversified. This is con-

[1] The Historical Magazine (1871), Vol. IX, Second Series, pp. 157 ff.
[2] For an interesting and novel view of the state of commerce under the Articles
of Confederation, see Channing, *History of the United States*, Vol. III, pp. 422 ff.

clusively shown by the petitions addressed to public bodies, by the number of influential men connected with the movement, and by the rapidity with which the new government under the Constitution responded to their demands.

CAPITAL INVESTED IN WESTERN LANDS. — Although companies had been formed to deal in western lands on a large scale before the Revolution, it was not until the close of the War that effective steps were taken toward settlement. At that time, says Professor Haskins, "the number of emigrants, the cheapness of the lands, and the lack of an established system of sale in small quantities offered many inducements for the formation of great land companies whose opportunities for speculation were increased by the depreciated currency and general ignorance concerning the West. . . . 'All I am now worth was gained by speculations in land,' wrote Timothy Pickering [a member of the Pennsylvania ratifying convention] in the same year [1796]; and many eminent men could have said the same, often with a later experience quite similar. Land speculation involved Washington, Franklin, Gallatin, Patrick Henry, Robert Morris, and James Wilson, as well as many less widely known." [1]

The situation was this: Congress under the Articles of Confederation adopted a policy of accepting certificates in part payment for lands; and it was hoped by some that the entire national debt might be extinguished in this way. However, the weakness of the Confederation, the lack of proper military forces, the uncertainty as to the frontiers kept the values of the large sections held for appreciation at an abnormally low price. Those who had invested their

[1] Haskins, *The Yazoo Land Companies*, p. 62. American Historical Association Papers for 1891. See also the lists printed in A. M. Dyer, *First Ownership of Ohio Lands* (1911).

funds in these lands or taken stocks in the companies felt
the adverse effects of the prevailing public policy, and fore-
saw the benefits which might be expected from a new and
stable government. Their view was tersely put by Williamson, a member of the Convention from North Carolina, in
a letter to Madison on June 2, 1788: "For myself, I conceive that my opinions are not biassed by private Interests,
but having claims to a considerable Quantity of Land in
the Western Country, I am fully persuaded that the Value
of those Lands must be increased by an efficient federal
Government." [1]

The weight of the several species of property in politics
is not determined by the amount, but rather by the opportunities offered to each variety for gain and by the degree
of necessity for defence against hostile legislation designed
to depreciate values or close opportunities for increments.
When viewed in this light the reason for the special pressure
of personalty in politics in 1787 is apparent. It was receiving attacks on all hands from the depreciators and it found
the way to profitable operations closed by governmental
action or neglect. If we may judge from the politics of
the Congress under the Articles of Confederation, two related groups were most active: those working for the establishment of a revenue sufficient to discharge the interest
and principal of the public debt, and those working for
commercial regulations advantageous to personalty operations in shipping and manufacturing and in western land
speculations. [2]

It should be remembered also that personalty is usually
more active than real property. It is centralized in the

---

[1] *Documentary History of the Constitution*, Vol. IV, p. 678.

[2] But see Madison's view as to the chief reason for calling the Convention,
below, p. 178.

towns and can draw together for defence or aggression with greater facility. The expectation of profits from its manipulation was much larger in 1787 than from real property. It had a considerable portion of the professional classes attached to it; its influence over the press was tremendous, not only through ownership, but also through advertising and other patronage.[1] It was, in short, the dynamic element in the movement for the new Constitution.

[1] A study of the newspapers of the period shows a large number of prominent advocates of the Constitution among the merchants and brokers advertising in the Federalist press.

CHAPTER III

THE MOVEMENT FOR THE CONSTITUTION

Dɪᴅ the system of government prevailing in the United States in 1787 affect adversely any of the economic interests enumerated in the preceding chapter? Furthermore, were the leaders in the movement which led to the adoption of the Constitution representatives of the interests so affected?

Fortunately, it is not necessary to devote any considerable attention to the first of these questions. It is answered in part above, and all of the standard treatises show conclusively that the legal system prevailing at the opening of 1787 was unfavorable to the property rights of four powerful groups above enumerated.[1] That system was, in brief, as follows. There was a loose union of thirteen sovereign states under the Articles of Confederation. The national government consisted of a legislature of one house in which the states had an equal voting power. There was no executive department and no general judiciary. The central government had no power to regulate commerce or to tax directly; and in the absence of these powers all branches of the government were rendered helpless. Particularly, money could not be secured to pay the holders of public securities, either their interest or principal. Under this system, the state legislatures were substantially without restrictions or judicial control; private rights in property were continually attacked by stay laws, legal tender laws,

[1] Bancroft, *op. cit.*, Book I, Chaps. II–VII; Fiske, *Critical Period;* Marshall, *Life of Washington* (1850 ed.), Vol. II, pp. 75 ff.

and a whole range of measures framed in behalf of debtors; and in New England open rebellion had broken out.

That the economic groups in question looked to a new national government as the one source of relief and advantage, is shown in a hundred contemporary pamphlets and newspaper articles. It was in fact the topic of the times.

For example, a letter from Philadelphia, under date of August 29, 1787, sums up concisely the interests which were turning to the new Constitution: "The states neglect their roads and canals, till they see whether those necessary improvements will not become the objects of a national government. Trading and manufacturing companies suspend their voyages and manufactures till they see how far their commerce will be protected and promoted by a national system of commercial regulations. The lawful usurer locks up or buries his specie till he sees whether the new frame of government will deliver him from the curse or fear of paper money and the tender laws. . . . The public creditor, who, from the deranged state of finances in every state and their total inability to support their partial funding systems, has reason to fear that his certificates will perish in his hands, now places all his hopes of justice in an enlightened and stable national government. The embarrassed farmer and the oppressed tenant, who wishes to become free . . . by emigrating to a frontier country, wait to see whether they shall be protected by a national force from the Indians." [1]

A final answer to the second question propounded above would require an exhaustive analysis of the " movement for the Constitution," in the following form: —

1. A study of the economic forces in the Revolution and particularly in the Continental Congress that drafted the Articles of Confederation.

---

[1] The Connecticut Courant, September 10, 1787.

2. An inquiry into the first signs of discontent with the prevailing system, their geographic distribution, and their economic sources.

3. An examination of the several attempts in the Congress under the Articles of Confederation to secure the power to regulate commerce and establish a revenue for discharging the debt.

4. A description of the economic interests of all the members who were most active in these attempts.

5. A description of the economic forces in the communities whose representatives in Congress were zealous in securing a revision of the Articles.

6. A study of the nature and distribution of the several legislative attacks on private rights in property between 1783 and 1787.

7. A minute study of the personnel of the movement for revision and the economic interests of the leading spirits in Congress and the state legislatures and outside of legislative chambers.

Any one superficially acquainted with the sources of American history will see at once the nature of the work which must be done to secure the raw materials for such a study. The enormous mass of unprinted papers of the Continental Congress in the Library at Washington would have to be thoroughly searched; proceedings in state legislatures during the years under consideration would have to be scrutinized; local archives and newspapers would have to be examined.

In the present state of our historical materials, therefore, all that can be attempted here is a superficial commentary on some of the outward aspects of the movement for the Constitution which are described in the conventional works on the subject. Many of the eminent men prominently

identified with the events which led up to the Convention
of 1787 were themselves members of that Assembly, and
their economic interests are considered below in Chapter V.
But it is not without significance to discover that some of
the leading men outside of the Convention who labored
for an overthrow of the old system were also directly interested in the results of their labors.

As early as January, 1781, General Philip Schuyler moved
in the senate of New York "to request the eastern states
to join in an early convention, which should form a perpetual league of incorporation, subservient, however, to
the common interest of all the states; invite others to accede to it; erect Vermont into a state; devise a fund for
the redemption of the common debts; substitute a permanent and uniform system for temporary expedients; and
invest the confederacy with powers of coercion."[1]   General
Schuyler was a large holder of depreciated securities.[2]

In February, 1781, Congress recommended to the states
that they vest in the national legislature a power to levy
a duty to pay the principal and interest of the debt. In
April, 1783, Congress again appealed to the states for
authority to lay duties for the purpose of supplying a
revenue with which to discharge the debt. Among the
leaders in Congress who favored this increase in power were
Gorham, Higginson, Ellsworth, Dyer, Boudinot, Fitzsimons,
Williamson, Izard, Johnson, and King, all of whom held
securities which were daily depreciating under the failure
of the government to meet its just obligations.[3]

In 1785, Governor Bowdoin, of Massachusetts, in his
inaugural address urged the necessity of a stronger union
with larger powers, and recommended a convention to de-

---

[1] Bancroft, *op. cit.*, Vol. I, p. 29.   [2] See below, p. 109.
[3] Elliot's *Debates*, Vol. I, p. 95. See below, Chaps. V and VII.

liberate upon the whole matter.[1]   Governor Bowdoin was
a large holder of public securities.[2]   The legislature of the
commonwealth, thereupon, resolved that the Articles of
Confederation were inadequate, and directed the representatives in Congress to take steps looking toward a
strengthening of the union; but they failed to act.

Men less eminent than Bowdoin and Schuyler were being
educated in Federalism by the march of events.   In Boston
merchants were petitioning Congress for relief from British
discriminations [3]; in the Virginia legislature the representatives of the commercial interests were learning their
lessons [4]; the demands for positive action were increasing
daily in number.   Every failure to find a remedy under the
Articles of Confederation only served to augment the ranks
of those who were ready for a complete reconstruction of the
prevailing system.

A few illustrations will serve to show how the demand for
reform was being fostered and also the connection between
the leaders in the agitation and the personnel of the public
bodies which later achieved the great work of framing and
ratifying the Constitution.   Even before the war was over
and the Articles of Confederation tested in a time of peace,
the inability of the government under it to afford defence
to commerce on the high seas was deplored by merchants
whose vessels were falling prey to the British.   In April,
1782, a number of prominent merchants presented a
petition to Congress in which they lamented the British
depredations on American trade and the want of adequate
naval protection at sea.[5]   Among the signers of this
petition were several men who were later known as warm

---

[1] Bancroft, op. cit., Vol. I, p. 190.   [2] See below, p. 263.
[3] See above, p. 46 n.   [4] Ambler, Sectionalism in Virginia, p. 48.
[5] Ms. Library of Congress: Papers of the Continental Congress (Memorials), No. 41,
Vol. VI, p. 283. Simpson, Eminent Philadelphians.

supporters of a strong federal government. One of them, Thomas Fitzsimons, was a member of the Convention which drafted the Constitution; another, John Barclay, was a member of the Pennsylvania convention and voted in favor of the ratification of the new system of government.

Six years before the Convention met in Philadelphia, the disordered financial system under the Confederation was the subject of protest by interested parties. In 1781, "divers inhabitants of the state of Pennsylvania," were petitioning Congress to take some action designed to put the credit of the country on a sound basis.[1] Thus runs the petition. "Humbly sheweth that whereas you thought fit heretofore in the course of your widsom to emit bills of credit for good and great purposes, but the same depreciating to such an amazing degree beyond the expectation of all living did therefore lay open wide door for the most monstrous and absurd injustices by fraudulent payments which we conclude is directly contrary to your good and great purposes in emitting the same, we therefore, not only firmly relying on the extraordinary clearness of the circumstances of our agrievances, but likewise on the uprightness of your understandings, Do therefore presume to pray your honors would be pleased to recommend to the several states to adopt such measures as they may think most likely to afford a safe and effectual redress to all such agrievances. . . ."[1] Among the signers to this petition are Thomas Bull, John Hannum, and Thomas Cheyney, who six years later as members of the Pennsylvania convention had the pleasure of voting for the ratification of an instrument of government that put an end to the evils against which they had so earnestly protested.

[1] *Ibid.*, No. 42, Vol. VI, p. 254.

The failure of repeated attempts in Congress to secure an amendment authorizing the laying of impost duties, the refusal of the states to pay the requisitions made by Congress, and the obvious impossibility of gaining their ends through the ordinary channels of ratification by state legislatures, drove the advocates of these measures to desperation. Republican government, as it had been tried out, had failed to secure for personalty that protection and opportunity for advancement which it enjoyed under monarchy. The despair of the representatives of the property interests thus jeopardized and their readiness for some heroic measures were fully manifest in the correspondence of the time.

Washington, who was not given to undue alarms, wrote to John Jay from Mount Vernon, on August 1, 1786, to the effect that men of leadership were ready for drastic action : "What astonishing changes," he said, " a few years are capable of producing. I am told that even respectable characters speak of a monarchical form of Government without horror. From thinking proceeds speaking, thence to acting is often but a single step. But how irrevocable and tremendous ! What a triumph for our enemies to verify their predictions — what a triumph for the advocates of despotism to find that we are incapable of governing ourselves, & that systems founded on the basis of equal liberty are merely ideal & fallacious ! Would to God that wise measures may be taken in time to avert the consequences we have but too much reason to apprehend." [1]

Later in that year, General Knox, who was a holder of public securities, wrote to Washington in the following strain : "The people who are the insurgents [Shaysites] have never paid any, or but very little taxes — But they see the weakness of government ; They feel at once their own

[1] *Documentary History of the Constitution*, Vol. IV, p. 20.

poverty, compared with the opulent, and their own force, and they are determined to make use of the latter, in order to remedy the former. Their creed is 'That the property of the United States has been protected from the confiscations of Britain by the joint exertions of all, and therefore ought to be the common property of all. And he that attempts opposition to this creed is an enemy to equity and justice, and ought to be swept from off the face of the earth.' In a word they are determined to annihilate all debts public and private and have agrarian Laws, which are easily effected by means of unfunded paper money which shall be a tender in all cases whatever —

"The numbers of these people may amount in Massachusetts to about one fifth part of several populous counties, and to them may be collected, people of similar sentiments, from the states of Rhode Island, Connecticut, and New Hampshire so as to constitute a body of 12 or 15000 desperate & unprincipled men — They are chiefly of the young and active part of the community, more easily collected than perhaps kept together afterwards — But they will probably commit overt acts of treason which will compel them to embody for their own safety — once embodied they will be constrained to submit to discipline for the same reason. Having proceeded to this length for which they are now ripe, we shall have a formidable rebellion against reason, the principle of all government, and the very name of liberty. This dreadful situation has alarmed every man of principle and property in New England. They start as from a dream, and ask what has been the cause of our delusion? what is to afford us security against the violence of lawless men? Our government must be braced, changed, or altered to secure our lives and property. We imagined that the mildness of our government and *the virtue* of the people were so correspondent, that we were not as other nations requiring brutal force to support the laws — But we find that we are men, actual men, possessing all the turbulent passions belonging to that anim[al] and that we must have a government proper and adequate for him. The people of Massachuse[tts] for instance, are far advanced in this doctrine, and the men of reflection, & principle, are determined to endev[or] to establish a government which shall have the power to protect them in their lawful pursuits, and which will be efficient in all cases of internal commotions or foreign invasions — They mean that liberty shall be the basis, a liberty resulting from the equal and firm administration of the laws. They wish for a general government of unity as they see the local legislatures must naturally and necessarily tend to retard and frustrate all general government." [1]

A few months later, Madison, writing to Edmund Pendleton from New York, the seat of the government, corroborated the views expressed by Washington and Knox and set forth what he conceived to be the desperate state of republican government. His letter, dated February 24, 1787, three days after Congress had issued the call for a national Convention, ran as follows: "In general I find men of reflection much less sanguine as to a new than despondent as to the present System. Indeed the Present System neither has nor deserves advocates; and if some very strong props are not applied will quickly tumble to the ground. . . . If the approaching Convention should not agree on some remedy, I am persuaded that some very different arrangement will ensue. The late turbulent scenes in Massachusetts & infamous ones in Rhode Island, have done inexpressible injury to the republican character in that part of the U. States; and a pro-

---

[1] *Documentary History of the Constitution*, Vol. IV, p. 30.

pensity towards Monarchy is said to have been produced by it in some leading minds. The bulk of the people will probably prefer the lesser evil of a partition of the Union into three more practicable and energetic Governments. The latter idea I find after long confinement to individual speculations & private circles, is beginning to show itself in the Newspapers."[1]

A few days after this letter was written by Madison, John Armstrong wrote to Washington from Carlisle that the suppression of the insurrection in Massachusetts had not allayed the fears of leading men in his state. "The alarming flame in Massachusetts," he says, "seems nearly extinguished, but if the subsequent measures of that State respecting the insurgents should be severe, amounting to *death*, Confiscation, or disfranchisement, the consequence may be bad, as tending to reinkindle the flame. Shall I tell you in *confidence*, I have now twice heard, nor from low authority (some principal men of that State) begin to talk of wishing one general *Head* to the Union, in the room of Congress !"[2]

By correspondence such as this just cited, by an increasing recognition of the desperate straights in which they were placed, a remarkable fusion of interested forces was effected. The wealth, the influence, and a major portion of the educated men of the country were drawn together in a compact group, "informed by a conscious solidarity of interests," as President Wilson has so tersely put it.[3]

Having failed to obtain relief through the regular channels of amendment by Congress ratified by the state legislatures, the leaders struck out on a new path. Operating through the Virginia legislature, they secured a resolution inviting

---

[1] *Ibid.*, Vol. IV, p. 83.   [2] *Ibid.*, Vol. IV, p. 88.
[3] *Division and Reunion*, p. 12.

the sister commonwealths to send delegates to a convention at Annapolis to take into consideration the trade and commercial system of the United States.[1] The convention duly met, but the attendance was so slim that, as Professor Burgess has put it, "a coup d'état attempted by so small a body could not but fail."[2]

Although the Annapolis convention was ostensibly concerned with commercial regulation primarily, there is no doubt that it was the creation of the men who had been working in Congress and out for a general revision of the whole system. There is no doubt also that it was not regarded as of much significance in itself, but rather as a preliminary to a national convention which would afford an opportunity for reconstructing the government. For this view we have a witness of high authority, James Madison, who in a letter of August 12, 1786, to Jefferson, written a month before the Annapolis conference, said: "Many gentlemen, both within and without Congress, wish to make this meeting subservient to a plenipotentiary Convention for amending the Confederation. Tho' my wishes are in favor of such an event, yet I despair so much of its accomplishment at the present crisis that I do not extend my views beyond a commercial Reform."[3]

Under the influence of Hamilton, the conference at Annapolis contented itself with merely recommending that another convention be called "to devise such further pro-

---

[1] James Monroe to James Madison. New York, September 3, 1786. "I consider the convention of Annapolis as a most important æra in our affairs — the eastern men be assur'd mean it as leading further than the object originally comprehended. If they do not obtain that things shall be arranged to suit them in every respect, their intrigues will extend to the objects I have suggested above — Pennsylvania is their object — upon succeeding or failing with her they will gain or lose confidence — I doubt not the emissaries of foreign countries will be on the ground." *Documentary History of the Constitution*, Vol. IV, p. 25.

[2] *Political Science and Constitutional Law*, Vol. I, p. 103.

[3] *Writings of James Madison* (1865), Vol. I, p. 246.

visions as shall appear to them necessary to render the constitution of the federal government adequate to the exigencies of the Union." Acting on this modest suggestion, Congress, in February, 1787, invited the states to send delegates to a Convention at Philadelphia for "the sole and express purpose of revising the Articles of Confederation."

Certain tentative conclusions emerge at this point.

Large and important groups of economic interests were adversely affected by the system of government under the Articles of Confederation, namely, those of public securities, shipping and manufacturing, money at interest; in short, capital as opposed to land.

The representatives of these important interests attempted through the regular legal channels to secure amendments to the Articles of Confederation which would safeguard their rights in the future, particularly those of the public creditors.

Having failed to realize their great purposes through the regular means, the leaders in the movement set to work to secure by a circuitous route the assemblying of a Convention to "revise" the Articles of Confederation with the hope of obtaining, outside of the existing legal framework, the adoption of a revolutionary programme.

Ostensibly, however, the formal plan of approval by Congress and the state legislatures was to be preserved.

CHAPTER IV

PROPERTY SAFEGUARDS IN THE ELECTION OF DELEGATES

UNDER the protection afforded by these outward signs of regularity, the leaders in the movement for the new Constitution set to work in their respective legislatures to secure the choice of delegates prepared to take the heroic measures which the circumstances demanded. The zealous and dynamic element, of course, was favored by the inertness, ignorance, and indifference of the masses, and the confidence of the legislatures in their ability to exercise the ultimate control through the ratifying power. No special popular elections were called to complicate the problem of securing the right kind of a Convention and the leaders were confronted with the comparatively simple task of convincing the legislatures of the advisibility of sending delegates. Naturally the most strenuous and interested advocates of change came forward as candidates.

The resolution of the Congress under the Articles of Confederation calling for the Convention provided that the delegates should be "appointed by the states." The actual selection was made in each case by the legislature, both houses participating, except in Georgia and Pennsylvania, which had unicameral assemblies. That is, the delegates to the federal Convention were selected in the same fashion as were United States Senators under the present Constitution, in all states, previous to the adoption of the principle of direct election. This fact in itself removed the choice of delegates one degree from the electorate.

A further safeguard against the injection of too much popular feeling into the choice of delegates to the Convention was afforded by the property qualifications generally placed on voters and members of the legislatures by the state constitutions and laws in force in 1787.[1] In order to ascertain the precise character of the defence afforded to property by this barrier to universal manhood suffrage, it is necessary to inquire in detail into the qualifications then imposed.[2]

The New Hampshire constitution of 1784 was in force when the call for the election of delegates came. It provided that "no person shall be capable of being elected a senator who is not of the Protestant religion, and seized of a freehold estate in his own right of the value of two hundred pounds."[3] Members of the lower house were required to possess an estate "of the value of one hundred pounds, one half of which to be a freehold." The suffrage was widely extended, for freeholders, tax payers, and even those who paid a poll tax could vote.

Massachusetts conferred the suffrage upon all males possessing a freehold estate of the annual income of three pounds, or any estate of the value of sixty pounds. A

[1] On the suffrage and elections in general in the eighteenth century, see the state constitutions in the well-known collections of Poore and Thorpe; A. E. McKinley, *The Suffrage Franchise in the Thirteen English Colonies;* Paullin's "The First Elections under the Constitution," Iowa Journal of History and Politics, Vol. II; Jameson, "Did the Fathers Vote," New England Magazine, January, 1890; Thorpe, *Constitutional History of the American People;* S. H. Miller, "Legal Qualifications for Office," *American Historical Association Report* (1899), Vol. I; F. A. Cleveland, *Growth of Democracy;* C. F. Bishop, *History of Elections in the American Colonies;* see below, Chap. IX.

[2] The data on the constitutions here given are taken from Thorpe's collection, *Charters, Constitutions,* etc.

[3] Senators were apportioned among the respective districts on the basis of public taxes paid by the said districts.

senator was required to be "seized in his own right of a freehold within this commonwealth, of the value of three hundred pounds at least, or possessed of a personal estate of the value of six hundred pounds at least, or of both to the amount of the same sum." Every member of the house of representatives was required to be "seized in his own right of a free hold of the value of one hundred pounds, within the town he shall be chosen to represent, or any ratable estate to the value of two hundred pounds; and he shall cease to represent the said town immediately on his ceasing to be qualified as aforesaid."

Like the neighboring state of Rhode Island, which sent no delegates to Philadelphia, Connecticut had continued after the Revolution under the old royal charter form of government without taking the trouble to draft a constitution. Under this old system, the suffrage was restricted to holders of real or personal property of a certain value. According to McKinley, "The forty-shilling freehold, translated later into seven dollars income from land, was retained as one of the alternative qualifications of the suffrage until the amendment in 1845 of the constitution of 1818."[1] The alternative qualification here spoken of was the ownership of forty pounds' worth of personal property, which was established in 1702 and remained until after the Revolution. The Connecticut Register of the time thus quaintly describes the franchise: "The qualifications for freemen are that they be at least twenty-one years of age, possessed of freehold estate to the value of 40s. per ann. or £40 personal estate in the general list of estates in that year wherein they desire to be admitted Freemen; or are possessed of estate as aforesaid and by law excused from putting it into the list; and being of quiet and peaceable behaviour."[2]

[1] *The Suffrage Franchise in the English Colonies*, p. 414.
[2] *Greene's Register for the State of Connecticut*, for the Year 1786, p. 4.

New York gave a special position to the rights of property
in the senate. Senators were required to be freeholders,
and were chosen by freeholders "possessed of freeholds of
the value of one hundred pounds." With regard to the
voter for members of the lower house, it was stipulated
that "he shall have been a freeholder, possessing a freehold
of the value of twenty pounds within said county, or have
rented a tenement therein of the yearly value of forty
shillings, and been rated and actually paid taxes to this
state." An exception to this rule conferred the suffrage
on all who were freemen in Albany, and in New York City,
on or before October 14, 1775.

These qualifications worked an extensive disfranchisement in New York. "The census of 1790 shows that out
of a population of thirty thousand [in New York City], there
were but 1,209 freeholders of £100 valuation or over; 1,221
of £20, and 2,661 'forty-shilling' freeholders. Property
interests — something like a landed aristocracy — controlled municipal elections." [1] Some notion of the extent
to which the adult males would have voted if permitted,
is afforded by the elections of 1788, at which members of the
state ratifying convention were chosen under the universal
manhood suffrage rule,[2] and members of the assembly
were chosen under the regular property qualifications.
For example, Richard Harrison received 2677 votes as
member of the convention, and 1500 votes as member of
the state assembly.[3] In Albany county the vote for members of the assembly ran about 1600 under that for members
of the convention.[4] It looks as if one could safely guess
that about one-third more voters would have been active

[1] Magazine of American History, April, 1893, p. 311.
[2] See below, p. 241.
[3] New York Journal, June 5, 1788.   [4] Ibid.

participants in elections if they had not been shut out by the prevailing property qualifications in New York.

New Jersey had a legislature of two houses, a council and a general assembly. Every member of the former had to be a freeholder and "worth at least one thousand pound proclamation money, or real and personal estate within the same county;" and every member of the latter body was required to possess at least half as much in real and personal property. As for the suffrage, the constitution provided "that all inhabitants of this colony, of full age, who are worth fifty pounds proclamation money clear estate in the same . . . shall be entitled to vote for Representatives in Council and Assembly."

The Delaware constitution of 1776 provided that members of both branches of the legislature should be chosen from among the freeholders of the county, and that "the right of suffrage in the election of members for both houses shall remain as exercised by law at present." The election law which then governed the suffrage in Delaware was the act of 1734 which enfranchised freeholders owning "fifty acres of land, with twelve acres cleared and improved, or otherwise worth £40 lawful money."[1]

The first constitution of Pennsylvania established in 1776 was the work of a radical party, and it provided for a single chambered legislature based on a widely extended suffrage. "Every freeman of the full age of twenty-one years," runs the instrument, "having resided in this state for the space of one whole year . . . and paid public taxes during that time, shall enjoy the right of an elector: *Provided* always that sons of freeholders of the age of twenty-one years shall be entitled to vote although they have not paid taxes."[2]

[1] McKinley, *The Suffrage Franchise in the English Colonies*, p. 270.

[2] Tench Coxe fixes the number of "taxables" in Pennsylvania at 39,765 in 1770 and 91,177 in 1793. *A View of the United States*, p. 413.

In Maryland a distinction was made between town and
county in the choice of delegates to the lower house of the
state legislature. Generally every freeman "having a freehold of fifty acres of land," or "having property in this
state above the value of thirty pounds current money"
could vote in the county in which he resided for members
of the house of delegates. All persons qualified by the
charter of Annapolis to vote for burgesses could vote for
delegates from that city ; and in Baltimore persons "having
the same qualifications as electors in the county" could vote
for delegates. County delegates in the state legislature
were required to possess "real or personal property above
the value of five hundred pounds current money." The
senators were chosen indirectly by electors selected by the
qualified voters for delegates. These senatorial electors
were to possess the qualifications of delegates, and senators
themselves had to possess "real and personal property above
the value of one thousand pounds current money."

The Virginia constitution of 1776 stipulated that members
of both houses of the legislature must be "freeholders or
duly qualified according to law ;" and added that "the right
of suffrage in the election of members of both houses shall
remain as exercised at present." Under this provision,
persons owning twenty-five acres of improved land or fifty
acres of unimproved land were admitted to the suffrage,
"together with certain artisans residing in Norfolk and
Williamsburg." [1]

At the time of choosing delegates to the Convention,
North Carolina was under the constitution of 1776 which
prescribed property qualifications for members of the legislature and for voters as well. Each member of the senate

[1] Ambler, *Sectionalism in Virginia*, p. 29, note 11; for details see McKinley, *op.
cit.*, pp. 40 ff.

was required to possess "not less than three hundred acres of land in fee," and each member of the lower house "not less than one hundred acres of land in fee or for the term of his own life." A freehold qualification of fifty acres of land was required of voters for senators, and the suffrage for voters for members of the lower house was extended to all freemen who paid "public taxes." In the towns entitled to representation the possession of a freehold or the payment of a public tax qualified for voting in the election of members of the lower house.

The legislature of South Carolina, that chose the representatives of that state to the Philadelphia Convention, was elected under the constitution of 1778 which prescribed high property qualifications.[1] "No person who resides in the parish for which he is elected shall take his seat in the senate, unless he possess a settled estate and freehold in his own right in the said parish or district of the value of two thousand pounds currency at least, clear of debt." Non-resident senators were required to be the holders of such an estate worth at least seven thousand pounds, clear of debt. The member of the lower house was required to possess an estate and slaves or realty worth one thousand pounds,[2] while each non-resident member of that house had to own a freehold estate worth at least three thousand five hundred pounds, clear of debt. The suffrage was restricted to persons owning fifty acres, or a town lot, or paying taxes equivalent to the taxes on fifty acres of land.

In 1787, the Georgia legislature consisted of one chamber, under the constitution of 1777, which stipulated that members of the house of representatives "Shall be of the Protestant religion, and of the age of twenty-one years, and

---

[1] Schaper, "Sectionalism in South Carolina," *American Historical Association Report* (1900), Vol. I, p. 368.   [2] *Statutes at Large* (S.C.), Vol. IV, p. 99.

shall be possessed in their own rights of two hundred and fifty acres of land or some property to the amount of two hundred and fifty pounds." The suffrage was widely extended to every white male having in his own right property "of ten pounds value and liable to pay tax" or "being of any mechanic trade."

From this review it is apparent that a majority of the states placed direct property qualifications on the voters, and the other states eliminated practically all who were not taxpayers. Special safeguards for property were secured in the qualifications imposed on members of the legislatures in New Hampshire, Massachusetts, New York, New Jersey, Maryland, North Carolina, South Carolina, and Georgia. Further safeguards were added by the qualifications imposed in the case of senators in New Hampshire, Massachusetts, New Jersey, New York, Maryland, North Carolina, and South Carolina.

While these qualifications operated to exclude a large portion of the adult males from participating in elections, the wide distribution of real property created an extensive electorate and in most rural regions gave the legislatures a broad popular basis.[1] Far from rendering to personal property that defence which was necessary to the full realization of its rights, these qualifications for electors admitted to the suffrage its most dangerous antagonists: the small farmers and many of the debtors who were the most active in all attempts to depreciate personalty by legislation. Madison with his usual acumen saw the inadequacy of such defence and pointed out in the Convention that the really serious assaults on property (having in mind of course, personalty) had come from the "freeholders."[2]

Nevertheless, in the election of delegates to the Conven-

[1] See below, p. 242.   [2] *Ibid.*, p. 167.

tion, the representatives of personalty in the legislatures were able by the sheer weight of their combined intelligence and economic power to secure delegates from the urban centres or allied with their interests. Happily for them, all the legislatures which they had to convince had not been elected on the issue of choosing delegates to a national Convention, and did not come from a populace stirred up on that question.[1] The call for the Convention went forth on February 21, 1787, from Congress, and within a few months all the legislatures, except that of Rhode Island, had responded. Thus the heated popular discussion usually incident to such a momentous political undertaking was largely avoided, and an orderly and temperate procedure in the selection of delegates was rendered possible.

[1] Some of the states selected delegates before Congress issued the call. Bancroft, *op. cit.*, Vol. I, pp. 269 ff.

CHAPTER V

THE ECONOMIC INTERESTS OF THE MEMBERS OF THE CONVENTION

HAVING shown that four groups of property rights were adversely affected by the government under the Articles of Confederation, and that economic motives were behind the movement for a reconstruction of the system, it is now necessary to inquire whether the members of the Convention which drafted the Constitution represented in their own property affiliations any or all of these groups. In other words, did the men who formulated the fundamental law of the land possess the kinds of property which were immediately and directly increased in value or made more secure by the results of their labors at Philadelphia? Did they have money at interest? Did they own public securities? Did they hold western lands for appreciation? Were they interested in shipping and manufactures?

The purpose of such an inquiry is not, of course, to show that the Constitution was made for the personal benefit of the members of the Convention. Far from it. Neither is it of any moment to discover how many hundred thousand dollars accrued to them as a result of the foundation of the new government. The only point here considered is: Did they represent distinct groups whose economic interests they understood and felt in concrete, definite form through their own personal experience with identical property rights, or were they working merely under the guidance of abstract principles of political science?

Unfortunately, the materials for such a study are very scanty, because the average biographer usually considers as negligible the processes by which his hero gained his livelihood. The pages which follow are, therefore, more an evidence of what ought to be done than a record of results actually accomplished. They would be meagre, indeed, were it not for the rich unpublished records of the Treasury Department which are here used for the first time in this connection; and they would doubtless have been fuller were it not for the fact that most of the books showing the central operations of the Treasury Department under Hamilton have disappeared. The names of the attending members of the Convention are given in alphabetical order.

Of *Abraham Baldwin's* private fortune there is little known. His father was evidently well-to-do, for he enjoyed the advantage of a classical education at Yale before he established himself in the practice of law at Savannah, Georgia. He soon rose to eminence in his profession, and was reckoned among the ablest and shrewdest lawyers of his adopted commonwealth. A short sketch of him states that by "his constant habits of economy and temperance," he accumulated enough to enable him to assist many young men in their education and establishment in business. When his father died, in 1787, he was able to pay the debts of the insolvent estate, and he educated his six half brothers and sisters "in a great measure at his own expense." [1]

Some portion of Baldwin's fortune was invested in public securities. He possessed a few thousand dollars worth of the stocks of the new government at its very inception, which doubtless represented old paper of the Confederation acquired by original subscription or by purchase. The ledgers and other principal records of Georgia are appar-

---

[1] Herring, *National Portrait Gallery*, Vol. IV.

ently unavailable — at all events a search at the Treasury Department failed to reveal them; but Baldwin held some paper which is entered on the books of his native state, Connecticut, in April, 1792: deferred 6 per cents, funded 6 per cents, and 3 per cents to the amount of about $2500.[1]

At later dates, 1797 and 1804, he appears on the Treasury Records for several thousand dollars worth of 6 per cents and 3 per cents, but the sources of these sums are not apparent.[2] It is probable, however, that these stocks were paper which Baldwin funded at the Treasury instead of a loan office. He was a member of Congress, and naturally would have transacted business with the agency nearest at hand. They may, of course, represent purchases for investment, made after the great appreciation had taken place.[3]

There is no exhaustive biography of *Richard Bassett*, of Delaware. A brief sketch of him relates that he "was born in 1745. He was the adopted son of Mr. Lawson, a lawyer, who married a Miss Inzer. The Inzer family was Herman's heir to Bohemia Manor. . . . Mr. Bassett was educated and trained for the profession of law by Mr. Lawson, whose heir he became. By this inheritance he came into possession of six thousand acres of Bohemia manor, which we are informed, embraced the fairest and best portion of

---

[1] Ms. Treasury Department: *Connecticut Loan Office, Ledger B, Assumed Debt,* folio 135; *ibid., Ledger C,* folio 135; *ibid., Ledger A,* folio 136.

[2] *Ibid., Ledger E, Treasury,* Vol. 44, folio 46; *Ledger C, Treasury,* 6 per cents, Vol. 42, folio 55; and Treasury Ledgers, *passim.* Consult Index.

[3] It is here assumed that when a member of the Convention appears upon the funding books of the new government he was a public creditor at the time of the Convention. Of course, it is possible that some of the members who are recorded as security holders possessed no paper when they went to Philadelphia, but purchased it afterward for speculation. But it is hardly to be supposed that many of them would sink to the level of mere speculators. There is plenty of evidence for the statement that many of the members did possess public paper *before* the meeting of the Convention, but the incompleteness of the old records prevents the fixing of the exact number. Those members who purchased after the Convention for speculation must have had idle capital seeking investment.

the Manor." [1]   Through his inheritance and his accumulations in the practice of law, he became one of the wealthy men of his state. Another biographer notes that "His fortune was large and he entertained lavishly at his three homes in Wilmington, Dover, and at Bohemia Manor." [2] He was on intimate terms with the leading financial men of the community; he was very active in securing a charter in Delaware for the Bank of North America when it was attacked by the Pennsylvania legislature, and was warmly thanked for his success by President Willing, in a letter dated February 6, 1786. [3]

Whether any considerable amount of Mr. Bassett's large fortune was invested in public securities at the inception of the new government it is impossible to ascertain, on account of the meagre records of the state of Delaware preserved in the Treasury Department. In the later documents of the central office of the Treasury there appears the remnant of "an old account" to the amount of a few hundred dollars worth of 3 per cents and 6 per cents under dates of 1796 and 1797. [4] A reasonable inference from the entry would be that Bassett, like other members of Congress, carried on his transactions directly with the Treasury (whose early records are missing), and that these holdings were based on paper originally funded.

Gunning Bedford, of Delaware, was the son of a "substantial land owner" [5] and a Bedford of that name appears on the tax lists of Newcastle county for the year 1776 for the amount of sixteen pounds, a moderate sum for those

---

[1] *Papers of the Delaware Historical Society*, No. XXIX (1900).

[2] *National Encyclopædia of Biography*, Vol. XI, p. 530.

[3] *History of the Bank of North America*, p. 68.

[4] Ms. Treasury Department: *Ledger E, Treasury*, Vol. 44, folio 26; and *ibid.*, *Ledger C, Treasury*, 6 per cents, Vol. 42, folio 33.

[5] *National Encyclopædia of Biography*, Vol. XI, p. 530.

days.[1] He was a lawyer, but the extent of his practice is not known. He was of high standing in the community, and was elected governor of his state a few years after the Convention met. He took an interest in the financial affairs of the state, and under his administration as governor the Bank of Delaware was organized. How far Bedford had an interest in public securities cannot be determined on account of the fact that only a few scraps of the loan office papers for Delaware seem to be preserved in the Treasury Department. An old loan office volume shows a Gunning Bedford down for one $400 certificate of May, 1779[2] and traces of the financial connections of the member of the Convention with the government are to be found in the Pennsylvania loan office records.[3]

John Blair, of Virginia, was born in that state about 1731. He received a collegiate education, prepared for the law, and "in a very few years rose to the head of his profession."[4] Pierce, in his notes on the men of the Convention, says: "Mr. Blair is one of the most respectable men in Virginia, both on account of his Family as well as fortune. He is one of the Judges of the Supreme Court of Virginia, and acknowledged to have a very extensive knowledge of the Laws. Mr. Blair is however no orator, but his good sense and most excellent principles compensate for other deficiencies."[5]

Blair took advantage of the excellent opportunity afforded by the formation of the new Constitution to profit by the rise of securities. He appears frequently in the

[1] Delaware Mss., *Tax Lists;* Library of Congress. This was probably the father of the member of the Convention.

[2] Ms. Treasury Department: *Loan Office, Delaware,* 1777–1784, see under date, May, 1779.

[3] *Journal C; Register of Certificates* (1777); and *Ledger C.*

[4] *Biographia Americana,* p. 48.

[5] Farrand, *Records,* Vol. III, p. 95.

fiscal transactions between the federal government and the Virginia loan office, of which a few illustrations need be given here. In March, 1791, he presented £577 : 16 : 7 in Virginia certificates toward the United States loan; and of these securities £249 had been invested by Blair himself in 1782. The remaining amount he had purchased on his own account.[1] In the same year an agent of Blair presented two small certificates which had evidently been purchased by the principal because they were issued to other parties in 1778.[2] In September of that year, Blair himself turned in nearly $10,000 worth of paper on the United States loan, of which a part was purchased and a part original issues to the holder.[3]

William Blount, of North Carolina, was the son of Jacob Blount who died in 1789, "leaving a large estate."[4] Of the younger Blount's property interests in 1787 it is impossible to speak in detail. Very early after the establishment of the new government he was connected with land speculations on a large scale.[5] In 1790 he was appointed by Washington to the post of governor of the Territory South of the Ohio and it seems that he did not consider the employment of public office for personal gain as incompatible with the discharge of his administrative duties. In July, 1797, President Adams sent a message to Congress asserting that there was a conspiracy in the southwest to wrest New Orleans and the Floridas from the King of Spain and transfer them to the English crown, and adding that Blount, who was then a Senator from Tennessee, was implicated in the plot. The United States Senate immediately took action, and

---

[1] Ms. Treasury Department: *Loan Office (Va.) Register of Subscriptions*, 1791, see date March 8, 1791.

[2] *Ibid., Register of Certificates of Public Debt Presented.*

[3] *Ibid., Virginia Loan Office*, 1791, under date September 30, 1791.

[4] *National Encyclopædia of Biography*, Vol. VII, p. 206.

[5] Haskins, *The Yazoo Companies*, p. 83.

after inquiry expelled him by a vote of twenty-five to one on the charge of "high misdemeanor inconsistent with public trust and duty." When the sergeant-at-arms went to arrest him and take him to Philadelphia for trial he refused to go; and in his refusal he was warmly supported by his friends, of whom he had a legion, for, as his biographer remarks, "He was a man of commanding presence, courtly yet simple manners, and having a large salary and large private means, he entertained lavishly at his house."[1]

It does not appear that Blount combined dealings in securities with speculations in land, for the loan office of North Carolina credits him with only a small holding, and the origin of that is not apparent.[2] It is true that the records of that state are incomplete, but Blount's appointment to the western post at the beginning of Washington's administration must have precluded extensive operations in securities.

David Brearley, of New Jersey, was the grandson of John Brearley, who "owned 1600 acres of land near Newton, N. J. . . . a hundred acre plantation on the Delaware . . . besides several thousand acres of land near Lawrenceville."[3] A brief sketch of him states that he "received the honors of Princeton at the age of eighteen. On leaving that celebrated seminary, he commenced the study of law, and in a few years stood foremost at the bar of his native state."[4] In 1779 he was appointed chief justice of New Jersey, a post which he held until 1789 when he resigned to accept a position as judge of the United States district court of that state.[5]

---

[1] *Encyclopædia of Biography,* Vol. VII, p. 206.
[2] Ms. Treasury Department: *Loan Office, N. C., 1791–1797,* folio 75.
[3] *The Brearley Family Genealogy* (Library of Congress).
[4] *Biographia Americana,* p. 49.
[5] L. Elmer, *Constitution and Government of New Jersey,* p. 274.

Brearley died in the summer of 1790 and consequently could not have established any fiscal relations with the new government. The incompleteness of the early loan office records for New Jersey, preserved in the Treasury Department, renders impossible a positive statement concerning Brearley's holdings of securities at the time of the Convention. Only one small entry appears in his name for a few hundred dollars in a certificate purchased in 1779 ;[1] his relatives, however, appear frequently on the loan office books of his state; but their aggregate holdings were small. Joseph Brearley's name occurs several times, for example in July, 1791, for $505.80 worth of 3 per cents ;[2] David Brearley had a son and a brother bearing that name.[3] Elizabeth Brearley is also among the small holders, and the Chief Justice's first and second wife and a daughter bore that name.[4] The name of Zerujah Brearley — a sister of the member of the Convention[5] — also appears.

Jacob Broom, of Delaware, was born at Wilmington, in 1752. His father "originally a blacksmith was regarded as one of 'the gentry' of the day, and was 'a man of considerable substance, in real estate, silver, and gold,' although not one of the very wealthiest of his class. 'Class' distinctions, arising from birth, education, and worldly possessions were not wholly ignored at that time by those who came to this land to find a home, a sanctuary, and liberty. And so in the transactions of the period we find James Broom, Jacob's father, referred to as James Broom, Gentleman; and Jacob Broom as Surveyor. And both of these men had

---

[1] Ms. Treasury Department: *Register — Loan Office, N. J.*, under date, Feb. 1779.

[2] *Ibid., Loan Office, N. J., Ledger* C/2, folio 38.

[3] *Brearley Family Genealogy* (L. C.).

[4] See records in Treasury for N. J. Loan Office, *passim*; also *Family Genealogy*.

[5] *Genealogy.*

lands and houses to rent and sell and gold and silver to loan on good security. And both of them sold and rented and loaned." [1]

Broom was a man of diversified financial resources. He was interested in cotton mills and other enterprises. He was one of the original stockholders of the Insurance Company of North America organized at Philadelphia in 1792. [2] He was also one of the organizers and original stockholders of the Delaware Bank established under Bedford's administration. [3] As mentioned above, the fragmentary records of Delaware in the Treasury Department throw little light on the public security holders of that state at the time of the formation of the Constitution; but the ledgers of the central Treasury show that Broom was a holder of a small amount of 3 per cents in 1797 and that this was a remnant of an older account. [4] Broom was also willing to serve the new government in an official capacity, for he applied to Madison in April, 1789, for an appointment as collector at Wilmington. [5]

Pierce Butler, of South Carolina, was a descendant of the Duke of Ormond and was very vain of his noble birth. [6] William Pierce in his notes on the members of the Convention records that Butler "is a gentleman of fortune and takes rank among the first in South Carolina." [7] He was a large slave holder, having thirty-one in his possession at the time of the first census. He also possessed some public securities, for he was a stockholder and director of the first United

[1] W. W. Campbell, *Life and Character of Jacob Broom*, Papers of the Historical Society of Delaware, Vol. LI, pp. 10, 26.

[2] *History of the Insurance Company of North America*, p. 138.

[3] Campbell, *op. cit.*, p. 26.

[4] Ms. Treasury Department: *Ledger E, Treasury*, 3%, Vol. 44, folio 57; also *ibid.*, *Ledger C, Treasury*, 6%, Vol. 42, folio 67.

[5] *Calendar Madison Correspondence*, under Broom.

[6] *National Encyclopædia of Biography*, Vol. II, p. 162.

[7] Farrand, *Records*, Vol. III, p. 97.

States Bank, and must have purchased his shares on the same basis as other stockholders, that is, by the exchange of securities. He does not appear on the records of South Carolina, however, but his daughter, Sarah, had in 1792 a small amount of the assumed debt.[1]

Daniel Carroll, of Maryland, is recorded by his contemporary, Pierce, as "a man of large fortune and influence in his state." [2] His interests were wide and varied. He was a stockholder in the Potomac Company;[3] and he favored the adoption of a protective tariff, for he was among the signers of the petition for such a measure laid before the first Congress under the new Constitution.[4] He was a holder of public securities, for his name occurs frequently in the Treasury records of the period.[5] His chief source of profit out of the new system was however in the location of the capitol at Washington, on land which he owned.[6] Incidentally, he was able to facilitate this last transaction, for he was a member of the Congress of 1789-1791 and was one of the commissioners appointed to lay out the District of Columbia.

George Clymer, of Pennsylvania, was the son of "a well-

---

[1] Ms. Treasury Department: *Loan Office, S. C., 1791–1797,* folio 128. The entry in the ledger notes the residence of Sarah Butler as Charleston; there was another Sarah Butler in South Carolina at the time, but according to the first Census she did not reside in that city. For the evidence that Sarah Butler was the daughter of Pierce Butler, see Salley, *South Carolina Marriages,* p. 108, for the record of her marriage.

[2] Farrand, *Records,* Vol. III, p. 93.

[3] Madison Ms: Letter to James Madison, October 28, 1787. Library of Congress.

[4] *State Papers: Finance,* Vol. I, p. 6.

[5] Ms. Treasury Department: *Loan Office, Maryland, 1790–1797,* folio 98; *Loan Office,* Penna., 1790–1791, folio 94; *Ledger C, 3% Stock (Pa.),* folio 54. *Alphabet to Dividend Book of Domestic Debt, Maryland,* under "C" (book not found). Charles Carroll was also a holder of securities. Ms. Treasury Department: *Maryland Loan Office, 1790–1797,* folios 157 and 226 for over $5000 worth of sixes and threes.

[6] Scharf, *History of Western Maryland,* Vol. I, p. 679; H. Crew, *History of Washington,* p. 108.

to-do merchant and ship builder of Philadelphia" who had augmented his fortunes by marrying the daughter of a fellow merchant of the same city.[1] On the early death of his parents he was placed under the guardianship of William Coleman, one of the first business men of his native city, whose counting house he entered to learn all the arts of mercantile pursuits and "the principal part of whose fortune he inherited."[2] Clymer's personal fortune was further enhanced by a happy marriage to Elizabeth Meredith, the daughter of Reese Meredith, "one of the principal merchants of Philadelphia."[3] He was thus a brother-in-law of Mr. Meredith the first treasurer of the Union, also a man of "large fortune."[4] For some time Clymer was associated in business with his father- and brother-in-law.[5]

Mr. Clymer's intimate associations were therefore mercantile and financial, and his large fortune and quick understanding of the needs of trade and commerce made him one of the first men of his city in the Revolution and gave him a wide influence during the critical period, the formation of the Constitution, and the establishment of the new government, which he served as a member of Congress and later in several official capacities.

In all financial matters he took a deep interest. He helped to create the temporary Bank of Pennsylvania in 1780, and subscribed £5000 to its capital stock. When the Bank of North America was organized he became one of the directors and later was president of the Philadelphia Bank.[6]

Clymer turned his extensive financial experience to some

[1] *Magazine of American History*, Vol. V, p. 196.
[2] Sanderson, *Biography of the Signers* (1831 ed.), Vol. III, p. 147.
[3] Sanderson, *ibid.*, p. 150.
[4] Simpson, *Lives of Eminent Philadelphians* (1859 ed.), p. 693.
[5] Sanderson, *ibid.*, p. 147.
[6] McMaster and Stone, *Pennsylvania and the Federal Constitution*, p. 705.

account in handling the securities of the new government which he had been instrumental in framing, for he is recorded in the Pennsylvania books as holding, in August, 1791, over $3000 worth of 3 per cent securities.[1] If he held sixes deferred and funded, as may be assumed, although the incomplete records apparently do not permit of a verification or denial of this, he had in all over $10,000 worth of the government paper.

Wm. R. Davie, of North Carolina, was born in England in 1756 and was brought to America in 1763 by his father, who left him in care of his maternal uncle, William Richardson, a Presbyterian clergyman, who took charge of his education and on his death bequeathed to him his estate.[2] Davie chose the profession of law, and by a lucrative practice "he quickly accumulated a large estate."[3] He was of counsel in the famous case of Bayard *v.* Singleton, and he had the satisfaction of securing from the court an opinion declaring an act of the state legislature unconstitutional.[4] He held a fine plantation at Tivoli and at his death left a considerable estate which was the subject of litigation as late as 1892 in the Supreme Court of the United States. His personal property certainly was not small for he was able to pay $5000 for a thorough-bred colt.[5] His connections with the landed proprietors of his region were intimate and extensive and he is reported to have drawn all the wills made during his time in that part of the state.[6]

---

[1] Ms. Treasury Department: *Ledger C*, 3% Stock, *Pa.*, folio 231; see also *Ledger E, Treasury*, 3%, Vol. 44, folio 170; and *Ledger C, Treasury*, 6%, Vol. 42, folio 114. The existence of this latter small account in sixes in 1797 is the basis for the surmise above that Clymer held also his quota of sixes. With his business acumen he might very well have disposed of most of this stock after "taking the rise" in 1787–1792, for he could have made more money in business than from the interest which the government paid.

[2] Peele, *Lives of Distinguished North Carolinians*, p. 59.

[3] *Ibid.*, p. 69.   [4] *Ibid.*, p. 69.

[5] *Ibid.*, p. 80.   [6] *Ibid.*, p. 78.

Jonathan Dayton, of New Jersey, was associated with, and agent for, John Cleves Symmes, in the purchase of an enormous tract of land in Ohio in July and October, 1787, the year of the Convention (formally consummated in 1788), and before the ensealing of the contract Symmes and his associates had paid into the Treasury $82,198 "one seventh in military rights and the residue in the public securities of the United States." The remainder was to be paid in gold or silver or the securities of the United States, and part (one seventh) in military rights. In 1792 Symmes and Dayton complained that on account of the "advanced price of certificates," they must have easier terms. It is apparent from this record,[1] that they were engaged in buying up military certificates and government securities about the time of the meeting of the Convention.

Afterward, by collusion with Ludlow, the official surveyor, and the inadvertence of Hamilton, Secretary of the Treasury, Symmes, Dayton, and associates secured "the advantage of paying almost two-sevenths of their contract and above one-half of their actual payments in military warrants of one acre for an acre and a half of the supposed million, instead of one-seventh part of the actual payments" at a loss to the United States of more than $30,000.[2] In March and April, 1800, Dayton purchased about 15,000 acres of public lands with military certificates.[3]

If further evidence were needed that Dayton was speculating vigorously in government securities and military certificates, it is to be found in a suit brought by him and his partner, Lawrence, against Childs, a member of their concern in 1800, which was carried before Chancellor Livingston and later withdrawn. In this case Childs ex-

---

[1] *State Papers: Public Lands*, Vol. I, pp. 104–106.
[2] *Ibid.*, p. 129.   [3] *Ibid.*, p. 118.

hibited sixteen letters from Dayton, showing that while the latter was Speaker of the House of Representatives he had been engaged in speculations in public land warrants. Dayton was not unaware of the improper character of such transactions, for in a letter of April 17, 1796, he wrote to Childs: "The contents of this letter are of such a nature as to render it improper to be seen by any except yourself; burn it therefore, when you have perused it." [1]

The conclusive evidence of Dayton's extensive operations in public securities during the period of the establishment of the new government and his term of service as Speaker is afforded by the records of the Treasury Department. Here he appears so frequently on the books of the loan offices of several states that some pages of this volume would be required to present the bare data of his transactions. However, a few examples of his dealings may be given by way of illustration. He appears on the loan office books of New York in February and March, 1791, for the following amounts: $17,060.82, $8530.40, $11,332.93, $7401.31, $3700.73, and $5100.61, totalling more than $50,000.[2] At another point he is recorded for more than $15,000;[3] and at another point for $6000.[4] Although Woods is not celebrated for the painstaking impartiality of his famous *History of Adams' Administration*, he is singularly accurate in one of his characterizations: "Jonathan Dayton, of New Jersey, the late speaker of Congress, is notorious from Boston to Georgia. The deeds of other members of Congress were scarcely known beyond the circle of their respective states, but the speculations of this man have rung throughout the western world."[5]

[1] John Wood, *Suppressed History of the Administration of John Adams*, pp. 149 ff.
[2] Ms. Treasury Department: *N. Y. Loan Office, 1791*, folio 130.
[3] *Ibid., N. Y. Office, Deferred 6%, 1790–1796*, folio 208.
[4] *Ibid., Ledger B, New York Office, Deferred 6% Stock, 1790*, folio 55.
[5] J. Wood, *Suppressed History of the Administration of John Adams* (1846 ed.), p. 145.

John Dickinson, of Delaware, was a member of one of the established landed families of the south. He was born in 1732, on a plantation in Talbot County, on the eastern shores of Maryland; and eight years after his birth, his father, Samuel Dickinson moved from Maryland to Delaware "where he purchased a large estate in Kent County, near Dover." [1] Dickinson was a student of law in the Middle Temple and took up the practice of his profession in Philadelphia in 1757.[2] Within five years he had acquired an extensive practice and won a respectable standing at the bar.

If his personal fortunes, however, had not been sufficient to assure him a satisfactory position in the business and professional world at Philadelphia, his marriage into one of the first and wealthiest commercial families would have more than made up for his deficiencies.

In 1770 he married Mary Norris, and for a time lived at the family estate, Fairhill, one of the show places of the day : "This house," says Simpson,[3] "was in its day a very grand mansion and a place of great celebrity, with a large front of sixty feet. It was surrounded by forest and evergreen trees of majestic growth and well-arranged shrubbery. It commanded a beautiful prospect of the city, with a distant view of the Delaware. . . . The mansion was two stories high and most substantially built, with a very wide hall running through its centre. The library was papered, but the parlors and hall were wainscotted with oak and red cedar unpainted, but polished with wax and kept in bright and handsome order by constant rubbing. The carriage way was finely graduated and wound through an extensive lawn, from its approach on the Germantown road which was bordered with shrubbery. The pleasure grounds,

---

[1] Stillé, *Life and Times of John Dickinson*, p. 14.
[2] *Ibid*, p. 35.   [3] *Eminent Philadelphians*, p. 747.

lawn, green house, and gardens, fish-ponds, and walks, embraced a large area of several acres in extent." It is true the vast estates bequeathed to Miss Norris by her father were transferred to collateral male heirs in order to preserve the family holding and name, but she retained the "considerable personal property" which her father left to her.[1] Dickinson was able to make a large gift to Dickinson College, named in his honor; and he and his wife were widely celebrated for their extensive benefactions.[2]

The meagreness of the Treasury records for Delaware make it impossible to determine whether Dickinson was engaged in fiscal operations along with his intimate friends, Robert Morris, Thomas Willing, George Clymer, and other prominent Philadelphia men of affairs. It is possible that he was not largely engaged in the public security transactions,[3] for he was an extremely cautious man in finances, and had got into serious discredit with the patriot party during the Revolution, because it was rumored that he had advised his brother against accepting the payment of debts in paper which was sure to depreciate. He was also unhappily involved with Robert Morris to the amount of £7000 at the time of the latter's embarrassment, and may not have wished to incur further risks.[4]

Oliver Ellsworth, of Connecticut, was the son of a clever Connecticut farmer who inherited a hundred pounds and "had the industry and the shrewdness to accumulate a considerable estate and to win the reputation of an excellent farmer."[5] Oliver was educated at Yale and Princeton and became a lawyer in spite of his father's determination to

---

[1] Stillé, p. 331.   [2] *Ibid.*, p. 327.
[3] The Index in the Treasury Department gives the name of John Dickinson among the security holders, but the volume referred to was not found.
[4] Morris Ms. in the Library of Congress, *Private Letter Book*, Vol. III, p. 160.
[5] G. Brown, *The Life of Oliver Ellsworth*, p. 11.

force him into the ministry. Though he was almost brief-
less during the early days of his practice, he had the good
fortune to wed the daughter of William Wolcott, of East
Windsor, "a gentleman of substance and distinction." [1]
He is described by his biographer as a man of great purpose,
persistency, and of little imagination, and he rose rapidly
to wealth and power at the bar of his native state. "It
is doubtful," says Brown, "if in the entire history of the
Connecticut bar any other lawyer has ever in so short a
time accumulated so great a practice. . . . Measured
either by the amount of his business or by his earnings, it
was unrivalled in his own day and unexampled in the history
of the colony. Naturally shrewd, and with nothing of the
spendthrift in his nature, he quickly earned a competence,
and by good management he increased it to a fortune which
for the times and the country was quite uncommonly large.
From a few documents still in existence it is clear that he
became something of a capitalist and investor. He bought
lands and houses and loaned out money at interest. He
was a stockholder in the Hartford Bank and one of the
original subscribers to the stock of the old Hartford Broad-
cloth Mill (1788)."

With that natural shrewdness and economy which his
latest biographer ascribed to him, Ellsworth accumulated
a by no means negligible amount in public securities from
which he profited by the rise of credit that accompanied
the establishment of the new government. He was among
the first citizens of Connecticut to have his paper funded
into the new government securities, for he appears in December, 1791, with $1330.50 in deferred sixes, $2660.98 in
funded sixes, and $1995.75 in 3 per cents.[2] His wife,

[1] Brown, *ibid.*, p. 23.
[2] Ms. Treasury Department: *Connecticut Loan Office, Ledgers A, B, and C*, folio 21 in each volume.

Abigail, and other members of her family, the Wolcotts, had also invested in securities.[1]

William Few, of Georgia, was almost unique among the members of the Convention in being a representative, in origin and education, of the small farming class. His father was a Maryland farmer who was led by a successive failure of crops to try his fortune in North Carolina, where young Few labored with the ax and plow. Even here the elder Few did not prosper, and he became so deeply involved in debt that his son had to take over the management of his property. William, afterward, in 1776, settled in Georgia, and soon became engaged in politics and the Revolutionary War.

At the close of the War, he relates, "I possessed not much property nor had I any expectation that I did not acquire by my own industry. I therefore determined to commence the practice of law, although I had never spent one hour in the office of an attorney to prepare for business, nor did I know anything of the practice." He adds, however, that his practice grew in spite of his deficiencies and that his "pecuniary prospects were very flattering," by the time he was elected a member of the Convention. At all events he acquired a plantation in Columbia County, and after the expiration of his term as Senator in 1793, he retired there and engaged in agricultural pursuits. In 1799 he left Georgia for New York, where he managed his small fortune in real and personal property, according to his own estimate, about $100,000.[2]

Few's personal interest in the new government was probably rather small, but the absence of the full records of Georgia from the books of the Treasury Department renders

[1] Consult same volumes through the Index.
[2] Facts here are taken from his *Autobiography,* in the Magazine of American History, Vol. VII, pp. 343 ff.

impossible a categorical statement. He was connected with the Georgia Union Company, which was involved in the Yazoo land deals;[1] and he presented for funding a certificate of the issue of 1779 to the amount of $2170 nominal value, which he had secured from one Spears.[2] His name appears occasionally on other records for small amounts, and the index in the office of the Register of the Treasury cites him as being among the security holders recorded in a volume not found.[3]

Thomas Fitzsimons, of Pennsylvania, was intimately identified with the mercantile interests of his city. He is described as "an extensive merchant," and his family connections were with people engaged in his own line. He married the daughter of Robert Meade, and established business relations with his brother-in-law "who was one of the prominent merchants and shipowners of Philadelphia."[4] It is recorded of him that "His influence in the country and especially among merchants was second to none. . . . Mr. Fitzsimons was one of those efficient and able men who laid the foundations of the commercial and financial systems of the United States."[5] It is not surprising to find that he was also a "conspicuous advocate of a protective tariff."[6]

Like his prominent associates in Philadelphia, Mr. Fitzsimons combined mercantile and financial operations. He was "for a long time a director in the Bank of North America and President of the Insurance Company of North America, in which latter office he continued until his death."[7] Indeed

[1] Haskins, *The Yazoo Land Companies*, p. 81.
[2] Ms. Treasury Department: *Register of Certificates of Public Debt Presented to the Auditor of the Treasury.*
[3] Volume 31, folio 346.
[4] McMaster and Stone, *Pennsylvania and the Federal Constitution*, p. 706.
[5] Simpson, *Eminent Philadelphians*, p. 373.
[6] McMaster and Stone, *op. cit.*, p. 707.
[7] Simpson, *op. cit.*, 373.

he was so extensively involved in the speculations of Robert Morris that his resources were seriously crippled by the failure of that gentleman.[1]

His intimate knowledge of finance and his immediate business connections doubtless invited him to deal in public securities; and Maclay sets him down among the speculators as follows : "The Speaker gives me this day his opinion that Mr. Fitzsimons was concerned in this business [of speculating] as well as Mr. Morris, and that they stayed away (from Congress) for the double purpose of pursuing their speculation and remaining unsuspected."[2]   It is probable that Maclay's version is correct, for in 1791 Fitzsimon's agent, Michael Conner, presented for him certificates of 1778 to the amount of nearly $12,000 nominal value which he had evidently bought up.[3] He appears also on the records of the 6 per cents and the threes for small amounts, and his operations extended beyond his native state.[4]

Fitzsimons was also involved extensively in land speculations with Robert Morris, for the latter in a letter of October 9, 1795, writes to James Marshall, their European agent, to the effect that Fitzsimons and he had put on sale in London "about 360,000 acres of land situated in Georgia."[5] But as pointed out above Fitzsimons' relations with Morris cost him dearly and snatched away from him all that he had made in public securities and more besides.

Benjamin Franklin, of Pennsylvania, in the midst of his

---

[1] Sumner, *The Financier and the Finances of the Revolution,* Vol. II, p. 294.

[2] Maclay, *Journal* (1890 ed.), p. 178.

[3] Ms. Treasury Department: *Register of Certificates of Public Debt Presented to the Auditor of the Treasury.*

[4] *Ibid.,* See *Ledger E, Treasury, 3%,* Vol. 44, folio 335. Also *Ledger C, Treasury, 6%,* Vol. 42, folio 300 for small entries.

[5] Morris Mss. in the Library of Congress: *Private Letter Book,* Vol. I, p. 529. Marshall (a brother of John Marshall) was the confidential and trusted agent of Morris in large transactions in land.

varied activities as printer, diplomat, statesman, and philosopher, managed withal by thrift and investments to accumulate a considerable fortune for his day, about $150,000.[1] At his great age on the assembling of the Convention, it would hardly have been practicable for him to have engaged in investments in public securities had he been so inclined; and he died in 1790, before the funding system went into effect. A short time before his death, however, he was interested in land speculations;[2] and in his will he bequeaths "lands near the Ohio" and three thousand acres granted by the State of Georgia to him.[3] He does not appear to have held any public paper.

Nicholas Gilman, of New Hampshire, was in public life from his youth until his death. He entered the army at the age of twenty-one, and after the War he served in Congress and in other public positions. He does not seem to have been a man of much weight either in private life or the Convention. A French observer remarks of his election as a member of the Federal Convention: "Cette circonstance prouve qu'il n'y a pas un grand choix à faire dans cet Etat, ou que du moins les hommes des plus sensés et les plus habiles ne sont pas assés riches pour accepter une place publique."[4]

In financial matters, there was no doubt of Gilman's ability. He managed to accumulate a considerable amount of public securities before the meeting of the Convention, and apparently added to his holdings later. In the Nicholas Gilman papers preserved in the Library of Congress there is a list of certificates of the liquidated debt to the amount of $5400.67, declared to be the property of Nicholas Gilman,

[1] Bigelow, *Life of Franklin*, Vol. III, p. 470.
[2] Haskins, *The Yazoo Land Companies*, p. 62.
[3] Bigelow, *Works*, Vol. X, pp. 206 ff.
[4] Farrand, *Records*, Vol. III, p. 232.

on December 9, 1786. This paper was bought up by Gilman, for the list of original holders is given. A receipt bearing the date of June 29, 1787, preserved in the above papers, shows Nicholas Gilman to have received interest on $6654.79 of the public debt. He and the various members of the Gilman family of New Hampshire were extensively engaged in transactions in public securities.[1] One entry in the Treasury books of the new government shows Nicholas Gilman to have $11,021.95 worth of 6 per cent Deferred Stock;[2] and he supplemented his purely fiscal operations by dealing in military certificates (that is, soldier's paper which could be bought from necessitous holders at a fraction of its value), and in public lands.[3]

  While Gilman was quick to look after his own interests, his devotion to his native state made him anxious for her towns to participate in the general prosperity enjoyed by holders of public securities after the formation of the Constitution. On September 3, 1787, he had already discovered the probable effect of the proposed Constitution, not yet ready to lay before the people, upon the securities of the government. On that day he wrote to the President of New Hampshire advising the towns to buy up public securities at the prevailing low price in order to have paper to transfer to the federal government in lieu of taxes and other charges. He says: "I find many of the states are making provision to buy in their quota's of the final settlements, and I must ardently wish that the towns in New Hampshire may be so far awake to a sense of their interest as to part with their property freely in order to purchase their several quota's of the public securities now in circula-

[1] Consult the Loan Office Records of New Hampshire in the Treasury Department, *passim*.
[2] Ms. Treasury Department: *Ledger C, Treasury, 6%*, Vol. 42, folio 368.
[3] *State Papers: Public Lands*, Vol. I, p. 118.

tion, while they are to be had at the present low rate; which is in this place, at two shillings and six pence on the pound. If they suffer the present opportunity to pass and we should be so fortunate as to have an efficient Government, they will be obliged to buy them of brokers, hawkers, speculators, and jockeys at six or perhaps eight times their present value." [1]

Elbridge Gerry, of Massachusetts, was born in Marblehead in 1744. His father was a merchant of good standing and comfortable estate. His biographer states that after his graduation from Harvard, Elbridge "turned his attention to that line of life in which his father's prosperity seemed to hold out the greatest inducements to a young and enterprising mind; and he plunged at once into the most active pursuits of commerce. His fairness, correctness, and assiduity, and the extensive knowledge of commercial concerns which he acquired from his father's experience and his own exertions were crowned with good fortune, and while yet young in business and in years he acquired a considerable estate and a very high standing at Marblehead." [2]

As a merchant, Gerry was closely in touch with the needs of commerce, and was deeply impressed with the necessity for national resistance to the discriminations of Great Britain. In April, 1784, he presented a report to Congress in which he called attention to the fact that Great Britain had adopted regulations destructive to American commerce in the West India Islands, and that these measures of discrimination were growing into a system. "Unless the United States in Congress assembled," he urged, "shall be vested with powers competent to the protection of commerce, they can never command reciprocal advantages in trade;

[1] Hammond, *State Papers of New Hampshire*, Vol. XVIII, p. 790.
[2] Sanderson, *Lives of the Signers* (1831 ed.), Vol. I, p. 197; Austin, *Life of Gerry*.

and without these, our foreign commerce must decline and eventually be annihilated." The West Indian trade affected New England particularly, and Gerry is thus reflecting a local interest in demanding a national system of commercial protection.[1]

In addition to his mercantile interests, Gerry was concerned in financial affairs. In the Convention he strongly urged inserting in the Constitution a clause conferring on the new government not only the power but also the obligation to provide fully for the holders of public securities. According to Madison's notes, "Mr. Gerry considered giving the power only, without adopting the obligation, as destroying the security now enjoyed by the public creditors of the United States. He enlarged on the merit of this class of citizens, and the solemn faith which had been pledged under the existing Confederation."[2] Later in the Convention, when Colonel Mason objected to making the full discharge of the debt obligatory, Gerry again took exceptions. He said, "that for himself he had no interest in the question, being not possessed of more of the securities than would by the interest pay his taxes. He would observe, however, that as the public had received the value of the literal amount, they ought to pay that value to somebody. The frauds on the soldiers ought to have been foreseen. These poor and ignorant people could not but part with their securities. There are other creditors who will part with anything rather than be cheated out of the capital of their advances. . . . If the public faith would admit, of which he was not clear, he would not object to a revision of the debt so far as to compel restitution to the ignorant and distressed who had been defrauded. As to the Stock-jobbers he saw no reason

[1] Sanderson, *Biography of the Signers*, Vol. I, p. 230.
[2] Farrand, *Records*, Vol. II, p. 356.

for the censures thrown on them. They kept up the value of the paper. Without them there would be no market." [1]

Gerry here explains to his colleagues that he is a holder of securities; but he modestly underestimates the amount, or his taxes were rather high, for the loan office records of Massachusetts show that the interest on his securities, issued pursuant to the act of Congress of April 28, 1784, was about $3500 a year, an amount which, even at the prevailing rate of depreciation,would have covered the taxes on a considerable estate.[2] The incompleteness of the records in the Treasury Department does not permit of an exact estimate of Gerry's holdings; but they must have been large, for the following items appear to his credit: $14,266.89 on the Liquidated Debt Book of the Massachusetts loan office,[3] $2648.50 worth of sixes and threes in 1790 on the Pennsylvania loan office books,[4] $409.50 in threes on the Pennsylvania ledger under the date of December 13, 1790,[5] and £3504 : 8 : 10 worth of old paper funded into federal securities in the Massachusetts loan office, August 24, 1791.[6] There may be of course some duplication of amounts but there can be no doubt that Gerry's interest income from confederate securities in one year shortly before the meeting of the Convention was about $3500, and also there can be no doubt that Gerry had bought largely with a view to speculation, for a very few of his certificates were issued to him originally. He had therefore more than an academic sympathy with the stockbrokers. Nevertheless, it should be

---

[1] *Ibid.*, 413.

[2] Ms. Treasury Department: *Mass. Loan Office, Register of Certificates of Interest Issued* (Vellum bound), folios 15 ff.

[3] *Ibid., Mass. Loan Office, Certificates for Liquidated Debt*, folios 3, 4, 5, 6, and 7. This paper had evidently been bought by Gerry for speculation.

[4] *Ibid., Loan Office, Pa., 1790–1791*, folio 60.

[5] *Ibid., Ledger C, 3% Stocks, Pa.*, folio 37.

[6] *Ibid., Massachusetts Loan Office, 1791*, Item 582; this was also paper bought up by Gerry for speculation.

noted that notwithstanding his large interests at stake, Gerry for several reasons strongly opposed the ratification of the Constitution.[1]

However, Gerry during his entire public career seems to have intermixed his official relations with his private economic affairs. While he was a member of Congress, before the adoption of the Constitution, he became interested in the public lands. On March 1, 1785, Timothy Pickering,[2] one of the leading land operators of the period, wrote to Gerry: "As you have expressed your wishes to be concerned in the purchase of lands on the other side of the Alleghany mountains thro' our agency, we think it very material to your interest as well as our own that we be informed, if possible, what plan Congress will probably adopt in disposing of those lands which lie west of the Ohio. If they mean to permit adventurers to make a scramble . . . it will behove us to engage seasonably with some enterprising, but confidential character, to explore the country and make locations. . . . If there must be a scramble, we have an equal right with others, and, therefore, the information

---

[1] Gerry was accused by Ellsworth (q.v.) of having turned against the new Constitution because the Convention refused to put the old continental paper money on the same basis as other securities. Toward the close of the Convention, "Gerry," says Ellsworth, "introduced a motion respecting the redemption of the old continental money — that it should be placed on a footing with other liquidated securities of the United States. As Mr. Gerry was supposed to be possessed of large quantities of this species of paper, his motion appeared to be founded in such bare-faced selfishness and injustice, that it at once accounted for all his former plausibility and concession, while the rejection of it by the convention inspired its author with the utmost rage and intemperate opposition to the whole system he had formerly praised." Ford, *Essays on the Constitution*, p. 174. Gerry indignantly denied that he ever made such a motion in the Convention, or that he held much continental money. *Ibid.*, p. 127. It does not appear in Farrand, *Records*, that any such motion was made in the Convention; and under the circumstances it seems not unjust to remark that Ellsworth's charges were made with very bad grace, particularly in view of the fact that he and members of his family and intimate friends held considerable amounts of public securities. "Bare-faced selfishness" was not monopolized by Gerry in the Convention.

[2] See above, p. 49.

desired in the beginning of this letter may be of essential importance. Your answer to this letter will much oblige your sincere friends who wish to advance your interest with their own." [1]

Gerry was then a member of Congress, which had under consideration the disposal of the western lands. If this land company, of course, could secure inside information, it would be advantageous to Mr. Gerry who contemplated speculating in those lands, as well as to Mr. Pickering's agency.

Gerry undoubtedly took advantage of the opportunity to invest in western enterprises, for he was a share-holder in the Ohio Company, proprietors of lands on the Muskingum River [2] — a concern in which he apparently became interested while a member of the Congress under the Articles of Confederation, during the organization of the Company and the procuring of the public grant.

Nathaniel Gorham, of Massachusetts, was a successful merchant at Charlestown, the place of his birth. He was prominent in the political life of his community, having served as a member of the legislature and the constitutional convention of his state.

In addition to his mercantile and political pursuits, Gorham engaged in land speculation on a large scale. In 1786, Massachusetts, by a compromise with New York, secured a large area of western country, and in April, 1788, "sold all this land to Nathaniel Gorham, of Charlestown, and Oliver Phelps, of Granville, for a million dollars, to be paid in three annual instalments in the scrip of Massachusetts, known as consolidated securities, which were then much below par. . . . Behind Phelps and Gorham there was a syndicate

---

[1] King, *Life and Correspondence*, Vol. I, p. 72.
[2] A. M. Dyer, *The Ownership of Ohio Lands*, p. 68.

of persons who desired to speculate in the lands, but who, in order not to compete with each other, had united and allowed these two to act for all." [1]

Robert Morris was one of Gorham's associates in this venture, and other prominent men were behind the project; but the projectors were unable to realize fully on their scheme, because the rise of Massachusetts scrip, after the adoption of the Constitution, made it impossible for them to fulfil the original terms of their contract. Consequently, they received only a portion of the original purchase.

The unhappy outcome of this venture apparently left Gorham without a very large fortune at his death in 1796. He does not seem to have combined any considerable transactions in continental securities with those in state scrip; although he was doubtless a holder in some amount because his will shows him to have been possessed of twenty shares in United States Bank stock.[2] Inasmuch as holders of this paper secured it in exchange for old securities and some specie, it may be surmised that Gorham must have had some of the continental paper at the time of the establishment of the Bank, although it may be that he purchased the stock as an investment. The tangled state of his affairs at his death makes this latter conclusion improbable at least.

We have now come to the colossal genius of the new system, *Alexander Hamilton.* It is true, that he had little part in the formation of the Constitution, but it was his organizing ability that made it a real instrument bottomed on all the substantial interests of the time. It was he who saw most keenly the precise character of the social groups which

---

[1] Sumner, *The Financier and the Finances of the Revolution*, Vol. II, pp. 253 ff. See Turner, *Pioneer History of the Holland Purchase of Western New York*, pp. 326 ff.

[2] T. Wyman, *Genealogies and Estates of Charlestown*, Vol. I, p. 424.

would have to be rallied to the new government in order to draw support away from the states and give the federal system a firm foundation. He perceived that governments were not made out of thin air and abstract principles. He knew that the Constitution was designed to accomplish certain definite objects, affecting in its operation certain definite groups of property rights in society. He saw that these interests were at first inchoate, in process of organization, and he achieved the task of completing their consolidation and attaching them to the federal government.

He saw, in the first place, that the most easily consolidated and timorous group was composed of the creditors, the financiers, bankers, and money lenders. He perceived that they were concentrated in the towns and thus were easily drawn together. He saw that by identifying their interests with those of the new government, the latter would be secure; they would not desert the ship in which they were all afloat. It has been charged that he leaned always on the side of the financial interest against the public as represented in the government; but it must be remembered that at the time the new system went into effect, the public had no credit, and financiers were not willing to forego their gains and profits for an abstraction. It is charged against him that he did not buy up government paper in behalf of the public at the most favorable terms; but to have done so would have diminished the profits of the very financiers whose good will was necessary to the continuance of the government.

The second group of interests which Hamilton saw ready for organization were the merchants and manufacturers who wished protective tariffs. He would have been blind, indeed, if he had not discovered and interpreted the widespread movement for protection which was swiftly gathering headway during the years preceding the formation of the Constitution. He was not blind. His first report on manufactures show how keenly alive he was to the extent and diversity of the groups whose financial advantage lay in a system of protection. Whether this was for the good of the whole people need not be argued here. Hamilton's relations were with the immediate beneficiaries. They were the men who were to throw their weight on the side of the new government. How persistently Hamilton sought to inform himself of the precise nature of the interests needing protection in the separate localities, from New Hampshire to Georgia, is evidenced by his unpublished correspondence with business men in all the commercial centres.[1]

The third interest which Hamilton consolidated was composed of the land speculators and promoters and embraced all the leading men of the time — Washington, Franklin, Robert Morris, James Wilson, William Blount, and other men of eminence.[2] This dealing in land was intimately connected with public securities, for a large portion of the lands were bought with land warrants purchased from the soldiers, and with other stocks bought on the open market at low prices. Hamilton saw clearly the connection of this interest with the new government, and his public land policies were directed especially to obtaining the support of this type of operators.[3]

Without the conciliation and positive support of these powerful elements in American society, the new government could not have been founded or continued. With keen insight, Hamilton saw this. He made no attempt to conceal it; for whatever may have been his faults he did not add the crime of demogogy. It is true that in private he often

---

[1] To be found in the Hamilton Mss., Library of Congress.
[2] Haskins, *The Yazoo Land Companies.*
[3] *State Papers: Finance,* Vol. I, p. 8.

expressed a contempt for popular rule which is absent from his public papers; but his public papers contain a plain statement of his policies, and show why he considered them necessary to the strength and stability of the government.

Thousands of small farmers and debtors and laboring mechanics were opposed to his policies, but they did not have the organization or consciousness of identity of interests which was necessary to give them weight in the councils of the new government. They were partly disfranchised under the existing laws, and they had no leaders worthy of mention. The road to power and glory did not yet lie in championing their cause. It required the astute leadership of Jefferson, and the creation of a federal machine under his direction, to consolidate the heterogeneous petty interests against the Federalist group.

But during Hamilton's administration, representatives of these smaller interests began to attack his policies as inimical to public interest, i.e., their own interests; and out of this attack grew the charge that Hamilton himself was privately engaged in augmenting his personal fortune by the methods which he had created for the advantage of public creditors and financiers generally. Although this charge, even if true, should not be allowed to obscure the real greatness of Hamilton's masterly mind, and has little bearing upon a scientific application of the economic interpretation to the period, it deserves examination at length.

Rumors that Hamilton was personally interested in securities were persistent from the beginning of his career as Secretary of the Treasury, and in his famous Reynolds pamphlet, published in 1797, he precisely states the charge against himself: "Merely because I retained an opinion once common to me and the most influential of those who opposed me, that the public debt ought to be provided for on the

basis of the contract upon which it was created, I have
been wickedly accused with wantonly increasing the public
burthen many millions in order to promote a stock-jobbing
interest of myself and friends." [1] That this heavy burden
was necessary to secure the support of the financial interests
concerned, and that their support was absolutely indispen-
able to the establishment of the new national system on a
substantial basis, was admitted by many of Hamilton's
worst enemies; but this did not prevent their attacking the
Secretary on mere rumors of private peculations.

It now remains to examine the evidence against Hamilton,
and state the case fairly so far as our existing records will
allow.   In 1793, Hamilton was accused of a criminal violation of the laws, and laid under the suspicion of being a
defaulter.   The House of Representatives was so impressed
with the charges that it appointed a committee to investigate
the conduct of the Treasury Department, particularly with
regard to the charge that Hamilton had made the public
moneys "subservient to loans, discounts, and accomoda-
tions" to himself and friends.

The result of this investigation was a vindication of the
Secretary by the committee on the basis of affidavits from
the officers and employees of the various banks involved,
public and private.   Hamilton cites the report of this committee of the House as containing the "materials of a complete exculpation." [2] But this investigation does not cover
the dealings which Hamilton might have had with stock
brokers and other persons handling public securities.
Evidences of such relations would not have been contained
in the public and private papers available to the committee.
Indeed, on account of his intimate business relations with
all the leaders who were buying and selling public securities,

[1] Hamilton, *Works* (Lodge ed.), Vol. VI, p. 453.
[2] *Ibid.*, Vol. VI, p. 454; *Annals of Congress*, Vol. III, pp. 900 ff.

and, on account of the fact that he could have seen them personally at New York and Philadelphia, it would not have been necessary for him to make any written record of such transactions. But of the larger charges brought against him in Congress we may regard this report as a complete vindication.

The direct charge, however, that Hamilton had violated the solemn obligations of his own office by buying up public securities, as distinct from the charge that he had employed his high authority in the interests of his friends and his class, first took on a serious form in 1797, when the notorious pamphleteer J. T. Callender, in his *History of the United States for the Year 1796* published a series of papers purporting to show that in 1791 and 1792 Hamilton had been engaged in speculative ventures with one James Reynolds and Mr. Duer.[1] It appears that in 1792 a Mr. Clingman, then in jail for a crooked transaction with the government, got into communication with Speaker Muhlenburg and hinted that a fellow-prisoner, Reynolds, had been associated with Hamilton in security operations, and had in his possession papers that would establish the facts in the case. Muhlenburg communicated with Monroe and Venable, and the three heard from Reynolds and his wife grave charges against the Secretary.

On learning of these serious charges, Muhlenburg, Venable, and Monroe confronted Hamilton with them and the Secretary explained that the whole charge of speculation was false and that his relations with the Reynolds grew out of an unhappy amour with Mrs. Reynolds. The three investigators accepted this explanation, although Monroe prosecuted further inquiries which resulted in his accumulating additional charges. The papers in the case, it was

[1] See below, p. 112.

agreed by Hamilton and his three investigators,[1] were to
be kept secret and out of the reach of publication. It
turned out, however, that Monroe, angered by the abuse
heaped upon him later by the Federalists, gave the documents out for publication, much to the scandal of the country.
Hamilton promptly replied in a pamphlet in which he denied
any improper financial relations with Reynolds, and explained in painful detail his affair with Reynolds' wife.[2]

When all the external and internal evidence is taken in
this case, and the documents connected with it are carefully
analyzed, it will be apparent that a decision will rest upon
the answer to this question: "Shall Hamilton's testimony
as to speculations outweigh that of an undoubted rascal and
his wife?" Mr. F. T. Fox, in a recent study of the matter,
attempts to convict Hamilton on the internal evidence of
his vindication; and apparently does so. But on an examination of Mr. Fox's brief against the Secretary, it soon
comes out that he has made a mistake in the crucial dates on
which turns his whole case.[3] Consequently, this particular
matter rests just where it did more than a hundred years
ago. Fair-minded men will be inclined to exonerate Hamilton of the charge brought in the Reynolds indictment.

That Hamilton himself made any money in stocks which
he held personally has never been proved by reference to
any authentic evidence. He did hold a small amount of
public securities, for in a letter of June 26, 1792, to William

---

[1] Mr. Lodge calls the three investigators "inquisitors," but this seems like a
strong word to apply to members of Congress engaged in running down rumors
relative to the official conduct of a government officer. *Works* (Lodge ed.), Vol. VI,
p. 450 note. The impropriety of Monroe's action in allowing the story to escape
is another matter.

[2] The pamphlet by Hamilton in his defence in printed in the Lodge edition, Vol.
VI, pp. 449 ff.

[3] Compare the date of the receipts on page 20 of Mr. Fox's *A Study in Hamilton*
with the date in the pamphlet (Lodge ed.), Vol. VI, p. 494.

Seton, he says, "All my property in the funds is about $800, 3 per cents. These at a certain period I should have sold, had I not been unwilling to give occasion to cavil." [1] The origin of this holding is not explained. Even if it was derived from the funding under the acts of August, 1790, and the 6 per cents, funded and deferred were added, it would not have made more than a trifling amount.

That Hamilton ever held any considerable sum in securities seems highly improbable, for he was at no time a rich man, and at his death left a small estate. Though he lived well, and had a large income apart from his paltry salary as Secretary, his earnings as an eminent lawyer may very well account for such sources of revenue as he may have enjoyed. Certainly, had he seen fit to employ his remarkable talents in private enterprise, he might have died one of the rich men of his day. However this may be, the question may be legitimately asked whether Hamilton had any personal connections with any of the security operations which were carried on during his administration of the Treasury?

Hamilton's defenders, in response to such an inquiry, will cite his famous reply to Henry Lee in 1789, when the latter asked him for his opinion about the probable rise of public securities: "I am sure you are sincere when you say that you would not subject me to an impropriety, nor do I know that there would be any in answering your queries; but you remember the saying with regard to Cæsar's wife. I think the spirit of it applicable to every man concerned in the administration of the finances of the country. With respect to the conduct of such men, suspicion is ever eagle-eyed, and the most innocent things may be misinterpreted." [2]

---

[1] *Works of Hamilton* (Lodge ed.), Vol. VIII, p. 268. Perhaps the remnant of an old account of Hamilton on the Treasury Books in 1797 refers to this petty holding. Ms. Treasury Department: *Ledger E, Treasury, 3%*, Vol. 44, folio 434.

[2] J. A. Hamilton, *Reminiscences*, p. 18.

On the other hand, Maclay, who, as United States Senator during the funding operations, had opportunities for first-hand information, answers the above question in the affirmative. He says, in his record of the Senate on February 1, 1790 : "If I needed proof of the baseness of Hamilton, I have it in the fullest manner. His price was communicated in manuscript as far as Philadelphia. Thomas Willing, in a letter to the speaker of the Representatives, after passing many eulogiums on Hamilton's plan, concludes, 'For I have seen in manuscript his whole price,' and it has been used as the basis of the most abandoned system of speculation ever broached in our country." [1] What Maclay doubtless means here is that Hamilton had communicated to one of the leading financiers of Philadelphia, a partner of Robert Morris and dealer in securities,[2] his proposed plans for redemption of the public debt in full, previous to their publication in the first report to the House on public credit, January 9, 1790. On the question as to how much credence should be given to the assertions of the querulous Maclay, students of history will differ, and impartial scholars will seek further evidence.

Far from admitting any truth in Maclay's allegations, Hamilton's friends would indignantly deny that he had any private connections with security operations in any form. Hamilton's son, in his *Reminiscences*, states that "Hamilton requested his father-in-law, General Schuyler, not to permit his son to speculate in the public securities lest it should be inferred that their speculations were made upon information furnished by Hamilton ; or were made in part on Hamilton's account. Schuyler inhibited any speculations; as Van Rensellaer Schuyler, my uncle, told me, complaining at

---

[1] W. Maclay, *Journal* (1890 ed.), p. 188.
[2] *State Papers: Finance*, Vol. I, p. 188.

the same time that, but for this inhibition, he would have made a large sum of money." [1]

The General, however, evidently did not regard this inhibition as binding upon himself, for he appears upon the records as one of the large dealers in public paper in New York. Examples of his extensive financial transactions can be readily found by reference to the old loan books in the Treasury Department; there appear in March, October, and November, 1791, the following amounts to his credit: $23,189.21; $15,594.61, $8036.50, $20,689.21. [2]

Neither did Hamilton deem it necessary to inhibit his brother-in-law, J. B. Church, from dealing in securities. During Hamilton's administration of the Treasury, Church was a large holder of public securities. [3] One entry credits him with $28,187.91 worth. Moreover, while Secretary of the Treasury, through his agents, Thomas Willing in Philadelphia, and Wm. Seton in New York, Hamilton bought and sold for his brother-in-law. In the Hamilton Mss. in the Library of Congress is preserved a letter from Thomas Willing bearing the date of February 24, 1790, and addressed to Hamilton, which shows that the former was then selling stocks under the latter's orders for Church. [4]

---

[1] *Reminiscences of J. A. Hamilton*, p. 18.

[2] Ms. Treasury Department: *N. Y. Loan Office, 1791*, folio 24. See also the volume of *N. Y. Loan Office Receipts* in the Mss. Division of the Library of Congress for General Schuyler's receipts for interest on securities. The intimate correspondence between Hamilton and General Schuyler during the period of the formation of the Constitution was destroyed by a son of one of the latter's executors. American Historical Review, Vol. X, p. 181. See Tuckerman, *Life of General Schuyler*.

[3] Ms. Treasury Department: *N. Y. Office, Deferred 6%, 1790–1796*, folio 325.

[4] PHILADELPHIA, Feby. 24$\frac{th}{}$, 1790.

[ALEXANDER HAMILTON, Esq.,

    Secretary of the Treasury at New York.]

SIR:

    I have had this day the honor of yours inclosing your power of substitution on behalf of Mr. Church. At present the sale of stock, and indeed every other money

At a later date, Hamilton was engaged in an extended correspondence with William Seton of the New York Bank, which shows that the latter was buying United States Bank stocks for Church, under Hamilton's orders. On November 21, 1793, Seton writes that he has not been able to make an investment for Mr. Church on account of the high price of bank stock.[1] Five days later Seton writes to Hamilton that he thinks it will be possible in a day or two to purchase stock for Mr. Church "under your limits;" and adds, after further remarks, "I therefore feel loth to enter into the market without further orders from you."[2] Here follows voluminous correspondence showing Seton's successful purchases.

Hamilton's operations for his brother-in-law, Church, also extended to speculations in public lands; for in the Hamilton Manuscripts there is a letter bearing the date of August 24, 1792, from William Henderson to him relative to the purchase of large quantities of land (45,000 acres).[3] It appears that Hamilton, Church, and General Schuyler were involved in this negotiation, and that Church was the principal.

Hamilton was also personally interested in western land schemes, for he held five shares of the Ohio Company, pro-

transaction is nearly at a stand. The produce of the State and the sale of Bills of Exchange will alone command it, untill we receive a supply from sea.

Mr. Constable has informed me of the purchase he had made of 20 shares and when they appear the transfer will be compleated.

I observe what you say respecting the sale of what remains of Mr. Church's shares and shall do whatever may be in my power to dispose of them, whenever I receive the certificates and your orders to make the sale. I am, Sir, with great respect,

Y: Obed: Serv:

Hamilton Mss., Vol. XXIII, p. 1.   THOS. WILLING.

[1] Library of Congress: *Hamilton Mss.*, Vol. XX, p. 180.

[2] *Ibid.*, Vol. XX, pp. 182 ff. Lodge omits references to this correspondence on Seton's part, although he gives selected letters from Hamilton to Seton. *Works of Alexander Hamilton*, Vol. VIII, pp. 231 ff.

[3] Library of Congress: *Hamilton Mss.*, Vol. XXIII, p. 180.

prietors of land on the Muskingum River.[1] Although this concern was organized before the formation of the Constitution, Hamilton as Secretary of the Treasury was called upon to pass upon the validity of claims involving thousands of acres. He felt the delicacy of this situation, for on May 9, 1792, he wrote to Washington that he regretted that he was required by law to decide a case in which he was an interested party, and stated that he had left the matter to be adjusted by the accounting officers of the Treasury acting under an opinion of the Attorney General.[2]

Although Hamilton showed great hesitancy in passing upon his own land claims while Secretary, he did not deem it incompatible with his official duties to communicate occasionally with friends as to the probable prices of public securities and bank stock.

For the communication to Willing, mentioned above,[3] we have, of course, only Maclay's testimony; and if his statement is true Hamilton transmitted official secrets of the most significant character to a financier who, however great his integrity, was in a position to take advantage of them, and was engaged in dealing in securities on his own account and for Hamilton's brother-in-law, Church, under Hamilton's orders. When we remember that Maclay's journal was private in its nature, not intended for publication, and not given to the world until long after all the men mentioned in it were dead, we are constrained to give some credence to his straightforward statements like the one in question, even though he was a bitter enemy of the Federalist leaders. But we are not constrained to attribute to Hamilton any improper motives. Those who assume that the Secretary of the Treasury could have carried out his

[1] A. M. Dyer, *The Ownership of Ohio Lands*, p. 69.
[2] Mss. Library of Congress: *Treasury Department, 1790-1792* (Washington papers), folio 291.   [3] P. 108.

enormous reorganization of the finances without conferring with the leading financiers of the time have only an elementary knowledge of Treasury administration.

As Secretary, he often found it necessary to set rumors at rest. An instance is afforded in a letter written by Hamilton, on August 17, 1791, to Rufus King, in which he mentioned having given out his opinion on prices to counteract an undue rise in script on the stock market, and concluded by giving King his standard of prices on that day, saying "I give you my standard that you may be able if necessary to contradict insinuations of an estimation on my part short of that standard for the purpose of depressing the funds." [1]

This letter from Hamilton was evidently drawn by one from King bearing the date of August 15, 1791, in which the latter cautions the former against giving out any statements which might affect prices, and informs him that his opinions had been quoted in efforts to depress stocks. [2]   King also adds that Duer had been injured in attempts to raise prices, but is of the opinion that "his conduct has been as correct as any buyer's and seller's could be."   King had little liking for popular vagaries in finance, for he tells Hamilton that "the fall of Bank certificates may have some good effects; it will operate to deter our industrious citizens from meddling in future with the funds, and teach them contentment in their proper avocations."

On the same day that Hamilton replied to King's letter which had informed him of Duer's danger, he wrote to Duer cautioning him against pushing prices too high and repeating earlier warnings. He says: "I will honestly own I had serious fears for you — for your purse and for your reputa-

---

[1] *Life and Correspondence of Rufus King*, Vol. I, p. 402.

[2] Library of Congress, *Hamilton Mss.*, Vol. XVI, p. 126.   The editor of King's letters says this letter is lost.

tion; and with an anxiety for both, I wrote you in earnest terms. You are sanguine, my friend. You ought to be aware of it yourself and to be on your guard against the propensity. . . . I do not widely differ from you about the real value of bank script. I should rather call it about 190, to be within bounds, with hopes of better things, and I sincerely wish you may be able to support it at what you mention." [1] There is of course, little beyond friendly advice in this, although Hamilton's enemies may see impropriety in his communicating his own price to a man deeply engaged in speculation.

There is some evidence, however, which may reasonably be interpreted to imply that Hamilton might have used his official power in behalf of Duer. In reply to a letter from Duer (after his disastrous failure) making some request which is not explained by Mr. Lodge, the Secretary says: "Your letter of the 11th got to hand this day. I am affected beyond measure at its contents, especially as it is too late to have any influence upon the event you were apprehensive of, Mr. Wolcott's instructions having gone off yesterday." [2] Wolcott was Hamilton's subordinate in the Treasury Department, and evidently he had issued some instructions which affected Duer's fortunes. Wolcott was the auditor of the Treasury whose duty it was under the act of September 2, 1789, "to receive all public accounts and after examination to certify the balance, and transmit the accounts with the vouchers and certificates to the Comptroller for his decision thereon." This connection with Duer is the sole piece of evidence of what might be termed the possible use of the Secretary's office in a private matter. The nature of this is not clear, and the plan was not carried out.

[1] Hamilton's *Works* (Lodge ed.), Vol. VIII, p. 234.
[2] *Ibid.*, Vol. VIII, p. 240, date March 14, 1792.

The conclusion to be reached from this evidence is that Hamilton did not have in 1787 any more than a petty amount of public securities which might appreciate under a new system; that he did have some western land; but that an extensive augmentation of his personal fortune was no consideration with him. The fact that he died a poor man is conclusive evidence of this fact. That he was swayed throughout the period of the formation of the Constitution by large policies of government — not by any of the personal interests so often ascribed to him — must therefore be admitted. Nevertheless, it is apparent from the additional evidence given here that it was no mere abstract political science which dominated his principles of government. He knew at first hand the stuff of which government is made.

William C. Houston, of New Jersey, was of no consequence in the Convention, and little is known of his economic interests. He was a Princeton graduate, and was for a time professor of mathematics and natural philosophy. He entered the practice of law at Trenton, and from 1784 until his death in 1788 he was clerk of the Supreme Court of his state. On account of ill health he was unable to remain through the sessions of the Convention. A search among the New Jersey loan office records in the Treasury Department failed to reveal Houston as a holder of securities; but the records for that state are incomplete and Houston's death in 1788 would have prevented his appearing on the Treasury Records of the new government. A William Houston is recorded in the New York books for small amounts of deferred sixes,[1] but, although William Churchill Houston had a son by that name, the identity of the son and the public creditor cannot be established.

[1] Ms. Treasury Department: *Ledger B, N. Y. Office, 1790, Deferred 6% Stock,* folio 260; also *N. Y. Office, Deferred 6%, 1790–1796,* folio 144.

Houston was, however, interested in the possibilities of western land speculations, for his biographer relates that he "joined with others in procuring for John Fitch, the steamboat inventor, the office of Deputy Surveyor. After the treaty of peace with England, the question of how the lands northwest of the Ohio should be disposed of was mooted in Congress. It was thought that they would be sold to pay the debts of the confederacy. Fitch was a land jobber and supposed that a good operation might be made by a presurvey of the country, so that when the Land Offices were opened, warrants might be taken out immediately for choice tracts. He found no difficulty in forming a company to forward such an enterprise. It was composed of Dr. John Ewing, Rev. Nathaniel Irwin, Wm. C. Houston. . . . These gentlemen put £20 each in a fund to pay expenses." [1] How far this venture was carried and whether Houston acquired lands through it is not related. As a member of the Congress under the Articles of Confederation, he doubtless learned of the advantages to be gained in the West.

William Houstoun, of Georgia, took some part in the proceedings of the Convention, but he was of little weight. He was the son of a royal officer in the government of Georgia; and he received his education in England and studied law at the Inner Temple. His colleague Pierce records that "Mr. Houstoun is an Attorney at Law, and has been a member of Congress for the state of Georgia. He is a gentleman of family, and was educated in England. As to his legal or political knowledge, he has little to boast of." [2] The meagre biographical details available do not permit a statement of his economic interests; and the paucity of the records of

---

[1] T. A. Glenn, *William Churchill Houston*, pp. 71-72 (Privately printed), copy in Library of Congress.
[2] Farrand, *Records*, Vol. III, p. 97.

the Georgia loan office in the Treasury Department makes it impossible to say whether he was among the beneficiaries through the appreciation of public securities. An index to a volume of Treasury Records not found (Vol. XXVI, folio 44) contains the name of William Houstown, but whether this holder of public debt and the member of the Convention were identical cannot be determined.

Jared Ingersoll, of Pennsylvania, was the son of Jared Ingersoll of Connecticut, sometime agent of that colony as commissioner in England and later admiralty judge in Pennsylvania. He graduated at Yale and studied in the Middle Temple. At the bar in Philadelphia he "soon rose to first rank. His practice was larger than any others. His opinions were taken on all important controversies, his services engaged in every great litigation." [1] Ingersoll was a man of considerable wealth, but he does not seem to be involved in the large transactions in public securities which engaged the attention of his intimate friends in the Convention.[2] He does not appear on the Pennsylvania books as a holder of securities. If he held any, his transactions must have been with the Treasury direct, and this would have been very convenient as it was located in Philadelphia during the funding process. Ingersoll was a son-in-law of Charles Pettit, one of the security operators in Philadelphia.[3]

Daniel of St. Thomas Jenifer, of Maryland, is reported by Pierce to have been "a gentleman of fortune" in his state.[4] He was a planter and a slave-holder; the census

---

[1] Simpson, *Eminent Philadelphians,* p. 596.

[2] His private fortune was much impaired by the failure of Robert Morris, for whom he had pledged his faith in several transactions. Morris Mss., Library of Congress: *Private Letter Book,* Vol. II, pp. 193, 261, 327, 351, 414.

[3] H. Binney, *Leaders of the Old Philadelphia Bar,* p. 83; *State Papers: Finance,* Vol. I, p. 81.

[4] Farrand, *Records,* Vol. III, p. 93.

of 1790 records his holding twenty slaves on one plantation under an overseer, but the number on his own plantation is illegible.[1] It is probable also that he held a small amount of public securities at the establishment of the new government. He died in the latter part of the year 1790, but his son,[2] Daniel Jenifer, Jr., appears on the loan office records as the holder of nearly six thousand dollars' worth of paper in December, 1790,[3] which he disposed of the following year.[4]

William Samuel Johnson, of Connecticut, was a son of Samuel Johnson, a clergyman of Stratford, Connecticut, and a gentleman of some means. He was a graduate of Yale, and entered the practice of law. He refused to aid in the Revolutionary cause, because he could not "conscientiously" take up arms against England, and he lived in retirement until the War was over. After the establishment of independence he resumed the prominent position in public life which he had enjoyed before the struggle; and according to his biographer he took "the highest rank in his profession and became the renowned and high-minded advocate who was always crowded with cases and had his clients in New York as well as in every part of Connecticut."[5] He added to his own patrimony by marrying the daughter of a "wealthy gentleman" of Stratford.

Johnson was a member of the first Senate under the new Constitution, and he was included by Jefferson in the list of men "operating in securities."[6] It is highly probable that he did not aid the Revolutionary cause by investing his money in the original paper; and he does not appear on the Treas-

---

[1] *Census of 1790: Heads of Families*, p. 51; consult Index.
[2] Appleton, *Encyclopædia of American Biography*, Vol. III, p. 426.
[3] Ms. Treasury Department: *Maryland Loan Office, 1790–1797*, folio 14.
[4] *Ibid.*, folio 134.
[5] Beardsley, *Life and Times of William Samuel Johnson*, pp. 8–9.
[6] *Writings of Jefferson* (Ford ed.), Vol. I, p. 223.

ury Books for large amounts of stock,[1] but there is every reason for believing that he carried on extensive operations through his son Robert Charles Johnson. The latter was speculating extensively in New York and Connecticut immediately after the establishment of the new government, and two entries show a credit to the father through the son.[2] The loan office books under the date of December 13, 1791, credit Robert Charles Johnson, of Stratford, Gentleman, with nearly fifty thousand dollars' worth of sixes and threes.[3] Connecticut loan office receipts confirm this evidence of his extensive holdings.   The New York loan office also shows large transactions in the name of Robert Charles Johnson.[4]

Rufus King, of Massachusetts, was born in Scarborough, Maine, then in the province of Massachusetts, March 24, 1755.   His father, in 1740, was "in prosperous business as a trader and factor for Ebenezer Thornton, one of the principal merchants in Boston for whom he purchased and prepared large quantities of timber."   On settling at Scarborough, his father became "both a farmer and a merchant, and in each capacity was so successful as to become the owner of three thousand acres of land divided into several valuable farms and to be the largest exporter of lumber from Maine."

[1] Ms. Treasury Department: *Ledger B, New York Office, Deferred 6%, 1790*, folios 10, 152, 457.

[2] Folios 152 and 457 of above *Ledger B*.

[3] Ms. Treasury Department: *Connecticut Loan Office, Ledger A*, folio 15; *Ledger B*, folio 15; *Ledger C*, folio 15.   *Connecticut Loan Office Receipts*, Library of Congress, Mss. Division.

[4] *Ibid., New York Loan Office, 6% Ledger, 1791-1797*, folio 161; *ibid., New York Office, Deferred 6%, 1790-1796*, folio 107 — two entries of about $25,000 each.   *Ledger B, New York Office, Deferred 6% Stock, 1790*, folios, 152, 457.   *Ledger E, Treasury, 3%*, Vol. 44, folio 529.   There can be no question of the identity of the Robert Charles Johnson who appears on the public security records and the Robert Charles Johnson who was the son of William Samuel.   The cross entries between father and son in the records constitute one piece of evidence.   The residence of Robert Charles in Stratford presents another, for that was the family place.   Furthermore, the signature to the Loan Office Receipts is the signature of Robert Charles, son of William Samuel Johnson.

Rufus was educated at Harvard. When his father died in 1775 he left a good estate which was divided among several children. Rufus King was also fortunate in his marriage; his wife was Mary Alsop. Her father at first sympathized with the movement against Great Britain, but, "taking umbrage at the manner in which the New York convention had conveyed their adhesion to the Declaration of Independence to the Congress, and besides unwilling to close the door of reconciliation with Great Britain," — he retired to Middletown, Connecticut, and stayed until after the War was over, when he returned to New York, resumed business, and became president of the Chamber of Commerce. According to King himself, his wife "was the only child of Mr. John Alsop, a very respectable and eminent merchant in this city [New York]. Mr. Alsop declined business in 1775 with a very handsome fortune." [1] King thus had extensive mercantile and other business interests which were largely managed for him by others, so that he was able to devote most of his time to politics.

Nevertheless, he did not neglect matters of private economy. Robert and Gouverneur Morris were engaged in 1788 in a plan to associate a number of Americans in a project to purchase up the debt (or portions thereof) of the United States due to France. Wadsworth, General Knox, Osgood, and Colonel Duer were involved in it. It was first proposed to send Gouverneur Morris as minister to Holland to further the scheme. The originators of the plan finally hit upon the appointment of Rufus King. King replied to the overture: "I told Col. Duer that I was not indisposed to a foreign appointment — that the honor and duties of such an office wd. be my sovereign rule of Cond. and that if in perfect consistence with the duties and dignity of the office, I cd.

---

[1] Rufus King, *Life and Correspondence*, Vol. I, 132.

promote the interest of my friends, it wd. be a great satisfaction to me.   But that I desired not to be considered as
giving an answer any way at present, that . . . the opinions
of Mr. Jay and Col. Hamilton were of consequence in my
mind.   That previous to any decision on my part I must be
ascertained of their opinions." [1]

Whether King engaged in this ambitious project or not,
there is evidence to show that he was a considerable holder
of government paper shortly after its establishment.   It
may be that a part of his fortune had been invested originally
in public securities, although this is not apparent from the
early loan office books in the Treasury Department.   Jefferson puts King down among the holders of bank stock
and public securities; [2] and he is correct in his statement.
King was director in the first United States bank. [3]   He
was also a large holder of government securities — one entry
records more than $10,000 worth to his credit. [4]   King
thought that speculations should be reserved to the experienced, and rejoiced in the hope that one of the crashes
would teach the ordinary industrious citizens "contentment
in their proper avocations." [5]

John Langdon, of New Hampshire, was born on the family
farm near Portsmouth in 1740, and "after a mercantile
education in the counting room of Daniel Rindge, he entered
upon a sea-faring life, but was driven from it by the revolutionary troubles."   He must have prospered, however,
before the War blighted his trade, for when the news of the
fall of Ticonderoga reached Exeter, he rose in the legislature

---

[1] *Life and Correspondence of King,* Vol. I, p. 624.

[2] *Writings* (Ford ed.), Vol. I, p. 223.   Maclay makes some quite uncompli-
mentary remarks about King, *Journal,* p. 315.

[3] Dunlap's Daily Advertiser, October 23, 1791.

[4] Ms. Treasury Department: *N. Y. Office, 6%, Ledger, 1791–1799,* folio 14.
Ibid., Ledger B, N. Y. Office, Deferred 6%, 1790, folio 60; *ibid., Deferred 6%,
1790–1796,* folio 14.   The Treasury Index gives a number of references to volumes
not found.   [5] See above, p. 112.

of which he was the speaker and said: "I have a thousand dollars in hard money; I will pledge my plate for three thousand more. I have seventy hogsheads of Tobago rum which will be sold for the most they will bring. They are at the service of the state. If we succeed . . . I will be remunerated; if we do not then the property will be of no value to me." [1]

After the war, Langdon's various mercantile and commercial enterprises took on new life, and there is every evidence that in his worldly affairs he was uniformly prosperous. A French report to the Ministry of Foreign Affairs on the Congress of 1788 speaks of John Langdon as a man of great wealth and pressing commercial interests: "M. L. a fait une grande fortune dans le commerce, c'est le Rob. Morris de son Etat, faisant une grande dépense et s'attachant beaucoup de citoyens par ses libéralités." [2]

John Langdon-Elwyn, grandson of John Langdon, in whose family were preserved the valuable private papers of the elder Langdon, wrote, sometime in the early part of the nineteenth century, a pamphlet on his celebrated grandfather. The author of this useful brochure "was nineteen years of age at the time of his grandfather's death. A critical observer of men and affairs, his opportunities as a member of the family of Governor Langdon give the production of his pamphlet a special significance." [3] This writer characterizes John Langdon as "a man that loved money, at an age when it gets the upper hand, that was prone to banking and funding, to whom such atmospheres were familiar and congenial, that knew how to make it and keep it, and felt no envy of others that did so too." [4]

[1] C. W. Brewster, *Rambles about Old Portsmouth* (1859), pp. 360–361.
[2] Farrand, *Records*, Vol. III, p. 233.
[3] Batchellor, *New Hampshire State Papers*, Vol. XXI, p. 804 note.
[4] *Ibid.*, Vol. XX, p. 868.

That Langdon was deeply concerned in the financial operations connected with the new government is evidenced in many sources. According to his grandson, quoted above, "He voted for this bank [the first United States Bank]; and was we suppose an original subscriber of some account. . . . We believe he had been concerned in the Bank of North America: the first real National Bank: He was an intimate friend of Robert Morris." [1]

Maclay also adds his testimony to that of Langdon's grandson. When he was a Senator, Langdon lodged in New York with a Mr. Hazard who followed the business of buying up government certificates of public debt which had been "issued in place of the paper money of the old Congress and bore interest for their face value," and had depreciated to even as low as seven cents on the dollar. Maclay writes, "Mr. Hazard told me he had made a business of it; it is easy to guess for whom. I told him, 'You are then among the happy few who have been let into the secret.' He seemed abashed and I checked by my forwardness much more information which he seemed disposed to give." [2]

The loan office books of New Hampshire show that Langdon was a large creditor of the new government, and indeed he was one of the heavy original contributors who risked their fortunes on the outcome of the War.[3] One entry in the New Hampshire ledger credits him with more than $25,000 worth of sixes and threes;[4] and there are other entries as well. His brother, Woodbury Langdon, was also among the holders of public paper.

With that patriotism to his state and thrift in her interest

---

[1] Batchellor, *New Hampshire State Papers*, Vol. XX, p. 872.

[2] *Journal of William Maclay* (1890 ed.), p. 178.

[3] Ms. Treasury Department: See *Loan Office Certificate Book*, New Hampshire (Loan of 1777 *passim*).

[4] *Ibid.*, *New Hampshire Loan Office, Journal A*, folio 4, date March, 1791, and *passim*.

that characterized his colleague, Gilman, Langdon sought to give the commonwealth some advantage in the various speculations in securities. On January 7, 1791, he wrote to the President of New Hampshire advising him of the approaching passage of the National Bank bill and advising that the state use its continental securities and some cash to buy stock in the new Bank. He says that the stock "would undoubtedly sell for specie at par at any time . . .; and in all probability it would soon sell above par, the state would therefore run no risque of looseing." [1]

John Lansing, of New York, was a lawyer at Albany and the mayor of that city. William Pierce, in his notes on the Convention, speaks of him in the following language: "His legal knowledge, I am told, is not extensive nor his education a good one. He is however a man of good sense, plain in his manners, and sincere in his friendships." [2] Lansing was one of the stout opponents of the Constitution and left the Convention early. He was there long enough however to learn (what was not a very deep secret) the certain effect of an efficient government on continental securities; for in January, 1791, immediately after the establishment of the new financial system, he appeared at the New York loan office with paper to fund to the amount of over seven thousand dollars. [3] All the members of the Lansing family in Albany seem to have taken advantage of the opportunity to augment their fortunes. [4]

William Livingston, of New Jersey, was a member of the distinguished Livingston family which was among the largest proprietors in New York. He graduated at Yale,

---

[1] Hammond, *State Papers of New Hampshire*, Vol. XVIII, p. 824.
[2] Farrand, *Records*, Vol. III, p. 90.
[3] Ms. Treasury Department: *New York Loan Office, 1791*, folio 97.
[4] Johannis, Garrit, Abraham, John J., Henry R., and other Lansings appear on *Ledger C, Funded 6%, 1790*, Ms. Treasury Department. Consult Index.

and in 1745 married Miss French "whose father had been a large proprietor of land in New Jersey." He entered the practice of law in 1748 "and soon became a prominent member of the bar and employed in most of the important legal controversies of that day in New York and New Jersey." He apparently accumulated a comfortable fortune, but had lost a portion of it in 1773 by the failure of his debtors, and the necessity of accepting depreciated continental currency.[1]

Whether Livingston held any of the securities of the confederacy, it is impossible apparently to determine, for his death in the summer of 1790, before the funding system went into effect, would have precluded his appearing on the Ledger records. It is probable, however, that he did not entertain views in regard to the relation of public and private affairs different from those of his eminent colleagues. This theory will seem justified when it is understood that his son and heir, Brockholst Livingston, a New York lawyer, was among the heaviest security holders in that city; and in view of the wide reaching ramifications of his operations and his connections with Le Roy and Bayard was reckoned among the princely speculators of his day. One entry in 1791 credits him with about $70,000 worth; another in the same year, in conjunction with Le Roy and Bayard, with nearly $30,000.[2] At a slightly later date, 1792 and 1793, his 6 per cents alone amount to more than $100,000,[3] and he appears frequently in the records of other states. How much of this was his own paper and how much was for friends who did not wish to appear among the records cannot be determined.

[1] L. Elmer, *The Constitution and Government of New Jersey* (1872), pp. 57–59.
[2] Ms. Treasury Department: *Ledger B, N. Y. Office, Deferred 6% Stock, 1790,* folios, 72, 306, etc.
[3] *Ibid., N. Y., 6%, Ledger, 1791–1797,* folio 123.

James Madison, of Virginia, was a descendant of one of the old landed families of Virginia whose wealth consisted principally of plantations and slaves, and whose personal property was relatively small in amount. Madison's father "was a large landed proprietor occupied mainly with the care and management of his extensive rural concerns." Madison graduated at Princeton and studied law, but the practice of his profession did not appeal to him. His inclinations were all toward politics, for which he was prepared by long and profound researches in history, law, and political economy. He was constantly in public life, and seems to have relied upon the emoluments of office and his father's generosity as a source of income. The postponement of his marriage until 1794 enabled him to devote himself to political pursuits rather than commercial or economic interests of any kind. He does not appear to have been a holder of public securities; for the small amounts credited to James Madison on the books of the Treasury Department [1] seem to have belonged to his father, also named James Madison. [2]

Having none of the public securities, Madison was able later to take a more disinterested view of the funding system proposed by Hamilton; and the scramble of politicians and speculators which accompanied the establishment of the new government did more than anything else to disgust him with the administration party and drive him into opposition. Writing to Jefferson in July, 1791, he said: "The subscriptions [to the Bank] are consequently a mere scramble for so much public plunder, which will be engrossed by those

---

[1] *Ibid., Virginia Loan Office, 1791,* under date of September 30, 1791; *Ledger A, Funded 6% Stock, 1790,* folio 123.

[2] In a letter of February 13, 1791, Madison advises his father to fund his Virginia certificates at Richmond: "I do not see what better you can do with your certificates than to subscribe them to the public fund at Richmond." *Writings of James Madison* (1865 ed.), Vol. I, p. 529.

already loaded with the spoils of individuals. . . . It
pretty clearly appears, also, in what proportions the public
debt lies in the Country, what sort of hands hold it, and by
whom the people of the United States are to be governed.
Of all the shameful circumstances of this business, it is among
the greatest to see the members of the legislature who were
most active in pushing this job openly grasping its emoluments. Schuyler is to be put at the head of the Directors,
if the weight of the New York subscribers can effect it.
Nothing new is talked of here. In fact, stock-jobbing
drowns every other subject. The Coffee-House is in an
eternal buzz with the gamblers." [1]

Alexander Martin, of North Carolina, was a graduate of
Princeton, and practised law. He was for a time governor
of his state. Later he served in the United States Senate,
and supported Adams and the alien and sedition laws;
but was defeated for election in 1799.[2] Martin was among
the well-to-do planters and slave-owners of his state;[3] but
his tastes do not seem to have turned to dealings in public
securities, for the Index to the holders of the public debt
preserved in the Treasury Department does not contain his
name, and a search among the papers of North Carolina
fails to reveal any record of his transactions.

Luther Martin, of Maryland, was a descendant of English
ancestors who had obtained "large grants of land in New
Jersey [and] removed their domestic establishment there
when a greater part of the colonial domain was a dense wilder-
ness." He was a graduate of Princeton and took up the
practice of law. Being the third of nine children, and having
little or no assistance from his parents, who were in pinched

[1] *Writings* (1865 ed.), Vol. I, p. 538.

[2] *National Encyclopædia of Biography,* Vol. IV, p. 420.

[3] *The Census of 1790 — Heads of Families,* p. 168, places the number of Martin's
slaves at 47.

circumstances, he was thrown upon his own resources. He commenced his career in Virginia "where he soon acquired a full and lucrative practice, amounting, as he informs us, to about one thousand pounds per annum ; which, however, was after a period diminished by the disturbance growing out of the American Revolution." [1]

Luther Martin's fortune was never very large, although he had among his clients men of great wealth and influence, like Robert Morris.[2] The census of 1790 records his owning only six slaves,[3] and his holdings of public securities were apparently meagre — a few thousand dollars at most. One entry of sixes and threes on June 15, 1791, credits him with $1992.67, and he occasionally appears in other records.[4] He was always more or less in sympathy with poor debtors, and was unwilling to preclude altogether the issue of paper money or moderate impairments of contract. He was accordingly a bitter opponent of the adoption of the Constitution in his state.[5]

George Mason, of Virginia, was born in 1725. He was the son of a rich slave owning and planting family of Dogue's Neck, and on account of the early death of his father he came into his vast estate on attaining his majority.[6] His family fortunes were augmented by speculations in western lands. He married the daughter of a Maryland merchant, from whom a large estate came into his family.[7] He was a member of the Ohio Company which was organized in 1749, and obtained a grant of "six hundred thousand acres of

---

[1] Herring, *National Portrait Gallery*, Vol. IV.

[2] See Index to *Private Letter Books* of Robert Morris, Library of Congress: Mss. Division.

[3] *Census of 1790 — Heads of Families*, Maryland, p. 18.

[4] Ms. Treasury Department: *Maryland Loan Office, 1790–1797*, folios, 80, 81, 194.   [5] See below, p. 205.

[6] Rowland, *The Life of George Mason*, Vol. I, pp. 48 ff, 55 ff.

[7] *Ibid.*, I, p. 56.

land, lying mostly west of the mountains and south of the
Ohio."[1] In 1754 he also secured a patent for about fifteen
hundred acres of land in Northern Neck.[2] He was constantly increasing his holdings,[3] and in 1769 "he seems to
have come into possession of two thousand acres of land in
the district of Kentucky."[4] As a member of the Virginia
legislature he drew a bill "to encourage the making of
hemp, woollen, linen, and other manufactures."[5]

His property at the time of the establishment of the Constitution was unquestionably large, for at his death in 1792
"he devised to his sons alone, some fifteen thousand acres,
the greater part of his own acquisition, of the very best land
in the Potomac region. Most of these estates were well
improved, with large and comfortable mansions and all
necessary outbuildings. But he left to be divided among
his children what was solely acquired by himself : sixty
thousand of among the finest acres in Kentucky, some
three hundred slaves, more than fifty thousand dollars'
worth of other personal property, and at least thirty thousand dollars of debts due on his books, while his own indebted-
ness was absolutely nothing."[6] Very little of this personal
property seems to have been in public securities, for a search
in the records of the Treasury Department shows one small
entry of a few hundred dollars' worth of threes and sixes to
his credit.[7]

Mason frankly admitted his personal interest in certain
landed property to be among his many objections to
the Constitution — which he refused to approve and the
adoption of which he bitterly opposed. Speaking on the

---

[1] Rowland, *The Life of George Mason*, Vol. I, p. 58.
[2] *Ibid.*, I, p. 60. [3] *Ibid.*, I, pp. 117, 154. [4] *Ibid.*, I, p. 119.
[5] *Ibid.*, I, p. 270. [6] *Ibid.*, Vol. II, p. 368.
[7] Ms. Treasury Department: *Ledger A, Funded 6% Stock, 1790*, folio 130;
see *Loan Office Virginia, 1790–1793*, folio 132. The Index gives references to other
volumes not found, Vols. 41, 43, 45, folios 93, 15, and 18 respectively.

dangers from the supremacy of the federal courts, in the Virginia ratifying convention, he said: "I am personally endangered as an inhabitant of Northern Neck. The people of that part will be obliged, by the operation of this power, to pay the quit rent of their lands. . . . Lord Fairfax's title was clear and undisputed. After the revolution we taxed his lands as private property. After his death, an act of Assembly was made, in 1782, to sequester the quit rents due, at his death, in the hands of his debtors. Next year an act was made restoring them to the executor of the proprietor. Subsequent to this, the treaty of peace was made, by which it was agreed that there should be no further confiscations. But after this an act of Assembly was passed, confiscating his whole property. As Lord Fairfax's title was indisputably good, and as treaties are to be the supreme law of the land, will not his representatives be able to recover all in the federal court? How will gentlemen like to pay an additional tax on lands in the Northern Neck?" [1]

Mason proposed to limit the judicial power in such a manner that it should "extend to no case where the cause of action shall have originated before the ratification of this Constitution, except in suits for debts due the United States, disputes between states about their territory, and disputes between persons claiming lands under grants of different states." He expressed a fear that under the Constitution as it stood the titles to all the country between the Blue Ridge and Alleghany Mountains would be upset in the federal courts and that the vast Indiana purchase would be rendered a subject of dispute.[2]

James McClurg, of Virginia, was an accomplished man of

---

[1] Elliot, *Debates* (1836 ed.), Vol. III, pp. 528–529.
[2] *Ibid.*, p. 529.

letters and distinguished physician of his native state. He was born there in 1747, studied at the college of William and Mary, and finished his training in medicine at Edinburgh and Paris. He established himself in the practice first at Williamsburg, and about 1783 he settled in Richmond, where he took first rank as a physician, scholar, and man of the world.[1]

McClurg's knowledge of government was not academic. He knew the subject practically, as well as theoretically ; for as early as November 23, 1790, he was engaged in operations in federal securities.[2]   And on February 17, 1791, he presented to the local loan office Virginia certificates to the amount of $26,819, all of which, except a few hundred pounds originally subscribed by himself, he had evidently bought for speculation.[3]   McClurg was also an investor in stock in the first United States Bank and one of the directors.[4]

James McHenry, of Maryland, received a classical education in Ireland, the country of his birth, and came to Baltimore in 1771. He studied medicine with Dr. Benjamin Rush at Philadelphia and became an army surgeon during the War. He was for a time secretary to Washington and later to Lafayette, and from 1783 to 1786 he was a member of Congress from Maryland.[5]

McHenry was the son of Daniel McHenry, a Baltimore merchant, who achieved "considerable financial success "[6] and was in business with his son, John, a brother of James, until his death in 1782. John and James began buying

---

[1] Duyckinck, *Cyclopædia of American Literature* (1855 ed.), Vol. I, p. 283.

[2] Ms. Treasury Department: *Ledger A, Funded 6% Stock, 1790*, folio 18.

[3] *Ibid., Loan Office: Register of Subscriptions, Virginia* (1791), see date, no folio given.

[4] Dunlap's Daily Advertiser, October 23, 1791.

[5] Magazine of American History, Vol. VII, p. 104.

[6] Steiner, *The Life and Correspondence of James McHenry*, p. 2.

town property, and when the former died in 1790, the latter inherited the entire estate, as John had never married. The death of James' father, says Steiner, left him financially independent.

McHenry's personal property must have been considerable. A casual letter of August 4, 1792, shows that one Dickinson owed him an amount secured by a bond for £5000.[1] He was one of the original stockholders of the Insurance Company of North America organized in 1792.[2] It is not apparent that he was among the original holders of federal securities, but an entry in 1797 records an old account to the amount of $6970.90, brought forward.[3]

McHenry's early mercantile interests left a deep impression on him, and he sympathized with the efforts made in his state to secure an adequate protective tariff. Indeed, he was among the signers of the memorial from Baltimore laid before Congress on April 11, 1789, praying for the protection and encouragement of American manufactures.[4]

John Francis Mercer, of Maryland, was born in Virginia and graduated at William and Mary College in 1775. He served in the army and after the war studied law with Jefferson. He moved to Maryland in 1786. He seems to have been a man of some fortune, for he held six slaves,[5] and a moderate amount of public securities.[6] His sympathies, however, were with the popular party in Maryland. He joined with Luther Martin in violent opposition to the adoption of the Constitution. In 1801 he was elected governor of the state, and as governor he attacked the property quali-

---

[1] *Hamilton Mss.*, Library of Congress, Vol. XXIII, p. 156.
[2] T. Montgomery, *History of the Insurance Company of North America*, p. 142.
[3] Ms. Treasury Department: *Ledger E, Treasury, 3%,* Vol. 45, folio 22.
[4] *State Papers: Finance,* Vol. I, p. 8.
[5] *Census of 1790 — Heads of Families, Maryland,* p. 41.
[6] Ms. Treasury Department: *Loan Office Maryland, 1790–1797, 3%,* folios 72, 135, and other loan office records of that state, *passim.*

fications on voters under the constitution of the commonwealth, at length securing the repeal of the provisions.

Thomas Mifflin, of Pennsylvania, was born in Philadelphia in 1744 and graduated at the College of Philadelphia,
where he distinguished himself as a student of the classics.
His father introduced him to a mercantile life by placing
him in the counting house of William Coleman, one of the
most eminent merchants of his native city. "When he
was twenty-one years of age he visited Europe to improve
his knowledge of commercial affairs, and after his return
home he entered into business with his brother, the connection continuing until after the Revolution." [1]

Mifflin was deeply interested in the protection of American
manufactures. He was prominently identified with the
Philadelphia Society for the Encouragement of Manufactures
and Useful Arts, organized in the summer of 1787. In fact,
he presided at the meeting at which it was established in
August of that year, during the sessions of the Convention.[2]

General Mifflin was a holder of public securities, but it
does not appear that his paper aggregated more than a
petty sum. He and Jonathan Mifflin are down for a few
hundred dollars' worth of continental paper in 1788; [3] and
he held in his own name another small account in 1791.[4]
It is, therefore, apparent that General Mifflin appreciated the
position of the powerful class of security holders who looked
to the Convention for relief, and had a more than abstract
interest in the establishment of public credit.

Gouverneur Morris, of Pennsylvania, was born in 1752 at
the family manor house at Morrisania. He "belonged by

---

[1] McMaster and Stone, *Pennsylvania and the Federal Constitution*, p. 701.

[2] *The American Museum*, Vol. II, p. 248.

[3] Ms. Treasury Department: *Pa. Loan Office Certificates, 1788*, folio 45.

[4] *Ibid.*: *Ledger C, 3% Stock, Pa.*, folio 48. John F. Mifflin was a holder of
paper to the amount of several thousand dollars funded in 1790. *Ibid., Loan Office,
Pa., 1790–1791*, folio 6; *Ledger C, 3% Stock, Pa.*, folio 6.

birth to that powerful landed aristocracy whose rule was known by New York alone among all the northern colonies." He graduated at King's College, entered the practice of law, and very soon began to take a hand in colonial politics, attacking with great vehemence the propositions of the paper money party. "He criticised unsparingly the attitude of a majority of his fellow citizens in wishing such a measure of relief, not only for their short-sighted folly, but also for their criminal and selfish dishonesty in trying to procure a temporary benefit for themselves at the lasting expense of the community." [1]

He was a member of the Continental Congress and was regarded as a considerable expert in financial affairs. He assisted Robert Morris in the establishment of the Bank of North America, and seems to have been able, in the midst of his public engagements, to augment his private fortunes and to engage in divers economic enterprizes. At the time of the formation of the Constitution, he had accumulated enough to purchase the family estate from his elder brother, and "he had for some time been engaged in various successful commercial ventures with his friend Robert Morris, including an East India voyage on a large scale, shipments of tobacco to France, and a share in iron works on the Delaware river, and had become quite a rich man." [2] He declared in the Convention that he did not hold any public securities, and the records seem to bear out his assertion, although his name does appear on an index to a volume of Treasury Records not found.

Of all the members of the Convention, *Robert Morris* of Pennsylvania, had the most widely diversified economic interests. He was born of humble parents in Liverpool in 1734, and came to America at an early age. The death of

---

[1] Roosevelt, *G. Morris*, pp. 1, 24. [2] *Ibid.*, p. 167.

his father, about 1750, left him a small estate of a few thousand dollars, which stood him in good stead in his relations with the Willings, whose counting house he had entered to learn mercantile arts, in which he showed an early proficiency.[1]

In the course of his long career he owned and directed ships trading with the East and West Indies, engaged in iron and several other branches of manufacturing, bought and sold thousands of acres of land in all parts of the country, particularly in the west and south, and speculated in lots in Washington as soon as he learned of the establishment of the capital there. He was instrumental in organizing the Bank of North America in Philadelphia, with Thomas Willing, his partner, as first President, and Thomas Fitzsimons, an associate in his land and speculative enterprises, as one of the directors,[2] and was in short a merchant prince, a captain of industry, a land speculator, a financier, and a broker combined.[3] Had he been less ambitious he would have died worth millions instead of in poverty and debt, after having served a term in a debtor's cell.

It is impossible to guage correctly the extent of his land speculations, for they ran into the millions of acres. Before and after the adoption of the Constitution, he was busy interesting his colleagues in every kind of enterprize that promised to be profitable. James Marshall, a brother of John Marshall, was his chief agent, and carried on operations for him in the United States and Europe. Marshall was given the power of attorney by Morris and his wife to sell enormous quantities of lands and other properties, and received from his principal letters of introduction to European

---

[1] Oberholtzer, *Robert Morris*, p. 4.

[2] *Ibid.*, p. 108.

[3] For his multifarious operations see Oberholtzer, *Robert Morris*; Sumner, *The Financier and the Finances of the American Revolution*, 2 vols.

capitalists and persons of prominence, including Mr. Pinckney, the representative of the United States in France.[1]

The exact extent of Morris' speculations in the securities of the new government is a matter beyond the scope of the present inquiry, but it is sufficient for our purposes to know that he held practically every kind of continental security, that his deals in stocks mounted upward into the tens of thousands of dollars,[2] and that in the Convention and in the first Senate under the Constitution, of which he was a member, he was uniformly strenuous in his support of public credit. No man of his time had such wide-reaching interests or involved in his personal affairs so many eminent men, like Hamilton, John Marshall, Thomas Fitzsimons, Thomas Willing, Gouverneur Morris, John Langdon, and Robert Clymer, all closely identified with the new system of government.

It may be truly said therefore that Morris was an effective representative of the speculative land operators, the holders of securities, the dealers in public paper, and the mercantile groups seeking protection for manufactures — in short every movable property interest in the country. It was fortunate for the new government to have in its support a man whose economic power and personal acquaintanceship extended from New Hampshire to Georgia. It seems fair to say that no man contributed more to the establishment of our

[1] Library of Congress: *Morris Mss.* Consult the Index to the three volumes of Morris' *Letter Books of Private Correspondence* for references, under "James Marshall." Only by turning over this enormous mass of correspondence can one gain a correct notion of the ramifications of Morris' interests and the number of prominent men involved in his schemes.

[2] *Hamilton Mss.*, Library of Congress, Vol. XXII, p. 179; two minor illustrations of his operations may be given: January 1, 1791, $7588.78, July 1, 1792, $26,408.66. See also the enormous transactions in the name of Willing and Morris scattered through the books of nearly every state. Ms. Treasury Department: *Ledger C, 3%, Pa.*, folio 334; *Register of Certificates of Public Debt Presented: Auditor of Treasury;* folios not given. Consult Index to holders of old securities in the Treasury Department.

Constitution and the stability of our national institutions
than Robert Morris, "the Patriot Financier."

Washington, therefore, showed his acumen when, as
first President of the United States, he selected Morris for
the office of Secretary of the Treasury; but the latter, on account of the pressing nature of his private business, was
unable to accept the post thus tendered. Indeed, he wisely
concluded that he could be more serviceable to the new
government in his capacity as senator from Pennsylvania;
and in this position he lent his powerful support to the
funding system, the new Bank, and the establishment of a
protective tariff. "Morris and Hamilton together worked
out a tariff bill," says Oberholtzer.[1] "But for the influence
of the Senator from Pennsylvania the measure, important
because it would provide the national government with
ample revenues, and because it had protective features
of utility in the development of the country industries, could
not have passed Congress in the form which would have
commended it to the Secretary of the Treasury. . . . All
witnesses agree that Robert Morris was a stupendous political force in Washington's administration, and his influence
did not decrease when, in December, 1790, the capital was
removed to Philadelphia, where he resumed his princely
entertainment of public men, surrendering his home on
Market Street to Washington, and becoming the President's
most intimate friend and closest companion."

William Paterson was born in the north of Ireland, came to
this country in 1747, graduated at Princeton in 1763, and
received his license to practise law in 1769. His father was a
merchant, and he was himself for a time engaged in the
mercantile business.[2] A by no means extensive search has

[1] *Op. cit.*, pp. 237 ff.
[2] L. Elmer, *The Constitution and Government of New Jersey*, p. 77.

failed to bring out any of Paterson's later economic interests.

William Pierce, of Georgia, does not seem to have made any considerable impression on his age, for the biographical material relating to him is meagre indeed. His economic interests do not appear to have been looked into, although it is known that he was "in business in Savannah as the head of the house of William Pierce and Company." [1] His private fortune was probably not large, for he applied to Madison in 1788 for a position as collector in his district. [2]

Charles Cotesworth Pinckney was the son of "Chief Justice Pinckney, a man of great integrity and of considerable eminence under the Provincial Government." He received a fine classical and legal education in England. He began the practice of law in the provincial courts in 1770, and very soon "began to acquire business and reputation." After the Revolutionary war "his business was large and its profits commensurate — reaching in one year the amount of four thousand guineas, a considerable sum for that day." He became "a considerable landholder in the city of Charleston. He had numerous tenants living on his property. . . . His benevolence was of the most enlarged character, and was experienced not only by the poor and such as were dependent on him, but in his liberal support of churches, seminaries of learning, and every object of public utility." [3] He also held a country estate at Pinckney Island, and is recorded in the first census as the owner of forty-five slaves. [4]

Pinckney had a large practice for the merchants of Charleston, and his knowledge of maritime law must have been

---

[1] American Historical Review, Vol. III, p. 312.
[2] *Calendar of Madison Correspondence*, Library of Congress. Mss.
[3] Herring, *National Portrait Gallery*, Vol. IV.
[4] *Census of 1790 — Heads of Families*, S.C., p. 33.

extensive.[1] Through this direct experience, he must have learned the importance of a national commercial system, not only to merchants and manufacturers, but also to those having occasion to appear in the courts. In the midst of the local conflict between the creditors and debtors, he took a firm stand against any weakening of public and private credit.

The significance and importance of the public credit he understood from first-hand knowledge, for his holdings of public securities were large when compared with the average holdings in the South. Shortly after the establishment of Hamilton's funding system, Pinckney is credited with over ten thousand dollars' worth of sixes and threes on the loan office books of his state.[2]

Charles Pinckney, like his distinguished cousin, was also an eminent lawyer in Charleston and enjoyed a large practice with the merchants. He was likewise a land-owner on a considerable scale, for the census of 1790 records the number of his slaves as fifty-two.[3]

Charles Pinckney was also identified with the conservative forces of the state in their fight against the debtor or paper money party, and he thoroughly understood the meaning of the sacredness of private and public obligations. He was a holder of government securities on a large scale, his transac-

---

[1] Speaking of the nature of the practice in Charleston just after the Revolution, Charles Fraser says, in *Reminiscences of Charleston*, p. 71: "It was stated by the Duc de Liancourt, who was well acquainted with most or all of the gentlemen named, that General Pinckney, Mr. Rutledge, Mr. Pringle, and Mr. Holmes, made from eighteen to twenty-three thousand dollars a year. . . . The extensive commercial business of Charleston at that time opened a wide field of litigation. Our courts were constantly employed in heavy insurance cases — in questions of charter party, foreign and inland bills of exchange, and in adjusting foreign claims. There was also a good deal of business in admiralty, and, occasionally, a rich prize case."

[2] Ms. Treasury Department: *Loan Office, S.C., 1791-1797*, folio 38. For other entries, *Loan Office, S.C.*, folio 70; a later entry of $8721.53 in trust for Mary Pinckney, *ibid.*, folio 152.

[3] *Census of 1790 — Heads of Families, S.C.*, p. 34.

tions early in the history of the new system amounting to more than fourteen thousand dollars.[1] In common with the men of his party he naturally feared the effect of popular lawmaking upon the value of personalty.[2]

Edmund Randolph was a grandson of Sir John Randolph, an English gentleman of ancient and honorable lineage. Through an uncle he inherited "three farms . . . negroes, and other property;" but this estate was burdened with debt.[3] As a lawyer, however, he enjoyed a magnificent practice which furnished him a considerable revenue. When charged with having defrauded the Treasury of the United States during his official service as Secretary of State, he advanced as a counter claim the fact that the condition of his fortune was evidence that he could not have engrossed any large government funds. He reported on that occasion (1801) that in money claims he had £14,200 Virginia currency which he traced "to the best of all resources, the independent labors of my own hands."[4] About that time, his other property which had come to him by way of inheritance amounted to "some seven thousand acres of land, several houses, and near two hundred negroes. The slaves had long been an incumbrance on account of his refusal to sell their increase and his inability while at Philadelphia to hire them properly."[5]

Indeed, Randolph was apparently never very prosperous. He held ten or fifteen thousand dollars' worth of public securities about the time of the establishment of the new government;[6] but he seems to have been in debt to Hamilton for

---

[1] Ms. Treasury Department: *Loan Office, S.C., 1791–1797*, folio 221.
[2] *Madison Mss.*, Library of Congress, under date of March 28, 1789.
[3] M. Conway, *Edmund Randolph*, p. 48.
[4] *Ibid.*, p. 372.
[5] *Ibid.*, p. 384.
[6] Ms. Treasury Department: *Current Accounts, Va., 1791–1796*, folios 6, 13, 21; *Ledger B, Assumed Debt, Va.*, folio 87.

a considerable sum that gave him some embarrassment.
On April 23, 1793, he wrote to Hamilton asking an extension of time on the paper, saying: "I am extremely
thankful to you for your readiness to accommodate me on
the subject of the bills. . . . The sum which I want to
sell is much less than £2600 stg. It is only £1300; as I
prefer waiting for a rise. . . ." [1]

George Read, of Delaware, was the grandson of a "wealthy
citizen of Dublin." His father had migrated to America
and established himself as "a respectable planter" in Delaware. George studied law under John Moland, a distinguished attorney in Philadelphia, and began business for
himself in Newcastle in 1754 where he soon acquired a
lucrative practice.[2] Although he surrendered all claim to
his father's estate on, the ground that he had received
his portion in his education,[3] Read managed to accumulate a modest competence.

Of his economic position, so far as it was reflected in his
style of living, a descendant writes: "The mansion of Mr.
Read commanded an extensive view of the river Delaware.
. . . It was an old-fashioned brick structure, looking very
comfortable but with no pretensions to elegance. . . . Here
Mr. Read resided for many years in the style of the colonial
gentry who, when having no more than the moderate income of Mr. Read, maintained a state and etiquette which
have long disappeared. . . . How could this be, Mr. Read
not being affluent? His income would buy more then than
now, and he had a small farm . . . and besides he generally
owned his servants." In addition to his income from
official positions and his practice, Read possessed some
capital for investment, because he appears among the sub-

---

[1] *Hamilton Mss.,* Library of Congress, Vol. XX, p. 57.
[2] Sanderson, *Biography of the Signers* (1831 ed.), Vol. III, p. 351.
[3] W. T. Read, *Life of George Read,* p. 575.

scribers to the stock of the Bank of North America issued in 1784.[1]

A small part of his worldly goods he had invested in the securities of the Continental Congress in 1779, during the dark days of the Revolution when the chances of ever recovering it were slight indeed. He was among those who risked their lives and fortunes in the Revolutionary cause, and has the honor of being one of the signers of the Declaration of Independence. The loan office of Delaware records that in March and April, 1779, Read subscribed for $2000 worth of certificates, and that Mary Read subscribed for $11,500 worth of the same paper.[2] The incompleteness of the records of Delaware in the Treasury department prevents the tracing of these securities, but an entry of 1797 shows Read as holding a small account (old) of threes.[3] At all events, Read had felt personally the inconveniences of depreciated paper, and knew the value of a stable government to every owner of personal property.

John Rutledge, of South Carolina, was the son of Dr. John Rutledge, a native of Ireland who settled in Carolina about 1735. He was educated under a classical tutor and pursued the study of law in the Temple. He opened his practice in Charleston in 1761, and a biographer relates that "instead of rising by degrees to the head of his profession, he burst forth at once the able lawyer and accomplished scholar. Business flowed in upon him. He was employed in the most difficult causes and retained with the largest fees that were usually given." [4]

[1] *History of the Bank of North America*, p. 147.

[2] Ms. Treasury Department: *Loan Office, Delaware, 1777–1784, passim.* His mother and daughter bore the name of "Mary." J. W. Reed, *The Reed Family*, pp. 433 and 436.

[3] *Ibid.*, *Ledger E, Treasury, 3%*, Vol. 45, folio 202. The Index gives references to several other volumes which were not found.

[4] Herring, *National Portrait Gallery*, Vol. IV.

Rutledge was elected president of South Carolina, under the first constitution, and when a new frame of government was made by the legislature, in some respects more democratic, he vetoed it, preferring "a compound or mixed government to a simple democracy, or one verging towards it." [1] "However unexceptionable democratic power may appear at first view," said Rutledge, "its defects have been found arbitrary, severe, and destructive."

He resigned because he was unable to prevent the adoption of the new constitution; but he was soon elected governor under it; and inasmuch as it provided that no person could be governor unless he held in his own right, on his election, "a settled plantation or freehold . . . of the value of at least ten thousand pounds currency, clear of debt," it must be assumed that Rutledge was the owner of a considerable plantation and a number of slaves. Indeed, the census of 1790 records the number at twenty-six, which, though small, was considerable for a man whose interests were not primarily in planting.[2] Unlike his other colleagues from South Carolina, John Rutledge does not seem to have invested in securities, though several members of the Rutledge family appear on the records.

Roger Sherman, the shoemaker of New Milford,[3] Connecticut, was one of the very few men of the Convention who had risen from poverty to affluence largely through his own efforts, and had none of the advantages of education and support which a family patrimony can give. But as his biographer remarks of him: "In regard to worldly circumstances, Mr. Sherman was very happily situated. Beginning life with-

---

[1] Flanders, *Lives of the Chief Justices*, Vol. I, p. 551.

[2] *Census of 1790 — Heads of Families*, S.C., p. 42.

[3] When Roger Sherman resided in Park Lane and ran a store in New Milford, Connecticut, he lost money through the depreciation of bills of credit, and he thereupon declared a war on paper money which he continued to the end of his days. *Proceedings of the American Antiquarian Society, 1906–1907*, pp. 214 ff.

out the aid of patrimonial wealth or powerful connections, with nothing but his good sense and good principles, he, by his industry and skilful management, always lived in a comfortable manner, and his property was gradually increasing." [1]

In common with other far-seeing business men of his day, Sherman seems to have invested a portion of his accumulations in public securities, for shortly after Hamilton's fiscal system went into effect he funded nearly eight thousand dollars' worth of paper at the loan office of his native state.[2]

Richard Dobbs Spaight, of North Carolina, was of respectable origin. His father had been secretary of the colony under the crown, and his mother was a sister of Dobbs, a royal governor of the colony. He came into his father's estate early; he studied in Ireland, and finished his education at the University of Glasgow. At the time of the Convention, he was, according to Pierce, a "worthy man, of some abilities, and fortune."[3] He was among the large planters of his state, and is recorded to have held seventy-one slaves.[4] He seems to have taken no share in the public security transactions. At least a search in the incomplete records does not reveal him as an original holder — but an old account of 3 per cents for the sum of a few dollars, shows that he was not unaware of the relations of public credit to stable institutions.[5] It was largely through his influence that Washington went to North Carolina to aid in the fight for the adoption of the Constitution by that state.

Caleb Strong, of Massachusetts, was the descendant of an old and honorable family of Northampton, the place of

[1] Sanderson, *Lives of the Signers*, Vol. II, p. 66.
[2] Ms. Treasury Department: *Loan Office: Connecticut, Ledgers A, B, and C, Threes and Sixes*, folio 28 in each; January, 1792.
[3] Farrand, *Records*, Vol. III, p. 95.
[4] *Census of 1790 — Heads of Families*, N.C., p. 130.
[5] Ms. Treasury Department: *Ledger E, Treasury, 3%*, Vol. 45, folio 308.

his birth. He was educated at Harvard and entered the practice of law.[1] He early began a public career for which he showed remarkable aptitudes, and was rewarded by election to the convention which drafted the constitution of his state, to the federal Convention, to the first United States Senate, and later to the office of governor of the commonwealth. Whether he inherited a fortune or accumulated considerable wealth in the practice of law is not recorded by his biographer, Senator Lodge,[2] but he took advantage of his superior knowledge of public affairs, and bought up £3271 : 0 : 6 worth of certificates of issues up to May, 1787, which he funded into federal securities in September, 1791.[3]

Washington, of Virginia, was probably the richest man in the United States in his time, and his financial ability was not surpassed among his countrymen anywhere. He possessed, in addition to his great estate on the Potomac, a large amount of fluid capital which he judiciously invested in western lands, from which he could reasonably expect a large appreciation with the establishment of stable government and the advance of the frontier.

Perhaps the best way to illustrate his economic interests is to give the data from the schedule of his property attached to his will, drawn up in 1799. He possessed in Virginia, counting the enormous holdings on the Ohio, and the Great Kenhawa, more than 35,000 acres, valued at $200,000; in Maryland, 1119 acres, at $9828; in Pennsylvania, 234 acres, at $1404; in New York, about 1000 acres, at $6000; in the Northwest Territory, 3051 acres, at $15,255; in Kentucky, 5000 acres, at $10,000; property in Washington, at $19,132; in Alexandria, at $4000; in Winchester, at $400; at Bath, $800. He held

---

[1] *Encyclopædia of National Biography*, Vol. I, p. 110.
[2] *Massachusetts Historical Society Proceedings, 1791-1835*, Vol. I, pp. 290 ff.
[3] Ms. Treasury Department: *Mass. Loan Office, 1791*, Vol. III, item No. 1284.

$6246 worth of United States securities; and of this holding he said: "These are the sums which are actually funded; and though no more in the aggregate than 7566 dollars, stand me in at least ten thousand pounds, Virginia money; being the amount of bonded and other debts due me and discharged during the war when money had depreciated in that rate — and was so settled by the public authority." He held $10,666 worth of shares in the Potomac Company presented to him by the state of Virginia (which he left to establish a national university); $500 worth of James River Company shares; $6800 worth of stock in the Bank of Columbia, and $1000 worth of stock in the Bank of Alexandria. His own slaves were to be emancipated on the death of his wife. His live-stock he estimated at $15,653 — making a grand total at a conservative estimate of $530,000.[1]

Washington was also a considerable money lender and suffered from the paper money operations of the Virginia legislature. He "had bonds and mortgages to 'nigh £10,000' paid off in depreciated paper currency worth at times as little as 2/6 in the pound, and when he attended the federal Convention he was in arrears for two years' taxes through having been unable to sell the products of his farms." [2]

If any one in the country had a just reason for being disgusted with the imbecilities of the Confederation it was Washington. He had given the best years of life to the Revolutionary cause, and had refused all remuneration for his great services. He was paid his personal expenses to the amount of $64,355.30 in paper that steadily depreciated. M. Otto writing to Vergennes on February 10, 1787, says of Washington's losses: "I have before me a letter of this

[1] Sparks, *Life of Washington*, Appendix, No. IX.
[2] W. C. Ford, *The Federalist*, p. xi, note 3.

honored man in which he complains of being obliged to sell at a rate of twenty for one the certificates which Congress sent to him in payment for the arrearages due him."[1]

Hugh Williamson, of North Carolina, was the son of "an industrious tradesman" of Dublin, who settled in America about 1730 — five years before Hugh was born. The latter received a fine education and graduated at the College of Philadelphia in 1757. About this time his father died, leaving him sole executor of the estate, the settlement of which required the greater part of two years.[2] He studied divinity, but later turned to medicine and went to Edinburgh to pursue his studies in that subject. He practised for a time in Philadelphia, but afterward went South to reside.

During the Revolutionary War he engaged in mercantile speculations in Charleston and later at Edenton, "from which he afterward traded to the neutral islands in the West Indies." While continuing his mercantile connections with his brother, "then also engaged in the West India trade, he determined to resume the practice of medicine; this he did with the same success as he had done formerly at Philadelphia." He was an opponent of the emission of paper money in North Carolina and published an essay against fiat currency.

He happily combined a theoretical and practical knowledge of finance, for he seems to have accumulated a large amount of public securities. He appears frequently on the records of the Treasury Department; for example in December, 1791, for $2444.84 worth of sixes and threes.[3] Furthermore, his correspondence with Hamilton and others shows that he had "the smallest of two large trunks" full of 6 per cents,

[1] Bancroft, *History of the Constitution* (1882 ed.), Vol. II, p. 411.
[2] D. Hosack, *Biographical Memoir of Hugh Williamson*, p. 18.
[3] Ms. Treasury Department: *Loan Office, N.C., 1791*, folio 3.

threes, and deferred stock which he had delivered to Hamilton for transfer to the New York loan office, in 1793.[1]

Williamson also engaged in western land speculations, and was not unaware of the advantage to that class of property which the new Constitution afforded. On June 2, 1788, he wrote to Madison from New York, "For myself, I conceive that my opinions are not biassed by private interests, but having claims to a considerable quantity of land in the Western Country, I am fully persuaded that the value of those lands must be increased by an efficient federal government."[2] After his long and assiduous public services, Williamson settled in New York, where he engaged in historical writing and the management of the considerable fortune which he had accumulated in the midst of his pressing public duties.[3]

James Wilson, of Pennsylvania, was born in Scotland in 1742 and received a fine classical education there. He came to America in 1766, began the study of law with John Dickinson, and was admitted to the bar in 1767. He developed a lucrative practice at Carlisle, where he first settled; but in 1778 he removed to Philadelphia where he established a close connection with the leading merchants and men of affairs including Robert Morris, George Clymer, and General Mifflin.[4] He was one of the directors of the Bank of North America on its incorporation in 1781;[5] and he also appears among the original stockholders of the Insurance Company of North America, organized in 1792.[6]

Wilson's largest interest seems to have been in public lands, for he was among the members of the Georgia Land

---

[1] *Hamilton Mss.*, Library of Congress, Vol. XXIV, pp. 70 ff.
[2] *Documentary History of the Constitution*, Vol. IV, p. 678.
[3] Hosack, *op. cit.*, p. 85.
[4] Simpson, *Eminent Philadelphians*, p. 966.
[5] Oberholtzer, *Robert Morris*, p. 108.
[6] *History of the Insurance Company of North America*, p. 146.

Company, a highly speculative concern tainted with fraud, to put it mildly, for ten shares, £25,000 cash and 750,000 acres.[1] Haskins says, "James Wilson, of the Supreme Court of the United States, held shares to the amount of at least one million acres and it is asserted was influential in securing the grants." [2]

Wilson does not appear to have been a large holder of public securities; for a search in the records of the Pennsylvania loan office preserved in the Department of the Treasury reveals only a trivial amount of 3 per cents to his credit, on June 2, 1791.[3] It may be that the extent of his other operations prevented his taking advantage of the opportunities offered in this line.

George Wythe, of Virginia, was born in 1726 on the shores of the Chesapeake in the colony of Virginia. "He was descended from a respectable family and inherited from his father, who was a farmer, an estate amply sufficient for all the purposes of ease and independence, although it was seriously impaired by the Revolution." He studied law, and "by reason of his extensive learning, correctness of elocution, and his logical style of argument, he quickly arrived at the head of the bar." [4] His second wife "was a lady of a wealthy and respectable family of Taliafero, residing near Williamsburg." He was a slave-owner, but he emancipated his slaves and made provisions to keep them from want. His public security holding was not large. On March 12, 1791, he presented Virginia certificates to the amount of £513 : 2 : 8 which he had acquired from their original owners.[5]

---

[1] *State Papers: Public Lands*, Vol. I, p. 141.

[2] *Yazoo Land Companies*, p. 83.

[3] Ms. Treasury Department: *Ledger C, 3% Stock, Pa.*, folio 195.

[4] Sanderson, *Biography of the Signers* (1831 ed.), Vol. IV, pp. 172 ff.

[5] Ms. Treasury Department: *Loan Office: Register of Subscriptions, Va., 1791,* see date. Also *Ledger A, Assumed Debt, Va.,* folio 32.

Robert Yates, of New York, was born in Schenectady, and received a classical education at New York City. He read law and began the practice at Albany where he soon built up an extensive business. He was made a judge of the Supreme Court under the state constitution of 1777, but his salary was small. "Indeed before the scale of depreciation of continental money had been settled, he received one year's salary in that money at its *nominal* value, the whole of which was just sufficient (as he humorously observed) 'to purchase a pound of green tea for his wife.'" He refused to enrich himself by speculating in confiscated estates, a favorite occupation of some of his friends, and "he died poor."[1] He opposed the adoption of the Constitution, and apparently took no part in the transactions in public securities; but several members of the Yates family, Richard, Adolphus, and Christopher were large operators.[2]

A survey of the economic interests of the members of the Convention presents certain conclusions:

A majority of the members were lawyers by profession.

Most of the members came from towns, on or near the coast, that is, from the regions in which personalty was largely concentrated.

Not one member represented in his immediate personal economic interests the small farming or mechanic classes.

The overwhelming majority of members, at least five-sixths, were immediately, directly, and personally interested in the outcome of their labors at Philadelphia, and were to a greater or less extent economic beneficiaries from the adoption of the Constitution.

1. Public security interests were extensively represented

---

[1] *Appendix to the Secret Proceedings and Debates of the Federal Convention* (1821, Albany).

[2] Records of the New York Loan Office in the Treasury Department.

in the Convention.[1] Of the fifty-five members who attended no less than forty appear on the Records of the Treasury Department for sums varying from a few dollars up to more than one hundred thousand dollars. Among the minor holders were Bassett, Blount, Brearley, Broom, Butler, Carroll, Few, Hamilton, L. Martin, Mason, Mercer, Mifflin, Read, Spaight, Wilson, and Wythe. Among the larger holders (taking the sum of about $5000 as the criterion) were Baldwin, Blair, Clymer, Dayton, Ellsworth, Fitzsimons, Gilman, Gerry, Gorham, Jenifer, Johnson, King, Langdon, Lansing, Livingston,[2] McClurg, R. Morris, C. C. Pinckney, C. Pinckney, Randolph, Sherman, Strong, Washington, and Williamson.

It is interesting to note that, with the exception of New York, and possibly Delaware, each state had one or more prominent representatives in the Convention who held more than a negligible amount of securities, and who could therefore speak with feeling and authority on the question of providing in the new Constitution for the full discharge of the public debt :

Langdon and Gilman, of New Hampshire.

Gerry, Strong, and King, of Massachusetts.

Ellsworth, Sherman, and Johnson, of Connecticut.

Hamilton, of New York. Although he held no large amount personally, he was the special pleader for the holders of public securities and the maintenance of public faith.

Dayton, of New Jersey.

Robert Morris, Clymer, and Fitzsimons, of Pennsylvania.

Mercer and Carroll, of Maryland.

Blair, McClurg, and Randolph, of Virginia.

Williamson, of North Carolina.

The two Pinckneys, of South Carolina.

Few and Baldwin, of Georgia.

[1] See above, p. 75, n. 3.

[2] See above, p. 124. Livingston's holdings are problematical.

2. Personalty invested in lands for speculation was represented by at least fourteen members: Blount, Dayton, Few, Fitzsimons, Franklin, Gilman, Gerry, Gorham, Hamilton, Mason, R. Morris, Washington, Williamson, and Wilson.

3. Personalty in the form of money loaned at interest was represented by at least twenty-four members: Bassett, Broom, Butler, Carroll, Clymer, Davie, Dickinson, Ellsworth, Few, Fitzsimons, Franklin, Gilman, Ingersoll, Johnson, King, Langdon, Mason, McHenry, C. C. Pinckney, C. Pinckney, Randolph, Read, Washington, and Williamson.

4. Personalty in mercantile, manufacturing, and shipping lines was represented by at least eleven members: Broom, Clymer, Ellsworth, Fitzsimons, Gerry, King, Langdon, McHenry, Mifflin, G. Morris, and R. Morris.

5. Personalty in slaves was represented by at least fifteen members: Butler, Davie, Jenifer, A. Martin, L. Martin, Mason, Mercer, C. C. Pinckney, C. Pinckney, Randolph, Read, Rutledge, Spaight, Washington, and Wythe.

It cannot be said, therefore, that the members of the Convention were "disinterested." On the contrary, we are forced to accept the profoundly significant conclusion that they knew through their personal experiences in economic affairs the precise results which the new government that they were setting up was designed to attain. As a group of doctrinaires, like the Frankfort assembly of 1848, they would have failed miserably; but as practical men they were able to build the new government upon the only foundations which could be stable: fundamental economic interests.[1]

---

[1] The fact that a few members of the Convention, who had considerable economic interests at stake, refused to support the Constitution does not invalidate the general conclusions here presented. In the cases of Yates, Lansing, Luther Martin, and Mason, definite economic reasons for their action are forthcoming; but this is a minor detail.

CHAPTER VI

THE CONSTITUTION AS AN ECONOMIC DOCUMENT

IT is difficult for the superficial student of the Constitution, who has read only the commentaries of the legists, to conceive of that instrument as an economic document. It places no property qualifications on voters or officers; it gives no outward recognition of any economic groups in society; it mentions no special privileges to be conferred upon any class. It betrays no feeling, such as vibrates through the French constitution of 1791; its language is cold, formal, and severe.

The true inwardness of the Constitution is not revealed by an examination of its provisions as simple propositions of law; but by a long and careful study of the voluminous correspondence of the period,[1] contemporary newspapers and pamphlets, the records of the debates in the Convention at Philadelphia and in the several state conventions, and particularly, *The Federalist*, which was widely circulated during the struggle over ratification. The correspondence shows the exact character of the evils which the Constitution was intended to remedy; the records of the proceedings in the Philadelphia Convention reveal the succes-

---

[1] A great deal of this valuable material has been printed in the *Documentary History of the Constitution*, Vols. IV and V; a considerable amount has been published in the letters and papers of the eminent men of the period; but an enormous mass still remains in manuscript form. Fortunately, such important papers as those of Washington, Hamilton, Madison, and others are in the Library of Congress; but they are not complete, of course.

sive steps in the building of the framework of the government under the pressure of economic interests; the pamphlets and newspapers disclose the ideas of the contestants over the ratification; and *The Federalist* presents the political science of the new system as conceived by three of the profoundest thinkers of the period, Hamilton, Madison, and Jay.

Doubtless, the most illuminating of these sources on the economic character of the Constitution are the records of the debates in the Convention, which have come down to us in fragmentary form; and a thorough treatment of material forces reflected in the several clauses of the instrument of government created by the grave assembly at Philadelphia would require a rewriting of the history of the proceedings in the light of the great interests represented there.[1] But an entire volume would scarcely suffice to present the results of such a survey, and an undertaking of this character is accordingly impossible here.

The Federalist, on the other hand, presents in a relatively brief and systematic form an economic interpretation of the Constitution by the men best fitted, through an intimate knowledge of the ideals of the framers, to expound the political science of the new government. This wonderful piece of argumentation by Hamilton, Madison, and Jay is in fact the finest study in the economic interpretation of politics which exists in any language; and whoever would understand the Constitution as an economic document need hardly go beyond it. It is true that the tone of the writers is somewhat modified on account of the fact that

---

[1] From this point of view, the old conception of the battle at Philadelphia as a contest between small and large states — as political entities — will have to be severely modified. See Professor Farrand's illuminating paper on the so-called compromises of the Constitution in the *Report of the American Historical Association, 1903,* Vol. I, pp. 73 ff. J. C. Welling, "States' Rights Conflict over the Public Lands," *ibid.* (1888), pp. 184 ff.

they are appealing to the voters to ratify the Constitution, but at the same time they are, by the force of circumstances, compelled to convince large economic groups that safety and strength lie in the adoption of the new system.

Indeed, every fundamental appeal in it is to some material and substantial interest. Sometimes it is to the people at large in the name of protection against invading armies and European coalitions. Sometimes it is to the commercial classes whose business is represented as prostrate before the follies of the Confederation. Now it is to creditors seeking relief against paper money and the assaults of the agrarians in general; now it is to the holders of federal securities which are depreciating toward the vanishing point. But above all, it is to the owners of personalty anxious to find a foil against the attacks of levelling democracy, that the authors of *The Federalist* address their most cogent arguments in favor of ratification. It is true there is much discussion of the details of the new frame-work of government, to which even some friends of reform took exceptions; but Madison and Hamilton both knew that these were incidental matters when compared with the sound basis upon which the superstructure rested.

In reading the pages of this remarkable work as a study in political economy, it is important to bear in mind that the system, which the authors are describing, consisted of two fundamental parts — one positive, the other negative:

I. A government endowed with certain positive powers, but so constructed as to break the force of majority rule and prevent invasions of the property rights of minorities.

II. Restrictions on the state legislatures which had been so vigorous in their attacks on capital.

Under some circumstances, action is the immediate interest of the dominant party; and whenever it desires to make an economic gain through governmental functioning, it must have, of course, a system endowed with the requisite powers.

Examples of this are to be found in protective tariffs, in ship subsidies, in railway land grants, in river and harbor improvements, and so on through the catalogue of so-called "paternalistic" legislation. Of course it may be shown that the "general good" is the ostensible object of any particular act; but the general good is a passive force, and unless we know who are the several individuals that benefit in its name, it has no meaning. When it is so analyzed, immediate and remote beneficiaries are discovered; and the former are usually found to have been the dynamic element in securing the legislation. Take for example, the economic interests of the advocates who appear in tariff hearings at Washington.

On the obverse side, dominant interests quite as often benefit from the prevention of governmental action as from positive assistance. They are able to take care of themselves if let alone within the circle of protection created by the law. Indeed, most owners of property have as much to fear from positive governmental action as from their inability to secure advantageous legislation. Particularly is this true where the field of private property is already extended to cover practically every form of tangible and intangible wealth. This was clearly set forth by Hamilton: "It may perhaps be said that the power of preventing bad laws includes that of preventing good ones. . . . But this objection will have little weight with those who can properly estimate the mischiefs of that inconstancy and mutability in the laws which form the greatest blemish in the character and genius of our governments. They will consider every institution calculated to restrain the excess of law-making, and to keep things in the same state in which they happen to be at any given period, as more likely to do good than harm. . . . The injury which may possibly be done by defeating a few good laws will be amply compensated by the advantage of preventing a number of bad ones." [1]

THE UNDERLYING POLITICAL SCIENCE OF THE CONSTITUTION [2]

Before taking up the economic implications of the structure of the federal government, it is important to ascertain what, in the opinion of *The Federalist*, is the basis of all government. The most philosophical examination of the foundations of political science is made by Madison in the tenth number. Here he lays down, in no uncertain language, the principle that the first and elemental concern of every government is economic.

1. "The first object of government," he declares, is the protection of "the diversity in the faculties of men, from which the rights of property originate." The chief business of government, from which, perforce, its essential nature must be derived, consists in the control and adjustment of conflicting economic interests. After enumerating the various forms of propertied interests which spring up inevitably in modern society, he adds: "The regulation of these various and interfering interests forms the principal task of modern legislation, and involves the spirit of party and faction in the ordinary operations of the government." [3]

2. What are the chief causes of these conflicting political forces with which the government must concern itself? Madison answers. Of course fanciful and frivolous distinctions have sometimes been the cause of violent conflicts; "but the most common and durable source of factions has

---

[1] *The Federalist*, No. 73.

[2] See J. A. Smith, *The Spirit of American Government.*

[3] See Noah Webster's consideration of the subject of government and property; Ford, *Pamphlets on the Constitution*, pp. 57 ff.

been the various and unequal distribution of property. Those who hold and those who are without property have ever formed distinct interests in society. Those who are creditors, and those who are debtors, fall under a like discrimination. A landed interest, a manufacturing interest, a mercantile interest, a moneyed interest, with many lesser interests grow up of necessity in civilized nations, and divide them into different classes actuated by different sentiments and views."

3. The theories of government which men entertain are emotional reactions to their property interests. "From the protection of different and unequal faculties of acquiring property, the possession of different degrees and kinds of property immediately results; *and from the influence of these on the sentiments and views of the respective proprietors, ensues a division of society into different interests and parties.*" Legislatures reflect these interests. "What," he asks, "are the different classes of legislators but advocates and parties to the causes which they determine." There is no help for it. "The causes of faction cannot be removed," and "we well know that neither moral nor religious motives can be relied on as an adequate control."

4. Unequal distribution of property is inevitable, and from it contending factions will rise in the state. The government will reflect them, for they will have their separate principles and "sentiments"; but the supreme danger will arise from the fusion of certain interests into an overbearing majority, which Madison, in another place, prophesied would be the landless proletariat,[1] — an overbearing majority which will make its "rights" paramount, and sacrifice the "rights" of the minority. "To secure the public good," he declares, "and private rights against the

[1] Farrand, *Records*, Vol. II, p. 203.

danger of such a faction and at the same time preserve the spirit and the form of popular government is then the great object to which our inquiries are directed."

5. How is this to be done? Since the contending classes cannot be eliminated and their interests are bound to be reflected in politics, the only way out lies in making it difficult for enough contending interests to fuse into a majority, and in balancing one over against another. The machinery for doing this is created by the new Constitution and by the Union. (a) Public views are to be refined and enlarged "by passing them through the medium of a chosen body of citizens." (b) The very size of the Union will enable the inclusion of more interests so that the danger of an overbearing majority is not so great. "The smaller the society, the fewer probably will be the distinct parties and interests composing it; the fewer the distinct parties and interests, the more frequently will a majority be found of the same party. . . . Extend the sphere, and you take in a greater variety of parties and interests; you make it less probable that a majority of the whole will have a common motive to invade the rights of other citizens; or if such a common motive exists, it will be more difficult for all who feel it to discover their strength and to act in unison with each other."

Q. E. D., "in the extent and proper structure of the Union, therefore, we behold a republican remedy for the diseases most incident to republican government."[1]

[1] This view was set forth by Madison in a letter to Jefferson in 1788. "Wherever the real power in a Government lies, there is the danger of oppression. In our Governments the real power lies in the majority of the Community, and the invasion of private rights is *chiefly* to be apprehended, not from acts of Government contrary to the sense of its constituents, but from acts in which the Government is the mere instrument of the major number of the constituents. This is a truth of great importance, but not yet sufficiently attended to, and is probably more strongly impressed upon my mind by facts, and reflections suggested by them, than on yours which has contemplated abuses of power issuing from a very different quarter. Wherever there is an interest and power to do wrong, wrong will

I. THE STRUCTURE OF GOVERNMENT OR THE BALANCE OF POWERS

The fundamental theory of political economy thus stated by Madison was the basis of the original American conception of the balance of powers which is formulated at length in four numbers of *The Federalist* and consists of the following elements:

1. No mere parchment separation of departments of government will be effective. "The legislative department is everywhere extending the sphere of its activity, and drawing all power into its impetuous vortex. The founders of our republic . . . seem never for a moment to have turned their eyes from the danger to liberty from the overgrown and all-grasping prerogative of an hereditary magistrate, supported and fortified by an hereditary branch of the legislative authority. They seem never to have recollected the danger from legislative usurpations, which, by assembling all power in the same hands, must lead to the same tyranny as is threatened by executive usurpations." [1]

2. Some sure mode of checking usurpations in the government must be provided, other than frequent appeals to the people. "There appear to be insuperable objections against the proposed recurrence to the people as a provision in all cases for keeping the several departments of power within their constitutional limits." [2] In a contest between the legislature and the other branches of the government, the former would doubtless be victorious on account of the ability of the legislators to plead their cause with the people.

3. What then can be depended upon to keep the govern-

generally be done, and not less readily by a powerful and interested party than by a powerful and interested prince." *Documentary History of the Constitution*, Vol. V, p. 88.

[1] *The Federalist*, No. 48.   [2] *Ibid.*, No. 49.

ment in close rein? "The only answer that can be given
is, that as all these exterior provisions are found to be inadequate, the defect must be supplied by so contriving the
interior structure of the government as that its several constituent parts may, by their mutual relations, be the means
of keeping each other in their proper places. . . . It is of
great importance in a republic not only to guard the society
against the oppression of its rulers, but to guard one part of
the society against the injustice of the other part. Different interests necessarily exist in different classes of citizens.
If a majority be united by a common interest, the rights of
the minority will be insecure." [1] There are two ways of
obviating this danger: one is by establishing a monarch
independent of popular will, and the other is by reflecting
these contending interests (so far as their representatives
may be enfranchised) in the very structure of the government itself so that a majority cannot dominate the minority
— which minority is of course composed of those who possess
property that may be attacked. "Society itself will be
broken into so many parts, interests, and classes of citizens,
that the rights of individuals, or of the minority, will be in
little danger from interested combinations of the majority." [2]

4. The structure of the government as devised at Philadelphia reflects these several interests and makes improbable
any danger to the minority from the majority. "The House
of Representatives being to be elected immediately by the
people, the Senate by the State legislatures, the President
by electors chosen for that purpose by the people, there
would be little probability of a common interest to cement
these different branches in a predilection for any particular
class of electors." [3]

5. All of these diverse interests appear in the amend-

[1] *The Federalist*, No. 51.   [2] *Ibid.*, No. 51.   [3] *Ibid.*, No. 60.

ing process but they are further reinforced against majorities. An amendment must receive a two-thirds vote in each of the two houses so constituted and the approval of three-fourths of the states.

6. The economic corollary of this system is as follows: Property interests may, through their superior weight in power and intelligence, secure advantageous legislation whenever necessary, and they may at the same time obtain immunity from control by parliamentary majorities.

If we examine carefully the delicate instrument by which the framers sought to check certain kinds of positive action that might be advocated to the detriment of established and acquired rights, we cannot help marvelling at their skill. Their leading idea was to break up the attacking forces at the starting point: the source of political authority for the several branches of the government. This disintegration of positive action at the source was further facilitated by the differentiation in the terms given to the respective departments of the government. And the crowning counterweight to "an interested and over-bearing majority," as Madison phrased it, was secured in the peculiar position assigned to the judiciary, and the use of the sanctity and mystery of the law as a foil to democratic attacks.

It will be seen on examination that no two of the leading branches of the government are derived from the same source. The House of Representatives springs from the mass of the people whom the states may see fit to enfranchise. The Senate is elected by the legislatures of the states, which were, in 1787, almost uniformly based on property qualifications, sometimes with a differentiation between the sources of the upper and lower houses. The President is to be chosen by electors selected as the legis-

latures of the states may determine—at all events by an
authority one degree removed from the voters at large.
The judiciary is to be chosen by the President and the
Senate, both removed from direct popular control and holding for longer terms than the House.

A sharp differentiation is made in the terms of the several
authorities, so that a complete renewal of the government
at one stroke is impossible. The House of Representatives
is chosen for two years; the Senators for six, but not at
one election, for one-third go out every two years. The
President is chosen for four years. The judges of the
Supreme Court hold for life. Thus "popular distempers,"
as eighteenth century publicists called them, are not only
restrained from working their havoc through direct elections,
but they are further checked by the requirement that they
must last six years in order to make their effects felt in the
political department of the government, providing they can
break through the barriers imposed by the indirect election
of the Senate and the President. Finally, there is the check
of judicial control that can be overcome only through the
manipulation of the appointing power which requires time,
or through the operation of a cumbersome amending
system.

The keystone of the whole structure is, in fact, the system
provided for judicial control — the most unique contribution to the science of government which has been made by
American political genius. It is claimed by some recent
writers that it was not the intention of the framers of the
Constitution to confer upon the Supreme Court the power
of passing upon the constitutionality of statutes enacted
by Congress; but in view of the evidence on the other side,
it is incumbent upon those who make this assertion to bring
forward positive evidence to the effect that judicial control

was not a part of the Philadelphia programme.[1] Certainly, the authors of *The Federalist* entertained no doubts on the point, and they conceived it to be such an excellent principle that they were careful to explain it to the electors to whom they addressed their arguments.

After elaborating fully the principle of judicial control over legislation under the Constitution, Hamilton enumerates the advantages to be derived from it. Speaking on the point of tenure during good behavior, he says: "In a monarchy it is an excellent barrier to the despotism of the prince; in a republic it is no less an excellent barrier to the encroachments and oppressions of the representative body. . . . If, then, the courts of justice are to be considered as the bulwarks of a limited Constitution against legislative encroachments, this consideration will afford a strong argument for the permanent tenure of judicial offices, since nothing will contribute so much as this to that independent spirit in the judges which must be essential to the faithful performance of so arduous a duty. . . . But it is not with a view to infractions of the Constitution only that the independence of the judges may be an essential safeguard against the effects of occasional ill humors in the society. These sometimes extend no farther than to the injury of private rights of particular classes of citizens, by unjust and partial laws. Here also the firmness of the judicial magistracy is of vast importance in mitigating the severity and confining the operation of such laws. It not only serves to moderate the immediate mischiefs of those which may have been passed, but it operates as a check upon the legislative body in passing them; who, perceiving that obstacles to the success of iniquitous intention are to be ex-

[1] Beard, *The Supreme Court and the Constitution.* See also the criticisms of this work by Professor W. F. Dodd, in the American Historical Review for January, 1913.

pected from the scruples of the courts, are in a manner compelled, by the very motives of injustice they meditate, to qualify their attempts. This is a circumstance calculated to have more influence upon the character of our governments than but few may be aware of." [1]

Nevertheless, it may be asked why, if the protection of property rights lay at the basis of the new system, there is in the Constitution no provision for property qualifications for voters or for elected officials and representatives. This is, indeed, peculiar when it is recalled that the constitutional history of England is in a large part a record of conflict over the weight in the government to be enjoyed by definite economic groups, and over the removal of the property qualifications early imposed on members of the House of Commons and on the voters at large. But the explanation of the absence of property qualifications from the Constitution is not difficult.

The members of the Convention were, in general, not opposed to property qualifications as such, either for officers or voters. "Several propositions," says Mr. S. H. Miller, "were made in the federal Convention in regard to property qualifications. A motion was carried instructing the committee to fix upon such qualifications for members of Congress. The committee could not agree upon the amount and reported in favor of leaving the matter to the legislature. Charles Pinckney objected to this plan as giving too much power to the first legislature. . . . Ellsworth objected to a property qualification on account of the difficulty of fixing the amount. If it was made high enough for the South, it would not be applicable to the Eastern States. Franklin was the only speaker who opposed the proposition to require property on principle, saying that 'some of the greatest rogues he was ever acquainted with were the richest rogues.' A resolution was also carried to require a property qualification for the Presidency. Hence it was evident that the lack of all property requirements for office in the United States Constitution was not owing to any opposition of the convention to such qualifications per se." [1]

Propositions to establish property restrictions were defeated, not because they were believed to be inherently opposed to the genius of American government, but for economic reasons — strange as it may seem. These economic reasons were clearly set forth by Madison in the debate over landed qualifications for legislators in July, when he showed, first, that slight property qualifications would not keep out the small farmers whose paper money schemes had been so disastrous to personalty; and, secondly, that landed property qualifications would exclude from Congress the representatives of "those classes of citizens who were not landholders," *i.e.* the personalty interests. This was true, he thought, because the mercantile and manufacturing classes would hardly be willing to turn their personalty into sufficient quantities of landed property to make them eligible for a seat in Congress.[2]

The other members also knew that they had most to fear from the very electors who would be enfranchised under a slight freehold restriction,[3] for the paper money party was everywhere bottomed on the small farming class. As Gorham remarked, the elections at Philadelphia, New York, and Boston, "where the merchants and mechanics vote, are at least as good as those made by freeholders only." [4] The fact emerges, therefore, that the personalty interests

---

[1] *American Historical Association Report* (1899), Vol. I, p. 108.
[2] Farrand, *Records*, Vol. II, pp. 123–124.
[3] *Ibid.*, pp. 201 ff.   [4] *Ibid.*, p. 216.

reflected in the Convention could, in truth, see no safe-guard at all in a freehold qualification against the assaults on vested personalty rights which had been made by the agrarians in every state. And it was obviously impossible to establish a personalty test, had they so desired, for there would have been no chance of securing a ratification of the Constitution at the hands of legislatures chosen by free-holders, or at the hands of conventions selected by them.

A very neat example of this antagonism between realty and personalty in the Convention came out on July 26, when Mason made, and Charles Pinckney supported, a motion imposing landed qualifications on members of Congress and excluding from that body "persons having unsettled ac-counts with or being indebted to the United States." In bringing up this motion Mason "observed that persons of the latter descriptions had frequently got into the state legis-latures in order to promote laws that might shelter their delinquencies; and that this evil had crept into Congress if report was to be regarded." [1]

Gouverneur Morris was on his feet in an instant. If qualifications were to be imposed, they should be laid on electors, not elected persons. The disqualification would fall upon creditors of the United States, for there were but few who owed the government anything. He knew that under this rule very few members of the Convention could get into the new government which they were establishing. "As to persons having unsettled accounts, he believed them to be pretty many. He thought, however, that such a discrimination would be both odious and useless and in many instances unjust and cruel. The delay of settlement had been more the fault of the public than of individuals. What will be done with those patriotic Citizens who have

[1] Farrand, *Records*, Vol. II, p. 121.

lent money or services or property to their country, without
having been yet able to obtain a liquidation of their claims?
Are they to be excluded?" On thinking it over, Morris
added to his remarks on the subject, saying, "It was a
precept of great antiquity as well as of high authority that
we should not be righteous overmuch. He thought we ought
to be equally on our guard against being wise overmuch. . . .
The parliamentary qualifications quoted by Colonel Mason
had been disregarded in practice; and was but a scheme
of the landed against the monied interest." [1]

Gerry thought that the inconvenience of excluding some
worthy creditors and debtors was of less importance than
the advantages offered by the resolution, but, after some
reflection, he added that "if property be one object of
government, provisions for securing it cannot be improper."
King sagely remarked that there might be a great danger in
imposing a landed qualification, because "it would exclude
the monied interest, whose aids may be essential in particular
emergencies to the public safety."

Madison had no confidence in the effectiveness of the
landed qualification and moved to strike it out, adding,
"Landed possessions were no certain evidence of real
wealth. Many enjoyed them to a great extent who were
more in debt than they were worth. The unjust laws of the
states had proceeded more from this class of men than any
others. It had often happened that men who had acquired
landed property on credit got into the Legislatures with a
view of promoting an unjust protection against their Creditors. In the next place, if a small quantity of land should
be made the standard, it would be no security; if a large
one, it would exclude the proper representatives of those
classes of Citizens who were not landholders." For these

[1] *Ibid.*, pp. 121–122.

and other reasons he opposed the landed qualifications and suggested that property qualifications on the voters would be better.[1]

The motion to strike out the "landed" qualification for legislators was carried by a vote of ten to one; the proposition to strike out the disqualification of persons having unsettled accounts with the United States was carried by a vote of nine to two. Finally the proposition to exclude persons who were indebted to the United States was likewise defeated by a vote of nine to two, after Pinckney had called attention to the fact that "it would exclude persons who had purchased confiscated property or should purchase Western territory of the public and might be some obstacle to the sale of the latter."

Indeed, there was little risk to personalty in thus allowing the Constitution to go to the states for approval without any property qualifications on voters other than those which the state might see fit to impose. Only one branch of new government, the House of Representatives, was required to be elected by popular vote; and, in case popular choice of presidential electors might be established, a safeguard was secured by the indirect process. Two controlling bodies, the Senate and Supreme Court, were removed altogether from the possibility of popular election except by constitutional amendment. Finally, the conservative members of the Convention were doubly fortified in the fact that nearly all of the state constitutions then in force provided real or personal property qualifications for voters anyway, and radical democratic changes did not seem perilously near.[2]

---

[1] Debate in Farrand, *Records*, Vol. II, pp. 123–124.

[2] See above, pp. 65 ff. The members of the Convention could not foresee the French Revolution which was to break out just as the new federal government was being put into operation in 1789.

II. THE POWERS CONFERRED UPON THE FEDERAL GOVERNMENT

1. The powers for positive action conferred upon the new government were few, but they were adequate to the purposes of the framers. They included, first, the power to lay and collect taxes; but here the rural interests were conciliated by the provision that direct taxes must be apportioned among the states according to population, counting three-fifths of the slaves. This, in the opinion of contemporaries eminently qualified to speak, was designed to prevent the populations of the manufacturing states from shifting the burdens of taxation to the sparsely settled agricultural regions.[1]

In a letter to the governor of their state, three delegates from North Carolina, Blount, Spaight, and Williamson, explained the advantage of this safeguard on taxation to the southern planters and farmers: "We had many things to hope from a National Government and the chief thing we had to fear from such a Government was the risque of unequal or heavy Taxation, but we hope you will believe as we do that the Southern states in general and North Carolina in particular are well secured on that head by the proposed system. It is provided in the 9th section of article the first that no Capitation or direct Tax shall be laid except in proportion to the number of inhabitants, in which number five blacks are only counted as three. If a land tax is laid, we are to pay the same rate; for example, fifty citizens of North Carolina can be taxed no more for all their Lands than fifty Citizens in one of the Eastern States. This must be greatly in our favour, for as most of their farms are small

---

[1] It was a curious turn of fortune that this provision prevented the agrarians and populists in 1894 from shifting a part of the burden of taxes to the great cities of the East. Thus the *Zweck im Recht* is sometimes reversed.

and many of them live in Towns we certainly have, one with another, land of twice the value that they possess.   When it is also considered that five Negroes are only to be charged the same Poll Tax as three whites, the advantage must be considerably increased under the proposed Form of Government.   The Southern states have also a better security for the return of slaves who might endeavour to escape than they had under the original Confederation." [1]

The taxing power was the basis of all other positive powers, and it afforded the revenues that were to discharge the public debt in full.   Provision was made for this discharge in Article VI to the effect that "All debts contracted and engagements entered into before the adoption of this Constitution shall be valid against the United States under this Constitution as under the Confederation."

But the cautious student of public economy, remembering the difficulties which Congress encountered under the Articles of Confederation in its attempts to raise the money to meet the interest on the debt, may ask how the framers of the Constitution could expect to overcome the hostile economic forces which had hitherto blocked the payment of the requisitions.   The answer is short.   Under the Articles, Congress had no power to lay and collect taxes immediately ; it could only make requisitions on the state legislatures.   Inasmuch as most of the states relied largely on direct taxes for their revenues, the demands of Congress were keenly felt and stoutly resisted.   Under the new system, however, Congress is authorized to lay taxes on its own account, but it is evident that the framers contemplated placing practically all of the national burden on the consumer.   The provision requiring the apportionment of direct taxes on a basis of population obviously implied that such taxes were to be viewed

[1] Clark, *The Records of North Carolina*, Vol. XX, p. 778.

as a last resort when indirect taxes failed to provide the required revenue.

With his usual acumen, Hamilton conciliates the freeholders and property owners in general by pointing out that they will not be called upon to support the national government by payments proportioned to their wealth.[1] Experience has demonstrated that it is impracticable to raise any considerable sums by direct taxation.   Even where the government is strong, as in Great Britain, resort must be had chiefly to indirect taxation.   The pockets of the farmers "will reluctantly yield but scanty supplies, in the unwelcome shape of impositions on their houses and lands; and personal property is too precarious and invisible a fund to be laid hold of in any other way than by the imperceptible agency of taxes on consumption."   Real and personal property are thus assured a generous immunity from such burdens as Congress had attempted to impose under the Articles; taxes under the new system will, therefore, be less troublesome than under the old.

2.   Congress was given, in the second place, plenary power to raise and support military and naval forces, for the defence of the country against foreign and domestic foes. These forces were to be at the disposal of the President in the execution of national laws; and to guard the states against renewed attempts of "desperate debtors" like Shays, the United States guaranteed to every commonwealth a republican form of government and promised to aid in quelling internal disorder on call of the proper authorities.

The army and navy are considered by the authors of *The Federalist* as genuine economic instrumentalities.   As will be pointed out below, they regarded trade and commerce as the fundamental cause of wars between nations; and the

[1] *The Federalist*, Number 12.

source of domestic insurrection they traced to class conflicts within society. "Nations in general," says Jay, "will make war whenever they have a prospect of getting anything by it";[1] and it is obvious that the United States dissevered and discordant will be the easy prey to the commercial ambitions of their neighbors and rivals.

The material gains to be made by other nations at the expense of the United States are so apparent that the former cannot restrain themselves from aggression. France and Great Britain feel the pressure of our rivalry in the fisheries; they and other European nations are our competitors in navigation and the carrying trade; our independent voyages to China interfere with the monopolies enjoyed by other countries there; Spain would like to shut the Mississippi against us on one side and Great Britain fain would close the St. Lawrence on the other. The cheapness and excellence of our productions will excite their jealousy, and the enterprise and address of our merchants will not be consistent with the wishes or policy of the sovereigns of Europe. But, adds the commentator, by way of clinching the argument, "if they see that our national government is efficient and well administered, our trade prudently regulated, our militia properly organized and disciplined, our resources and finances discreetly managed, our credit re-established, our people free, contented, and united, they will be much more disposed to cultivate our friendship than provoke our resentment."[2]

All the powers of Europe could not prevail against us. "Under a vigorous national government the natural strength and resources of the country, directed to a common interest, would baffle all the combinations of European jealousy to restrain our growth. . . . An active commerce, an ex-

---

[1] *The Federalist*, No. 4.   [2] *Ibid.*

tensive navigation, and a flourishing marine would then be the offspring of moral and physical necessity. We might defy the little arts of the little politicians to control or vary the irresistible and unchangeable course of nature."[1] In the present state of disunion the profits of trade are snatched from us; our commerce languishes; and poverty threatens to overspread a country which might outrival the world in riches.

The army and navy are to be not only instruments of defence in protecting the United States against the commercial and territorial ambitions of other countries; but they may be used also in forcing open foreign markets. What discriminatory tariffs and navigation laws may not accomplish the sword may achieve. The authors of *The Federalist* do not contemplate that policy of mild and innocuous isolation which was later made famous by Washington's farewell address.[2] On the contrary — they do not expect the United States to change human nature and make our commercial classes less ambitious than those of other countries to extend their spheres of trade. A strong navy will command the respect of European states. "There can be no doubt that the continuance of the Union under an efficient government would put it within our power, at a period not very distant, to create a navy which, if it could not vie with those of the great maritime powers, would at least be of respectable weight if thrown into the scale of either of two contending parties. . . . A few ships of the line sent opportunely to the reinforcement of either side, would often be sufficient to decide the fate of a campaign, on the event of which interests of the greatest mag-

[1] *The Federalist*, No. 11.

[2] Washington's farewell address which was partially written by Hamilton is one of the most ingenious partisan documents ever written. It, too, has its economic interpretation.

nitude were suspended. Our position is, in this respect, a
most commanding one. And if to this consideration we
add that of the usefulness of supplies from this country,
in the prosecution of military operations in the West Indies,
it will be readily perceived that a situation so favorable
would enable us to bargain with great advantage for commercial privileges. A price would be set not only upon
our friendship, but upon our neutrality. By a steady adherence to the Union, we may hope, ere long, to become
the arbiter of Europe in America, and to be able to incline the
balance of European competitions in this part of the world
as our interest may dictate." [1]

As to dangers from class wars within particular states,
the authors of *The Federalist* did not deem it necessary
to make extended remarks : the recent events in New England were only too vividly impressed upon the public mind.
"The tempestuous situation from which Massachusetts
has scarcely emerged," says Hamilton, "evinces that dangers
of this kind are not merely speculative. Who can determine what might have been the issue of her late convulsions,
if the malcontents had been headed by a Cæsar or by a
Cromwell." [2]   The strong arm of the Union must be available
in such crises.

In considering the importance of defence against domestic
insurrection, the authors of *The Federalist* do not overlook
an appeal to the slave-holders' instinctive fear of a servile
revolt. Naturally, it is Madison whose interest catches
this point and drives it home, by appearing to discount it.
In dealing with the dangers of insurrection, he says : "I
take no notice of an unhappy species of population abound-
ing in some of the states who, during the calm of regular
government are sunk below the level of men ; but who, in

¹ *The Federalist*, No. 11.   ² *Ibid.*, No. 21.

the tempestuous scenes of civil violence, may emerge into human character and give a superiority of strength to any party with which they may associate themselves." [1]

3. In addition to the power to lay and collect taxes and raise and maintain armed forces on land and sea, the Constitution vests in Congress plenary control over foreign and interstate commerce, and thus authorizes it to institute protective and discriminatory laws in favor of American interests,[2] and to create a wide sweep for free trade throughout the whole American empire. A single clause thus reflects the strong impulse of economic forces in the towns and young manufacturing centres. In a few simple words the mercantile and manufacturing interests wrote their *Zweck im Recht;* and they paid for their victory by large concessions to the slave-owning planters of the south.[3]

While dealing with commerce in *The Federalist*[4] Hamilton does not neglect the subject of interstate traffic and intercourse. He shows how free trade over a wide range will be to reciprocal advantage, will give great diversity to commercial enterprise, and will render stagnation less liable by offering more distant markets when local demands fall off. "The speculative trader," he concludes, "will at once perceive the force of these observations and will acknowledge that the aggregate balance of the commerce of the United States would bid fair to be much more favorable than that of the thirteen states without union or with partial unions."

4. Another great economic antagonism found its expression in the clause conferring upon Congress the power to dispose of the territories and make rules and regulations for their government and admission to the Union. In this contest, the interests of the states which held territories came

---

[1] *The Federalist*, No. 43. [2] *Ibid.*, No. 35.
[3] See the entire letter of Blount, Spaight, and Williamson, cited above, p. 169.
[4] No. 11.

prominently to the front; and the ambiguity of the language used in the Constitution on this point may be attributed to the inability of the contestants to reach precise conclusions.[1] The leaders were willing to risk the proper managem᷊nt of the land problem after the new government was safely launched; and they were correct in their estimate of their future political prowess.

These are the great powers conferred on the new government: taxation, war, commercial control, and disposition of western lands. Through them public creditors may be paid in full, domestic peace maintained, advantages obtained in dealing with foreign nations, manufactures protected, and the development of the territories go forward with full swing. The remaining powers are minor and need not be examined here. What implied powers lay in the minds of the framers likewise need not be inquired into; they have long been the subject of juridical speculation.

None of the powers conferred by the Constitution on Congress permits a direct attack on property. The federal government is given no general authority to define property. It may tax, but indirect taxes must be uniform, and these are to fall upon consumers. Direct taxes may be laid, but resort to this form of taxation is rendered practically impossible, save on extraordinary occasions, by the provision that they must be apportioned according to population — so that numbers cannot transfer the burden to accumulated wealth. The slave trade may be destroyed, it is true, after the lapse of a few years; but slavery as a domestic institution is better safeguarded than before.

Even the destruction of the slave trade had an economic basis, although much was said at the time about the ethics

[1] J. C. Welling, "States' Rights Conflict over the Public Lands," *Report of the American Historical Association* (1888), pp. 174 ff.

of the clause. In the North where slavery, though widespread, was of little economic consequence, sympathy with the unfortunate negroes could readily prevail. Maryland and Virginia, already overstocked with slaves beyond the limits of land and capital, had prohibited the foreign trade in negroes, because the slave-holders, who predominated in the legislatures, were not willing to see the value of their chattels reduced to a vanishing point by excessive importations. South Carolina and Georgia, where the death rate in the rice swamps and the opening of adjoining territories made a strong demand for the increase of slave property, on the other hand, demanded an open door for slave-dealers.

South Carolina was particularly determined,[1] and gave northern representatives to understand that if they wished to secure their commercial privileges, they must make concessions to the slave trade. And they were met half way. Ellsworth said: "As slaves multiply so fast in Virginia and Maryland that it is cheaper to raise than import them, whilst in the sickly rice swamps foreign supplies are necessary, if we go no farther than is urged, we shall be unjust towards South Carolina and Georgia. Let us not intermeddle. As population increases; poor laborers will be so plenty as to render slaves useless." [2]

General Pinckney taunted the Virginia representatives in the Convention, some of whom were against slavery as well as importation, with disingenuous interestedness. "South Carolina and Georgia cannot do without slaves. As to Virginia she will gain by stopping the importations. Her slaves will rise in value and she has more than she wants. It would be unequal to require South Carolina and Georgia to confederate on such unequal terms."

---

[1] Farrand, *Records*, Vol. II, p. 371.
[2] *Ibid.*, p. 371.

III. RESTRICTIONS LAID UPON STATE LEGISLATURES

Equally important to personalty as the positive powers conferred upon Congress to tax, support armies, and regulate commerce were the restrictions imposed on the states.[1] Indeed, we have the high authority of Madison for the statement that of the forces which created the Constitution, those property interests seeking protection against omnipotent legislatures were the most active.

In a letter to Jefferson, written in October, 1787, Madison elaborates the principle of federal judicial control over state legislation, and explains the importance of this new institution in connection with the restrictions laid down in the Constitution on laws affecting private rights. "The mutability of the laws of the States," he says, "is found to be a serious evil. The injustice of them has been so frequent and so flagrant as to alarm the most steadfast friends of Republicanism. I am persuaded I do not err in saying that the evils issuing from these sources contributed more to that uneasiness which produced the Convention, and prepared the public mind for a general reform, than those which accrued to our national character and interest from the inadequacy of the Confederation to its immediate objects. A reform, therefore, which does not make provision for private rights must be materially defective." [2]

Two small clauses embody the chief demands of personalty against agrarianism: the emission of paper money is pro-

---

[1] There are, of course, some restrictions on Congress laid down in the Constitution; but the powers of the national legislature are limited and the restrictions are not of the same significance. Radical action on the part of the national legislature was anticipated in the structure of the government itself, but specific provision had to be made against the assaults of popular majorities in state legislatures on property rights.

[2] *Writings of James Madison* (1865), Vol. I, p. 350. This entire letter deserves careful study by anyone who would understand the Constitution as an economic document.

hibited and the states are forbidden to impair the obligation of contract. The first of these means a return to a specie basis — when coupled with the requirement that the gold and silver coin of the United States shall be the legal tender. The Shays and their paper money legions, who assaulted the vested rights of personalty by the process of legislative depreciation, are now subdued forever, and money lenders and security holders may be sure of their operations. Contracts are to be safe, and whoever engages in a financial operation, public or private, may know that state legislatures cannot destroy overnight the rules by which the game is played.

A principle of deep significance is written in these two brief sentences. The economic history of the states between the Revolution and the adoption of the Constitution is compressed in them. They appealed to every money lender, to every holder of public paper, to every man who had any personalty at stake. The intensity of the economic interests reflected in these two prohibitions can only be felt by one who has spent months in the study of American agrarianism after the Revolution. In them personalty won a significant battle in the conflict of 1787–1788.

The authors of *The Federalist* advance in support of these two clauses very substantial arguments which bear out the view here expressed. "The loss which America has sustained since the peace, from the pestilential effects of paper money on the necessary confidence between man and man, on the necessary confidence in the public councils, on the industry and morals of the people, and on the character of republican government, constitutes an enormous debt against the States chargeable with this unadvised measure, which must long remain unsatisfied; or rather an accumulation of guilt which can be expiated no otherwise than by a voluntary sacrifice on the altar of justice of the power which has been the instrument of it." Speaking on the contract clause — that "additional bulwark in favor of personal security and private rights" — Madison is sure that the "sober people of America are weary of the fluctuating policy which has directed the public councils," and will welcome a reform that will "inspire a general prudence and industry and give a regular course to the business of society."[1]

Hamilton on several occasions laid great stress on the contract clause as one of the features of the Constitution which had warmly commended it to its supporters. In a communication to Washington, dated May 29, 1790, he wrote: "This, to the more enlightened part of the community, was not one of the least recommendations of that Constitution. The too frequent intermeddlings of the state legislatures in relation to private contracts were extensively felt and seriously lamented; and a Constitution which promised a preventative was, by those who felt and thought in that manner, eagerly embraced."[2]

There was not a little discussion of the obligation of contract clause in the contemporary press during the period of ratification, and there can be no doubt that it was favorably viewed by the supporters of the Constitution as an added safeguard against paper money and stay laws. A writer in the New Hampshire Spy, on November 3, 1787, in commending the new frame of government to his fellow citizens, calls particular attention to this provision: "It also expressly prohibits those destructive laws in the several states which alter or impair the obligation of contracts; so that in future anyone may be certain of an exact fulfilment

---

[1] *The Federalist*, No. 44.
[2] Ms. Library of Congress: *Treasury Department Letters, 1789–1790* (Washington Papers), folio 297.

of any contract that may be entered into or the penalty that may be stipulated for in case of failure."

Another writer of the period approves the same principle with more vigor. "My countrymen, the devil is among you. Make paper as much as you please. Make it a tender in all *future* contracts, or let it rest on its own credit — but remember that *past* contracts are sacred things — and that legislatures have no right to interfere with them— they have no right to say, a debt shall be paid at a discount, or in any manner which the parties never intended. . . . To pay *bona fide* contracts for cash, in paper of little value, or in old horses, would be a dishonest attempt in an individual: but for legislatures to frame laws to support and encourage such detestable villainy, is like a judge who should inscribe the arms of a rogue over the seat of justice." [1]

The full import of the obligation of contract clause was doubtless better understood by Chief Justice Marshall than by any man of that generation. He had taken an active part in the adoption of the Constitution in his state, and he had studied long and arduously the history of the period for his classic defence of Federalism, *The Life of Washington.* In more than one decision he applied the clause with great effect, and voiced the views of his Federalist contemporaries on this point, explaining the deep-seated social antagonism which is reflected in it.[2] And when at length, in his declining years, he saw it attacked in the legislatures by Jacksonian democracy, and beheld the Supreme Court itself surrendering the position which he had earlier taken, he spread on record in a dissenting opinion a warning and a protest which for cogency and vigor equals any of his great dissertations delivered in the name of the Court.

In the case of Ogden *v.* Saunders, decided in the January

---

[1] *The American Museum,* Vol. I, p. 118.   [2] See below, p. 295.

term of 1827, the Supreme Court was compelled to pass upon the issue: "Does a bankrupt law which applies to contracts made *after* its passage impair the obligation of those contracts?" The newer school on the bench, Washington, Johnson, Trimble, and Thompson were of opinion that such a law did not impair the obligation of contract and was valid. Marshall, Duvall, and Story dissented. The Chief Justice took the high ground that the obligation of a contract inhered in the contract itself, and could not be changed by any external legislation whatever. Therefore, obviously, legislation affecting adversely the obligation of future contracts was just as unconstitutional as legislation attacking contracts already made. In other words, Marshall, who ought to have known what the framers of the Constitution intended better than any man on the supreme bench, believed that it was designed to bring under the ban substantially all legislation which affected personalty adversely — in other words that it was similar in character to the due process clause of the Fourteenth Amendment.

Speaking on the contract clause he said with great solemnity: "We cannot look back to the history of the times when the august spectacle was exhibited of the assemblage of the whole people by their representatives in convention, in order to unite thirteen independent sovereignties under one government, so far as might be necessary for the purposes of union, without being sensible of the great importance attached to the tenth section of the first article. The power of changing the relative situation of debtor and creditor, of interfering with contracts, a power which comes home to every man, touches the interest of all, and controls the conduct of every individual in those things which he supposes to be proper for his own exclusive management, had been used to such an excess by the state legislatures as to break in upon the ordinary intercourse of society, and destroy all confidence between man and man. The mischief had become so great, so alarming as not only to impair commercial intercourse, and threaten the existence of credit, but to sap the morals of the people, and destroy the sanctity of private faith. To guard against the continuance of the evil was an object of deep interest with all the truly wise, as well as virtuous, of this great community, and was one of the important benefits expected from a reform of the government." [1]

THE ECONOMICS OF INTERNATIONAL POLITICS

The authors of *The Federalist* carry over into the field of international politics the concept of economic antagonisms which lie at the basis of their system of domestic politics. Modern wars spring primarily out of commercial rivalry, although the ambitions of princes have often been a source of international conflict. "Has commerce hitherto done anything more than change the objects of war?" asks Hamilton. "Is not the love of wealth as domineering and enterprising a passion as that of power or glory? Have there not been as many wars founded upon commercial motives, since that has become the prevailing system of nations, as were before occasioned by the cupidity of territory or dominion? Has not the spirit of commerce, in many instances, administered new incentives to the appetite, both for the one and for the other?" [2] Let history answer. Carthage, a commercial republic, was an aggressor in a war that ended in her destruction. The furious contests of Holland and England were over the dominion of the sea. Commerce has been for ages the predominant pursuit of England, and she has been constantly engaged in wars.

---

[1] Ogden *v.* Saunders, 12 Wheaton, pp. 213 ff.   [2] *The Federalist*, No. 6.

Even the Hapsburg-Bourbon wars have in a large measure grown out of commercial considerations.

In this world-wide and age-long conflict of nations for commercial advantages, the United States cannot expect to become a non-resistant, an idle spectator. Even were pacific ideals to dominate American policy, she could not overcome the scruples of her ambitious rivals. In union, therefore, is strength against aggression and in support of offensive operations. Moreover, the Union will be better able to settle disputes amicably because of the greater show of power which it can make. "Acknowledgements, explanations, and compensations are often accepted as satisfactory from a strong united nation, which would be rejected as unsatisfactory if offered by a state or a confederacy of little consideration or power." [1]

Turning from the material causes of foreign wars the authors of *The Federalist* examine the possible sources of danger from domestic discord among the states, regarded as independent sovereignties. And how may such domestic discord arise? The North will probably grow strong and formidable and be tempted to despoil the South: nor "does it appear to be a rash conjecture," says Jay, "that its young swarms might often be tempted to gather honey in the more blooming fields and milder air of their luxurious and more delicate neighbors." [2]

Then the apple of discord may be thrown among the states by foreign countries if several confederacies take the place of union. And what is this apple of discord? Each of the proposed confederacies, says Jay, "would have its commerce with foreigners to regulate by distinct treaties; and as their productions and commodities are different and proper for different markets, so would those treaties

[1] *The Federalist*, No. 3.   [2] *Ibid.*, No. 5.

be essentially different." Treaties are subject to the law of greatest economic pressure. "Different commercial concerns," he continues, "must create different interests, and of course different degrees of political attachment to and connection with different foreign nations."[1] The degrees of political attachment also follow the law of greatest economic pressure ; and if foreign nations come to blows among themselves, their allies in America are likely to be drawn into the conflict. Thus domestic discord may arise among the states indirectly through their material connections with other countries.

But internecine warfare will more probably arise from causes operating within the states ; and what may be the real sources of such conflict ? asks Hamilton.[2] They are numerous : lust for power and dominion, the desire for equality and safety, the ambitions of leaders. Has it not invariably been found, he adds, "that momentary passions, and immediate interests have a more active and imperious control over human conduct than general and remote considerations of policy, utility, or justice ? . . . Has commerce hitherto done anything more than change the objects of war ? Is not the love of wealth as domineering and enterprizing a passion as that of power or glory ? Have there not been as many wars founded upon commercial motives since that has become the prevailing system of nations, as were before occasioned by the cupidity of territory or dominion ?"

Of course such acute observers as the authors of *The Federalist* do not omit to remark that the personal ambitions of monarchs have been a cause of wars, and the passions of men for leadership have been a source of domestic insurrections. But they are quick to add that the ag-

[1] *Ibid.*   [2] *Ibid.*, No. 6.

grandizement and support of their particular families are among the motives that have led monarchs to undertake wars of conquest;[1] and as to personal element in domestic insurrections, Hamilton expresses a doubt whether Massachusetts would recently have been plunged into civil war "if Shays had not been a *desperate debtor*."[2]

Turning from the question as to the extent of the economic motive in the personal element, Hamilton makes an inquiry into the more probable sources of wars among the states in case a firmer union, endowed with adequate powers, is not established.   These he enumerates:[3]

1. "Territorial disputes have at all times been found one of the most fertile sources of hostility among nations." The several states have an interest in the Western Territories, and "to reason from the past to the future, we shall have good ground to apprehend that the sword would sometimes be appealed to as the arbiter of their differences."

2. "The competitions of commerce would be another fruitful source of contention."   Each state will pursue a policy conducive to its own advantage, and "the spirit of enterprize, which characterizes the commercial part of America, has left no occasion of displaying itself unimproved.   It is not at all probable that this unbridled spirit would pay much respect to those regulations of trade by which particular states might endeavor to secure exclusive benefits to their own citizens."   The economic motive will thus probably override all considerations of interstate comity and all considerations of international law.   But that is not all; says Hamilton, in italics, "*We should be ready to denominate injuries those things which were in reality the justifiable acts of independent sovereignties consulting a distinct interest.*"   Com-

---

[1] *The Federalist*, No. 4.   [2] *Ibid.*, No. 6.
[3] *Ibid.*, No. 7.

merce will have little respect for the right of other peoples to protect their interests, and it will stigmatize as an "injury" anything which blocks its enterprise.

3. "The public debt of the Union would be a further cause of collision between the separate states or confederacies." Some states would oppose paying the debt. Why? Because they are "less impressed with the importance of national credit, or because their citizens have little, if any, immediate interest in the question." But other states, "a numerous body of whose citizens are creditors to the public beyond the proportion of the state in the total amount of the national debt, would be strenuous for some equitable and effective provision." In other words, citizens who had nothing at stake would be indifferent, and those who had something to lose would clamor. Foreign powers also might intervene, and the "double contingency of external invasion and internal contention" would be hazarded.

4. "Laws in violation of private contracts, as they amount to aggressions on the rights of those states whose citizens are injured by them, may be considered as another probable source of hostility." Had there not been plenty of evidence to show that state legislatures, if unrestrained by some higher authority, would attack private rights in property? And had there not been a spirit of retaliation also? "We reasonably infer that in similar cases, under other circumstances, a war, not of *parchment*, but of the sword, would chastise such atrocious breaches of moral obligation and social justice."

These, then, are the four leading sources of probable conflict among the states if not united into a firm union: territory, commerce, the national debt, and violations of contractual rights in property — all as severely economic as could well be imagined.

To carry the theory of the economic interpretation of the Constitution out into its ultimate details would require a monumental commentary, such as lies completely beyond the scope of this volume. But enough has been said to show that the concept of the Constitution as a piece of abstract legislation reflecting no group interests and recognizing no economic antagonisms is entirely false. It was an economic document drawn with superb skill by men whose property interests were immediately at stake; and as such it appealed directly and unerringly to identical interests in the country at large.

CHAPTER VII

HAVING examined the economic implications of the Constitution in the light of the greatest of all commentaries,
The Federalist, it is now interesting to inquire whether
the members of the Convention at large entertained substantially identical views as to the political science of the
system. There are several difficulties in the way of such
an investigation. Not all of the delegates, indeed not all
of the most influential, were speech makers or writers or
philosophers. As intensely practical men they were concerned with tangible results, not with the manner in which
political scientists might view the details of their operations.
There is, accordingly, a considerable danger of attempting
too much in making generalizations, and to obviate this as
far as possible, the method of taking the members in alphabetical order is adopted, and the evidence of the views
entertained by each is fully documented.[1]

The leaders in politics and political philosophy in the
eighteenth century were not far removed from that frank
recognition of class rights which characterized English
society, and they were not under the necessity of obscuring
— at least to the same extent as modern partisan writers —
the essential economic antagonisms featuring in law and
constitution making. Their clarity of thought was greatly
facilitated by the disfranchisement of the propertyless,

---

[1] A few whose views were not ascertained are omitted.

which made it unnecessary for political writers to address themselves to the proletariat and to explain dominant group interests in such a manner as to make them appear in the garb of "public policy."

There does not appear, of course, in the writings of American political scientists in the eighteenth century, that sharp recognition of class rights which characterizes the feudal legists, because within the propertied interests politically represented in the government, there were divisions which had to be glossed over; and there were also mutterings of unrest on the part of the disfranchised which later broke out in the storm that swept away the property qualifications on voters and introduced political equalitarianism. Under these circumstances the supporters of the Constitution had to be somewhat circumspect in the expression of their views; but, happily for science, the proceedings at Philadelphia during the drafting of the Constitution were secret, and they were able to discuss with utmost frankness the actual politico-economic results which they desired to reach. Fortunately, also, fragmentary reports of these proceedings have come down to us, and have been put in a definitive form by Professor Farrand.

Abraham Baldwin, of Georgia, did not indulge in any lengthy disquisitions on government in the Convention, and his literary remains are apparently very meagre. However, his view that the Senate of the United States ought to represent property came out in the debate on June 29, over a motion by Ellsworth to the effect that the "rule of suffrage in the second branch be the same as that established by the Articles of Confederation." Baldwin immediately opposed the proposition, saying, "He thought the second branch ought to be the representation of property, and that in forming it therefore some reference ought to be had to the relative wealth of their constituents, and to the principles on which the senate of Massachusetts was constituted." [1] At the time the senate of that commonwealth rested upon special freehold and personalty qualifications,[2] and the members were apportioned among the several districts on the basis of the amount of taxes paid by each. It is thus apparent that Baldwin wished the Senate of the new government to be based frankly upon property.

Gunning Bedford, of Delaware, did not participate extensively in the debates of the Convention, but it seems from the character of the few remarks that he made that he favored a more democratic form than was finally adopted, although he signed the Constitution. This inference is drawn from a brief notice of his objection to the establishment of a council of revision composed of the executive and a certain number of the judiciary to exercise a sort of censorship over the acts of Congress. Madison records as follows : "Mr. Bedford was opposed to every check on the Legislative, even the Council of Revision first proposed. He thought it would be sufficient to mark out in the Constitution the boundaries to the Legislative Authority, which would give all the requisite security to the rights of the other departments. The Representatives of the People were the best judges of what was for their interest, and ought to be under no external controul whatever. The two branches would produce a sufficient controul within the Legislature itself." [3]

Jacob Broom was among those who wished to "lessen the dependence of the general government on the people," to use Jefferson's phrase, by lengthening the terms of public officers. He seconded Read's motion to increase the term

---

[1] Farrand, *Records*, Vol. I, p. 469.
[2] Above, p. 65.   [3] Farrand, *Records*, Vol. I, p. 100.

of Senators to nine years; [1] he opposed the election of the
executive by popular vote, and supported Luther Martin's
resolution in favor of election by electors appointed by the
legislatures of the several states; [2] he wished to give life tenure
to the executive, that is, during good behavior, [3] and he
favored the suggestion that Congress should be given a
negative over state legislatures. [4]   Broom seldom spoke in
the Convention, but there is no doubt that he believed in
a restricted and well "balanced" democracy.

Pierce Butler, of South Carolina, on more than one occasion
urged the desirability of making property at least
one of the elements in the distribution of representation.
On June 6, when Charles Pinckney moved that the lower
house of the national legislature should be chosen by the
state legislatures and not by the people, Butler said: "I
am against determining the mode of election until the ratio
of representation is fixed — if that proceeds on a principle
favorable to wealth as well as numbers of free inhabitants,
I am content to unite with Delaware (Mr. Read) in abolishing
the state legislatures and becoming one nation instead
of a confederation of republics." [5]   In connection with a
discussion of the Senate, "he urged that the second branch
ought to represent the states according to their property." [6]
Later in the sessions of the Convention he again "warmly
urged the justice and necessity of regarding wealth in the apportionment
of representation." [7]   He was also particularly
solicitous about slave property, and he declared that "the
security which the southern states want is that their negroes
may not be taken from them." [8]

Daniel Carroll favored the popular election of the execu-

[1] Farrand, *Records*, Vol. I, p. 421.
[2] *Ibid.*, Vol. II, p. 32.
[3] *Ibid.*, Vol. II, p. 33.
[4] *Ibid.*, Vol. II, p. 390.
[5] *Ibid.*, Vol. I, p. 144.
[6] *Ibid.*, p. 529.
[7] *Ibid.*, p. 562.
[8] *Ibid.*, p. 605.

tive, but he advocated a three-fourths vote in Congress to overcome the executive veto. Speaking on this point, "He remarked that as a majority was now to be the quorum, seventeen in the larger and eight in the smaller house might carry points. The advantage that might be taken of this seemed to call for greater impediments to improper laws." [1] Carroll did not indulge in any philosophic reflections in the Convention so that his "political science," if he had worked out any definite system, is not apparent in the records.

George Clymer entertained the notions of government which were common to the Federalists of his time. He held that "a representative of the people is appointed to think *for* and not *with* his constituents"; [2] and invariably, during the course of his career, he "showed a total disregard to the opinions of his constituents when opposed to the matured decisions of his own mind." It was on these principles that he "warmly opposed the proposition introducing a clause in the Constitution which conferred upon the people the unalienable right of instructing their representatives." [3]

W. R. Davie, although he is reputed to have been an accomplished orator and profound student, does not figure extensively in Madison's meagre records. At no point does he expound any philosophy of government. His views were always practical. On the proposition to count slaves in apportioning representation, he threw down the gauntlet to the Convention, and declared that if the rate was not at least three-fifths, North Carolina would not federate. [4] As to the basis of government Davie "seemed to think that wealth or property ought to be represented in the second branch; and numbers in the first branch." [5]

---

[1] *Ibid.*, Vol. II, p. 300. [2] Sanderson, *op. cit.*, p. 168. [3] *Ibid.*, p. 169.
[4] Farrand, *Records*, Vol. I, p. 593. [5] *Ibid.*, Vol. I, p. 542.

Davie fully understood the significance of the obligation of contract clause which was designed as a check on the propensities of popular legislatures to assault private rights in property, particularly personalty. Speaking in the convention of North Carolina on this clause, he said: "That section is the best in the Constitution. It is founded on the strongest principles of justice. It is a section, in short, which I thought would have endeared the Constitution to this country."[1] Davie undoubtedly understood and approved the doctrines of balanced classes in the government, as expounded in Adams' *Defence of American Constitutions*.[2]

At no time does Davie appear to have courted popular favor in his native state, for a writer speaking of his candidacy for the legislature in 1798 says: "The 'true Whigs,' as they styled themselves, dined together under the oaks and toasted Mr. Jefferson. The other party, who were called 'aristocrats,' ate and drank in the house on entirely different principles. General Davie dined in the house with the 'aristocrats.' The 'true Whigs' took offence at this and resolved to oppose his selection, and it was only with much address that they were kept quiet. . . . If any person had had the impudence to dispute the election, General Davie would certainly not have been returned. The rabble, which in all places is the majority, would have voted against him."[3]

John Dickinson, of Delaware, frankly joined that minority which was outspoken in its belief in a monarchy—an action that comported with his refusal to sign the Declaration of Independence and his reluctance to embark upon the stormy sea of Revolution. At the very opening of the Convention,

---

[1] Farrand, *Records*, Vol. III, p. 350.

[2] McRee, *Life and Correspondence of James Iredell*, Vol. II, pp. 161, 168.

[3] Peele, *Lives of Distinguished North Carolinians*, p. 75. Davie's great collection of papers was destroyed in Sherman's raid. *Ibid.*, p. 78.

on June 2, he expressed his preference for a regal government, although he admitted that the existing state of affairs would not permit its establishment in America. Madison records him as saying: "A limited Monarchy he considered as one of the best Governments in the world. It was not certain that the same blessings were derivable from any other form. It was certain that equal blessings had never yet been derived from any of the republican form. A limited monarchy, however, was out of the question."[1]

Dickinson was also among the members of the Convention who wished to establish a property qualification for voters because he thought no other foundation for government would be secure. In the debate on this subject on August 7, according to Madison's notes: "Mr. Dickinson had a very different idea of the tendency of vesting the right of suffrage in the freeholders of the Country. He considered them as the best guardians of liberty; And the restriction of the right to them as a necessary defence agst. the dangerous influence of those multitudes without property & without principle, with which our Country like all others, will in time abound. As to the unpopularity of the innovation it was in his opinion chemirical. The great mass of our Citizens is composed at this time of freeholders, and will be pleased with it."[2]

According to King's notes: "Dickinson — It is said yr. restraining by ye Constitution the rights of Election to Freeholders, is a step towards aristocracy — is this true, No. — we are safe by trusting the owners of the soil — the Owners of the Country — it will not be unpopular — because the Freeholders are the most numerous at this Time — The Danger to Free Governments has not been from Freeholders, but those who are not Freeholders — there is no

[1] Farrand, *Records*, Vol. I, p. 86. [2] *Ibid.*, Vol. II, p. 202.

Danger — because our Laws favor the Division of property — The Freehold will be parcelled among all the worthy men in the State — The Merchants & Mechanicks are safe — They may become Freeholders besides they are represented in ye State Legislatures, which elect the Senate of the U.S.[1]

No member of the Convention distrusted anything savoring of "levelling democracy" more than *Oliver Ellsworth.* Later as Chief Justice he denounced from the bench Jefferson and the French party as "the apostles of anarchy, bloodshed, and atheism."[2] In the Convention, he opposed the popular election of the President[3] and favored associating the judges with the executive in the exercise of a veto power over acts of Congress.[4] He believed in the restriction of the suffrage to those who paid taxes.[5] He was a warm advocate of judicial control, in general, and thoroughly understood the political significance of the system.[6]

Thomas Fitzsimons, the wealthy merchant and stockbroker from Pennsylvania, was, after his kind, not a loquacious man, but rather a man of action — a practical man; and the records of the Convention contain no lengthy speech by him. When Gouverneur Morris, on August 7, proposed to restrain the right to vote to freeholders, Fitzsimons seconded the motion, apparently without saying anything on the point.[7] While he thus sympathized with the movement to set the Constitution frankly on a property basis, Fitzsimons was naturally more interested in such matters as protection to manufactures and harbor improvements.[8]

---

[1] Farrand, *Ibid.*, Vol. II, p. 207.
[2] H. J. Ford, *Rise and Growth of American Politics*, p. 113.
[3] Farrand, *Records*, Vol. II, pp. 57, 58, 63, 101, 108, 111.
[4] *Ibid.*, Vol. II, p. 73.   [5] *Ibid.*, Vol. II, p. 207.
[6] Beard, *The Supreme Court and the Constitution*, pp. 71–72.
[7] Farrand, *Records*, Vol. II, p. 201.   [8] *Ibid.*, pp. 362, 529, 589.

Benjamin Franklin, who at the time of the Convention was so advanced in years as to be of little real weight in the formation of the Constitution, seems to have entertained a more hopeful view of democracy than any other member of that famous group. He favored a single-chambered legislature,[1] opposed an absolute veto in the executive,[2] and resisted the attempt to place property qualifications on the suffrage.[3] He signed the Constitution when it was finished, but he was accounted by his contemporaries among the doubters, and was put forward by the opponents of ratification in Pennsylvania as a candidate for the state convention, but was defeated.[4]

Elbridge Gerry, of Massachusetts, participated extensively in the debates of the Convention, but his general view of government was doubtless stated in his speech on May 31, when he expressed himself as not liking the election of members of the lower house by popular vote. He said on this point: "The evils we experience flow from the excess of democracy. The people do not want virtue; but are the dupes of pretended patriots. In Massts. it has been fully confirmed by experience that they are daily misled into the most baneful measures and opinions by the false reports circulated by designing men, and which no one on the spot can refute. One principal evil arises from the want of due provision for those employed in the administration of Governnt. It would seem to be a maxim of democracy to starve the public servants. He mentioned the popular clamour in Massts. for the reduction of salaries and the attack made on that of the Govr. though secured by the spirit of the Constitution itself. He had, he said, been too republican heretofore: he was still, however, republican,

---

[1] *Ibid.*, Vol. I, p. 48; Vol. III, p. 297.
[2] *Ibid.*, Vol. I, pp. 94, 99.   [3] *Ibid.*, Vol. II, p. 204.
[4] Scharf and Wescott, *History of Philadelphia*, Vol. I, p. 447.

but had been taught by experience the danger of the levilling spirit." [1]

When the proposition that Senators should be elected by the state legislatures was up for consideration, "Mr. Gerry insisted that the commercial and monied interest wd. be more secure in hands of the State Legislatures, than of the people at large. The former have more sense of character, and will be restrained by that from injustice. The people are for paper money when the Legislatures are agst. it. In Massts. the County Conventions had declared a wish for a depreciating paper that wd. sink itself. Besides, in some States there are two Branches in the Legislature, one of which is somewhat aristocratic. There wd. therefore be so far a better chance of refinement in the choice." [2]

Nicholas Gilman was by temper and interest a man of affairs, more concerned with the stability of public securities and the development of western land schemes than with political theorizing. From Madison's record he does not appear to have said anything in the Convention.

Nathaniel Gorham was opposed to property qualifications on the suffrage in the federal Constitution and the association of the judiciary with the executive in the exercise of the veto power.[3] Speaking on the latter point, however, he said, "All agree that a check on the legislature is necessary. But there are two objections against admitting the judges to share in it which no observations on the other side seem to obviate. The 1st is that the judges ought to carry into the exposition of the laws no prepossessions with regard to them ; 2d that as the judges will outnumber the executive, the revisionary check would be thrown entirely out of the executive hands, and instead of enabling him to defend himself would enable the judges to sacrifice him."

[1] Farrand, *Records*, Vol. I, p. 48.   [2] *Ibid.*, Vol. I, p. 154.
[3] *Ibid.*, Vol. II, p. 122 and pp. 73–79.

Alexander Hamilton had a profound admiration for the British constitution. "The House of Lords," he said in the Convention, "is a noble institution. Having nothing to hope for by a change and a sufficient interest by means of their property, in being faithful to the national interest, they form a permanent barrier against every pernicious innovation whether attempted on the part of the Crown or of the Commons." [1] Doubtless his maturely considered system of government was summed up in the following words : "All communities divide themselves into the few and the many. The first are the rich and well born, the other the mass of the people. The voice of the people has been said to be the voice of God ; and however generally this maxim has been quoted and believed, it is not true in fact. The people are turbulent and changing ; they seldom judge or determine right. Give therefore to the first class a distinct, permanent share in the government. They will check the unsteadiness of the second, and as they cannot receive any advantage by a change, they therefore will ever maintain good government. Can a democratic assembly who annually revolve in the mass of the people, be supposed steadily to pursue the public good ? Nothing but a permanent body can check the imprudence of democracy. . . . It is admitted that you cannot have a good executive upon a democratic plan." [2] In consonance with these principles Hamilton outlined his scheme of government which included an assembly to consist of persons elected for three years by popular vote, a senate chosen for life or during good behavior by electors chosen by the voters, and a president also elected for life or during good behavior by electors chosen by the voters. The Convention failed to adopt his programme, and he entertained a rather uncertain view of the

[1] *Ibid.*, Vol. I, p. 288.   [2] *Ibid.*, Vol. I, pp. 299 ff.

Constitution as it was finally drafted, doubting its stability and permanency.

William Houstoun, of Georgia, seems to have spoken only once or twice; but he gave an indication of his political science in a remark which he made to the effect that the Georgia constitution "was a very bad one, and he hoped it would be revised and amended."[1] The constitution to which he alludes was the radical instrument made in 1777, which provided for a legislature with a single chamber and an unusually wide extension of the suffrage.[2]

Jared Ingersoll, in spite of his great abilities as a student and lawyer, seems to have taken no part at all in the debates of the Convention. Such at least is the view to which Madison's records lead. Something is known, however, of the political principles which he entertained. Though he became intimately associated with President Reed on his migration to Philadelphia in 1778, he never accepted the extreme democratic principles embodied in the constitution of that state in 1776.[3] His biographer, after making an exception of Ingersoll's services in the Convention, says: "I am not aware that he held or sought a position in any popular or representative body whatever. He was what is called conservative in politics; that is to say, he was not by constitutional temper a rebuilder or reconstructor of anything that had been once reasonably well built; nor was his favorite order of political architecture, the democratic. After the great subversion in 1801 he was found as rarely as anybody in Pennsylvania on the side of the majority. He was known to be inclined to the contrary, so far that with or without his consent he was selected in that state, in the year 1812, as the opposition or anti-Madisonian candidate for the office of Vice-President of the United States."[4]

[1] Farrand, *op. cit.*, Vol. II, p. 48.   [2] See above, p. 70.
[3] H. Binney, *Leaders of the Old Bar of Philadelphia*, p. 86.   [4] *Ibid.*, p. 87.

Rufus King correctly understood the idea of a balanced government independent of "popular whims" and endowed with plenty of strength. He favored a long term for the President, and speaking on the executive department in the Convention he "expressed his apprehensions that an extreme caution in favor of liberty might enervate the government we were forming. He wished the house to recur to the primitive axiom that the three great departments of governments should be separate and independent: that the executive and the judiciary should be so, as well as the legislative: that the executive should be equally so with the judiciary. . . . He [the executive] ought not to be impeachable unless he hold his office during good behavior, a tenure which would be most agreeable to him; provided an independent and effectual forum could be devised; But under no circumstances ought he to be impeachable by the legislature. This would be destructive of his independence and of the principles of the constitution. He relied on the vigor of the executive as a great security for the public liberties."[1] King also believed in the principle of judicial control — that most effective check on the popular attacks on property through legislatures.[2]

It was largely on King's initiative that the prohibition against interference with contracts was placed in the Constitution.[3]

William Livingston took a middle ground between the "high-toned" system of John Adams and the simple democracy of such writers as "Centinel" of Pennsylvania.[4] *The Defence of the Constitutions* he impatiently characterized as "rubbage"; and a "Humiliating and mortify-

---

[1] Farrand, *Records*, Vol. II, p. 66.
[2] Beard, *The Supreme Court and the Constitution*, p. 29.
[3] Farrand, *Records*, Vol. II, p. 439.
[4] See below, p. 312.

ing acknowledgement that man is incapable of governing himself." But for the opposite party that would set up a simple democratic government through legislative majorities, Livingston had just as little patience. "The security of the liberties of a people or state depends wholly on a proper delegation of power. The several component powers of government should be so distributed that no one man, or body of men, should possess a larger share thereof than what is absolutely necessary for the administration of government. . . . The people ever have been and ever will be unfit to retain the exercise of power in their own hands; they must of necessity delegate it somewhere. . . . But it has been found from experience that a government by representation, consisting of a single house of representatives, is in some degree liable to the same inconveniences which attend a pure democracy; a few leading men influence the majority to pass laws calculated not for the public good, but to promote some sinister views of their own. To prevent this, another representative branch is added: these two separate houses form mutual checks upon each other; but this expedient has not been found to be altogether effectual. If the legislative power, even tho' vested in two distinct houses is left without any controul, they will inevitably encroach upon the executive and judicial; . . . But further, as prejudices always prevail, more or less, in all popular governments, it is necessary that a check be placed somewhere in the hands of a power not immediately dependent upon the breath of the people, in order to stem the torrent, and prevent the mischiefs which blind passions and rancorous prejudices might otherwise occasion. The executive and judicial powers should of course then be vested with this check or controul on the legislature; and that they may be enabled fully to effect this beneficial purpose, they should be rendered as independent as possible. . . . Tho' it is so short a time since our governments have been put in motion, yet examples have not been wanting of the prevalence of this dangerous thirst after more power in some of our legislatures; a negative therefore lodged in the hands of the executive and judicial powers, is absolutely necessary in order that they may be able to defend themselves from the encroachments of the legislature." [1] Livingston thought that there were some grave defects in the Constitution as drafted at Philadelphia and proposed some emendations. He believed that the President should enjoy the appointing power without any control by the Senate; he thought the Chief Justice should hold office during good behavior and be empowered to appoint his colleagues; and he further held that the President, the Chief Justice, and a Superintendent of Finance should be organized into a council of revision to pass upon the acts of Congress.

James McClurg, of Virginia, left the Convention during the early part of August, and was silent on most of the questions before that body. On July 17th, he proposed that the term of the executive should be changed from seven years to "good behavior"; [2] and he was particularly anxious to have the executive independent of the legislature. He said that he "was not so much afraid of the shadow of monarchy as to be unwilling to approach it; nor so wedded to republican government as not to be sensible of the tyrannies that had been and may be exercised under that form. It was an essential object with him to make the executive

---

[1] *Observations on Government, Including Some Animadversions on Mr. Adams's Defence of the Constitutions of Government of the United States of America*, etc., published in 1787, by Livingston, under the pen-name of "A Farmer of New Jersey." The pamphlet is sometimes ascribed to J. Stevens, but there is good authority for believing that Livingston is the author. It is not inconsistent with his notions on judicial control; see American Historical Review, Vol. IV, pp. 460 ff.

[2] Farrand, *Records*, Vol. II, p. 33.

independent of the legislature; and the only mode left for effecting it, after the vote destroying his ineligibility the second time, was to appoint him during good behavior." [1] That McClurg had small respect for legislatures in general is shown by a letter which he wrote to Madison from Virginia on August 7, 1787, in which he said: "The necessity of some independent power to controul the Assembly by a negative, seems now to be admitted by the most zealous Republicans—they only differ about the mode of constituting such a power. B. Randolph seems to think that a magistrate annually elected by the people might exercise such a controul as independently as the King of G. B. I hope that our representative, Marshall, will be a powerful aid to Mason in the next Assembly. He has observ'd the continual depravation of Mens manners, under the corrupting influence of our Legislature; & is convinc'd that nothing but the adoption of some efficient plan from the Convention can prevent Anarchy first, & civil convulsions afterwards." [2]

James McHenry belonged to the conservative party of his state and opposed "radical alterations" in the constitution of that commonwealth as it stood in November, 1791.[3]

Writing in February, 1787, on the property qualifications placed on voters and representatives in Maryland, McHenry explained that "These disabilities, exclusions, and qualifications have for their object an upright legislature, endowed with faculties to judge of the things most proper to promote the public good." He was warmly opposed to the doctrine that the people had a right to instruct their representatives.[4] Democracy was, in his opinion, synonymous with "confusion and licentiousness."[5]

---

[1] Farrand, *Records*, Vol. II, p. 36.
[2] *Documentary History of the Constitution*, Vol. IV, p. 245.
[3] Letter to Hamilton, Library of Congress, *Hamilton Mss.*, Vol. XXIII, p. 93.
[4] *American Museum*, Vol. IV, p. 333. [5] Steiner, *Life and Correspondence*, p. 527.

James Madison was the systematic philosopher of the Convention and set forth his views with such cogency and consistency on so many different topics that no short quotations will suffice to state his doctrines. His general scheme of political science was, however, embodied in the tenth number of *The Federalist* which has been discussed above and need not be reconsidered here.[1]

Alexander Martin was among the silent members of the Convention, for Madison records only an occasional and incidental participation by him in the proceedings.

Luther Martin was the champion of the extreme states' rights' view, and entertained rather democratic notions for his time, although, in arguing against the clause prohibiting Congress to issue paper money, he held that, "considering the administration of the government would be principally in the hands of the wealthy," there could be little danger from an abuse of this power. Martin was in fact a champion of paper money in his state, and he opposed that part of the Constitution which prohibited the emission of bills of credit. As a representative of the more radical section of his community, he was against the clauses restricting the states to the use of the gold and silver coin of the United States, and was opposed to the clause forbidding the impairment of the obligation of contract. Speaking on the latter point he said: "There might be times of such great public calamities and distress, and of such extreme scarcity of specie, as should render it the duty of a government for the preservation of even the most valuable part of its citizens in some measure to interfere in their favor, by passing laws totally or partially stopping the courts of justice, or authorizing the debtor to pay by installments, or by delivering

---

[1] Above, p. 156. Mr. E. W. Crecraft, of Columbia University, has in preparation a dissertation on Madison's political philosophy.

up his property to his creditors at a reasonable and honest valuation. The times have been such as to render regulations of this kind necessary in most or all of the states, to prevent the wealthy creditor and the moneyed man from totally destroying the poor, though even industrious debtor. Such times may again arrive. . . . I apprehend, Sir, the principal cause of complaint among the people at large, is the public and private debt with which they are oppressed, and which in the present scarcity of cash threatens them with destruction, unless they can obtain so much indulgence in point of time that by industry and frugality they may extricate themselves." [1]

As might have been expected, a man entertaining such radical notions about the power and duty of a government to interfere with the rights of personalty in behalf of the debtor could not have accepted the instrument framed at Philadelphia. In fact, Martin refused to sign the Constitution; he wrote a vehement protest against it to the legislature of his state; he worked assiduously against its ratification; and as a member of the state convention, he voted against its approval by his commonwealth — but in vain.

George Mason thoroughly understood the doctrine of a balanced government. Speaking in the Convention on the function of the upper house, he said: "One important object in constituting the senate was to secure the rights of property. To give them weight and firmness for this purpose a considerable duration in office was thought necessary. But a longer term than six years would be of no avail in this respect, if needy persons should be appointed. He suggested therefore the propriety of annexing to the office a qualification of property. He thought this would

[1] Farrand, *Records*, Vol. III, pp. 214 ff.

be very practicable; as the rules of taxation would supply a scale for measuring the degree of wealth possessed by every man." [1] On another occasion, he presented a motion requiring "certain qualifications of landed property, in members of the legislature." [2] Although Mason refused to sign the Constitution, his reasons were based on personal economic interests, not on any objections to its checks on democratic legislatures. [3]

J. F. Mercer, of Maryland, who opposed the Constitution in its final form and became the belligerent anti-federalist leader in that state, does not appear to have been so warmly devoted to the "people's cause," behind the closed doors of the Convention, for he took exceptions to the proposition that the determination of the qualifications of voters should be left to the several states. But his particular objection was "to the mode of election by the people. The people cannot know and judge of the characters of candidates. The worst possible choice will be made." [4]

Thomas Mifflin took no part worthy of mention in the proceedings of the Convention, and expounded no views of government during the debates.

Gouverneur Morris, of Pennsylvania, was the leader of those who wanted to base the new system upon a freehold suffrage qualification; and, on August 7, he made a motion to this effect. In the course of the discussion which followed, Morris said: "He had long learned not to be the dupe of words. The sound of Aristocracy, therefore, had no effect on him. It was the thing, not the name, to which he was opposed, and one of his principal objections to the Constitution as it is now before us, is that it threatens this Country with an Aristocracy. The Aristocracy will grow out of

---

[1] Farrand, *Records*, Vol. I, p. 428.   [2] *Ibid.*, Vol. II, p. 121.
[3] See above, p. 128.   [4] Farrand, *Records*, Vol. II, p. 205.

the House of Representatives. Give the votes to people who have no property, and they will sell them to the rich who will be able to buy them. We should not confine our attention to the present moment. The time is not distant when this Country will abound with mechanics & manufacturers who will receive their bread from their employers. Will such men be the secure & faithful Guardians of liberty? Will they be the impregnable barrier agst. aristocracy? — He was as little duped by the association of the words, 'taxation & Representation' — The man who does not give his vote freely is not represented. It is the man who dictates the vote. Children do not vote. Why? because they want prudence, because they have no will of their own. The ignorant & the dependent can be as little trusted with the public interest. He did not conceive the difficulty of defining 'freeholders' to be insuperable. Still less that the restriction could be unpopular. 9/10 of the people are at present freeholders and these will certainly be pleased with it. As to Merchts. &c. if they have wealth & value the right they can acquire it. If not they don't deserve it." [1]

In all the proceedings of the Convention, Morris took a deep interest and expressed his views freely, always showing his thorough distrust of democratic institutions. As his biographer, Mr. Roosevelt puts it, "He throughout appears as the *advocatus diaboli*; he puts the lowest interpretation upon every act, and frankly avows his disbelief in all generous and unselfish motives. His continual allusions to the overpowering influence of the baser passions, and to their mastery of the human race at all times, drew from Madison, although the two men generally acted together, a protest against his 'forever inculcating the utter political depravity of men, and the necessity of opposing one vice and interest as the only possible check to another vice and interest.'"[1] This protest from Madison, however, betrays inconsistency, for on more than one occasion in the Convention he expounded principles substantially identical with those which he reprobated in Morris.[2] Indeed, what appeared to be cynical eccentricity on the part of the latter was nothing more than unusual bluntness in setting forth Federalist doctrines.

Robert Morris, the merchant prince and speculator of Pennsylvania, seems to have broken his rule of absolute silence only two or three times in the Convention, and he apparently made no speech at all. He nominated Washington as president of the assembly, and seconded Read's motion that Senators should hold office during good behavior.[3] There is no doubt that Morris appreciated the relative weight of speeches and private negotiations.[4]

In the proceedings of the Convention, *William Paterson* was chiefly concerned with protecting the rights of small states; but he signed the Constitution, and after its adoption became an ardent Federalist, serving as an associate justice of the Supreme Court. On the bench he was one of the most scholarly and eminent supporters of the doctrine of judicial control over legislation.[5]

William Pierce took little part in the proceedings of the Convention. On the question of states' rights he held a broad view, saying, "state distinctions must be sacrificed so far as the general government shall render it necessary — without, however, destroying them altogether. Al-

---

[1] Roosevelt, *Gouverneur Morris*, p. 140.

[2] See *The Federalist*, No. 51.

[3] Farrand, *Records*, Vol. I, p. 409.

[4] For an example see *ibid.*, p. 11, note. He also entertained Washington during the sessions of the Convention. *American Historical Association Report* (1902), Vol. I, p. 92.

[5] Beard, *The Supreme Court and the Constitution*, p. 37.

though I am here as a representative from a small state, I consider myself as a citizen of the United States, whose general interest I will always support."[1] On no occasion, apparently, did Pierce indulge in any general reflections on the basis of all government. He did not sign the Constitution, but he explained this fact by saying, "I was absent in New York on a piece of business so necessary that it became unavoidable. I approve of its principles and would have signed it with all my heart had I been present. To say, however, that I consider it as perfect would be to make an acknowledgement immediately opposed to my judgment."[2]

Charles Pinckney was among the members of the Convention who thought that it was desirable to fix the property qualifications of members of the national legislature firmly in the Constitution. Speaking on the subject of property and government he said: "The Committee as he had conceived were instructed to report the proper qualifications of property for the members of the Natl. Legislature; instead of which they have referred the task to the Natl. Legislature itself. Should it be left on this footing, the first Legislature will meet without any particular qualifications of property; and if it should happen to consist of rich men they might fix such qualifications as may be too favorable to the rich; if of poor men, an opposite extreme might be run into. He was opposed to the establishment of an undue aristocratic influence in the Constitution, but he thought it essential that the members of the Legislature, the Executive, and the Judges — should be possessed of competent property to make them independent & respectable. It was prudent when such great powers were to be trusted to connect the tie of property with that of reputation in securing a faithful administration. The Legislature would have the fate of the Nation put into their hands. The President would also have a very great influence on it. The Judges would have not only important causes between Citizen & Citizen but also where foreigners were concerned. They will even be the Umpires between the U. States and individual States as well as between one State & another. Were he to fix the quantum of property which should be required, he should not think of less than one hundred thousand dollars for the President, half of that sum for each of the Judges, and in like proportion for the members of the Natl. Legislature. He would however leave the sum blank. His motion was that the President of the U. S., the Judges, and members of the Legislature should be required to swear that they were respectively possessed of a clear unincumbered Estate to the amount of —— in the case of the President, &c &c —"[1]

Pinckney, in fact, had no confidence in popular government, for on March 28, 1788, he wrote to Madison: "Are you not . . . abundantly impressed that the theoretical nonsense of an election of Congress by the people in the first instance is clearly and practically wrong, that it will in the end be the means of bringing our councils into contempt."[2]

General Charles Cotesworth Pinckney entertained views with regard to the special position that should be enjoyed by property, which were substantially identical with those held by his cousin. He proposed that no salary should be paid to members of the Senate. As this branch, he said, "was meant to represent the wealth of the country, it ought to be composed of persons of wealth; and if no allowance

[1] *Ibid.*, Vol. II, p. 248.
[2] *Madison Mss.*, Library of Congress; date of March 28, 1788.

was to be made the wealthy alone would undertake the service."[1] General Pinckney also wished to extend property qualifications not only to members of the legislature, but also to the executive and judicial departments.[2]

Edmund Randolph was not only fully aware of the distress to which property had been put under the Articles of Confederation, but he also understood the elements of a "balanced" government. Speaking on the subject of the structure of the Senate, he said: "If he was to give an opinion as to the number of the second branch, he should say that it ought to be much smaller than that of the first, so small as to be exempt from the passionate proceedings to which numerous assemblies are liable. He observed that the general object was to provide a cure for the evils under which the U. S. Laboured; that in tracing these evils to their origin every man had found it in the turbulence and follies of democracy: that some check therefore was to be sought for agst. this tendency of our governments: and that a good Senate seemed most likely to answer the purpose. . . . Mr. Randolph was for the term of 7 years. The Democratic licentiousness of the State Legislatures proved the necessity of a firm Senate. The object of this 2d. branch is to controul the democratic branch of the Natl. Legislature. If it be not a firm body, the other branch being more numerous, and coming immediately from the people, will overwhelm it. The Senate of Maryland constituted on like principles had been scarcely able to stem the popular torrent. No mischief can be apprehended, as the concurrence of the other branch, and in some measure, of the Executive, will in all cases be necessary. A firmness & independence may be the more necessary also in this branch, as it ought to guard the Constitution agst. encroachments of the Executive who will be apt to form combinations with the demagogues of the popular branch." [1]

George Read was most outspoken in his desire to see the Articles of Confederation completely discarded. He said that "he was against patching up the old federal system: he hoped the idea would be dismissed. It would be like putting new cloth on an old garment. The Confederation was founded on temporary principles. It cannot last; it cannot be amended." [2] He favored vesting an absolute veto power in the executive; [3] and he proposed that Senators should hold office during good behavior. [4]

John Rutledge held that the apportionment of representatives should be on a basis of wealth and population. [5] He favored a property qualification for the legislative, executive, and judicial departments; [6] and he thought that Senators should not be paid. [7] In fact, he was one of the most ardent champions of the rights of property in government in the Convention. He was strictly opposed to the introduction of sentimental considerations in politics, for, speaking on an aspect of slavery and the Constitution, he said: "Religion & humanity had nothing to do with this question — Interest alone is the governing principle with Nations — The true question at present is whether the Southn. States shall or shall not be parties to the Union. If the Northern States consult their interests they will not oppose the increase of Slaves which will increase the commodities of which they will become the carriers." [8]

Roger Sherman believed in reducing the popular influence in the new government to the minimum. When it was proposed that the members of the first branch of the national

[1] *Ibid.*, Vol. I, p. 51 and p. 218.
[2] *Ibid.*, Vol. II, p. 200.
[6] *Ibid.*, Vol. I, p. 582.
[7] *Ibid.*, Vol. I, p. 211.
[3] *Ibid.*, Vol. I, p. 136.
[4] *Ibid.*, Vol. I, p. 409.
[5] *Ibid.*, Vol. II, p. 249.
[8] *Ibid.*, Vol. II, p. 364.

legislature should be elected, Sherman said that he was "opposed to the election by the people, insisting that it ought to be by the state legislatures. The people, he said, immediately should have as little to do as may be about the government. They want information and are constantly liable to be misled." [1]

Richard Dobbs Spaight does not seem to have made any very lengthy speeches in the Convention, but his occasional motions show that he was not among those who believed in "frequent recurrence to the people." On September 6, he moved that the length of the President's term be increased to seven years, and finding this lost he attempted to substitute six years for four. [2] Spaight was the one member of the Convention, however, who came out clearly and denounced judicial control; [3] but he nevertheless proved a stout champion of the Constitution in North Carolina — defending it warmly against charges to the effect that it was aristocratic in character. [4]

Caleb Strong carried into the Convention the old Massachusetts tradition in favor of frequent elections. He favored a one year term for representatives, [5] voted against a seven year term for President, [6] and also opposed a seven year term for Senators. [7] He supported the Constitution, however, in his native state, and was a member of the convention that ratified it.

George Washington's part in the proceedings of the Convention was almost negligible, and it does not appear that in public document or private letter he ever set forth any coherent theory of government. When he had occasion to dwell upon the nature of the new system he indulged in the

---

[1] Farrand, *Records*, Vol. I, p. 48; also p. 154.   [2] *Ibid.*, Vol. II, p. 525.
[3] Beard, *The Supreme Court and the Constitution*, p. 53.
[4] Elliot, *Debates*, Vol. IV, p. 207.   [5] Farrand, *Records*, Vol. I, 361.
[6] *Ibid.*, p. 72.   [7] *Ibid.*, p. 219.

general language of the bench rather than that of the penetrating observer. For example, in his Farewell Address, which was written largely by Hamilton, he spoke of the government's being "the offspring of our own choice, uninfluenced and unawed, adopted upon full investigation, and mature deliberation, completely free in its principles, in the distribution of its powers, uniting security with energy." [1] He feared, however, the type of politics represented by the Democratic Societies which sprang up during his administration, and looked upon criticism of the government as akin to sedition.[2] Like Jefferson, he also viewed with apprehension the growth of an urban population, for in a letter to La Fayette at the time of the French Revolution, he said, "The tumultuous populace of large cities are ever to be dreaded. Their indiscriminate violence prostrates for the time all public authority." [3]

Hugh Williamson was against placing property qualifications on voters for members of Congress;[4] and he was opposed to the association of the judges with the executive in the exercise of the veto power.[5] He preferred to insert a provision requiring a two-thirds vote for every "effective act of the legislature." [6] He was, however, an opponent of the paper money party in North Carolina [7] and in the Convention he supported a proposition forbidding the states to pass ex post facto laws, on the ground that "the judges can take hold of it." [8]

James Wilson was among the philosophers of the period who had seriously pondered on politics in its historical and practical aspects. In the Convention he took a democratic

[1] *Writings* (Sparks ed., 1848), Vol. XII, p. 222; see below, p. 299.
[2] *Ibid.*, Vol. X, p. 429.   [3] *Ibid.*, Vol. X, p. 179.
[4] Farrand, *Records*, Vol. II, pp. 201, 250.
[5] *Ibid.*, Vol. I, p. 140.   [6] *Ibid.*, Vol. I, p. 140.
[7] Above, p. 146.   [8] Farrand, Vol. II, 376.

view on several matters. He favored the annual election
of representatives by the people,[1] he advocated the popular
election of United States Senators,[2] and he believed also in
the popular election of the President.[3] He furthermore
opposed the proposition to place property qualifications on
voters.[4] His check on popular legislation was to be found in
judicial control, at first in the association of the judges
with the executive in its exercise, and later in its simple,
direct form.[5] In fact, Wilson shared the apprehensions of
his colleagues as to the dangers of democratic legislatures,
though he did not frankly advocate direct property checks.[6]
He doubtless believed that judicial control would be
sufficient.

George Wythe was a representative of the old school of
lawyers in Virginia, and he was a profound student of historical jurisprudence, although he apparently made no
attempt to apply his learning to any of the general political
questions before the Convention. He was a warm advocate
of the doctrine of judicial control and gave practical effect
to principles while on the bench in Virginia.[7]

The conclusion seems warranted that the authors of *The
Federalist* generalized the political doctrines of the members
of the Convention with a high degree of precision, in spite
of the great diversity of opinion which prevailed on many
matters.

[1] Farrand, *Records*, Vol. I, p. 49 and *passim*.
[2] *Ibid.*, p. 52 and *passim*.   [3] *Ibid.*, p. 68 and *passim*.
[4] *Ibid.*, Vol. I, p. 375; Vol. II, p. 125 and *passim*.
[5] *Ibid.*, Vol. I, p. 98; Beard, *The Supreme Court and the Constitution*, p. 42.
[6] *Lectures on Law* (1804 ed.) Vol. I, pp. 398 ff.
[7] Beard, *The Supreme Court and the Constitution*, p. 48.

CHAPTER VIII

On the 17th day of September, 1787, the Convention at Philadelphia finished its work and transmitted the new Constitution to Congress, with the suggestion that "it should afterwards be submitted to a convention of delegates chosen in each state by the people thereof, under the recommendation of its legislature for their assent and ratification; and that each convention assenting to and ratifying the same should give notice thereof to the United States in Congress assembled." The Philadelphia Convention further proposed that when nine states had ratified the new instrument, it should go into effect as between the states ratifying the same. Eleven days later, on September 28, the Congress, then sitting in New York, resolved to accept the advice of the Convention, and sent the Constitution to the state legislatures to be transmitted by them to conventions chosen by the voters of the respective commonwealths.

This whole process was a departure from the provisions of the then fundamental law of the land — the Articles of Confederation — which provided that all alterations and amendments should be made by Congress and receive the approval of the legislature of every state. If to-day the Congress of the United States should call a national convention to "revise" the Constitution, and such a convention should throw away the existing instrument of government entirely and submit a new frame of government to a popular referendum, disregarding altogether the process of amendment now provided, we should have something analogous to the great political transformation of 1787–89. The revolutionary nature of the work of the Philadelphia Convention is correctly characterized by Professor John W. Burgess when he states that had such acts been performed by Julius or Napoleon, they would have been pronounced *coups d'état.*[1]

This revolutionary plan of procedure was foreshadowed in the Virginia proposals at the opening of the Convention, and was, therefore, contemplated by some of the leaders from the beginning. When it was under consideration on June 5, Sherman, of Connecticut, opposed it on the ground that it was unnecessary and that regular provisions were already made in the Articles for amendments. Madison wanted to establish the Constitution on some foundation other than mere legislative approval. Gerry "observed that in the Eastern states the Confederation had been sanctioned by the people themselves. He seemed afraid of referring the new system to them. The people in that quarter have, at this time, the wildest ideas of government in the world. They were for abolishing the senate in Massachusetts." King thought that "a convention being a single house, the adoption may be more easily carried through it than through the legislatures where there are several branches. The legislatures also being to lose power will be most likely to raise objections."[2]

---

[1] "What they [the Convention] actually did, stripped of all fiction and verbiage, was to assume constituent powers, ordain a constitution of government and of liberty, and demand a *plébiscite* thereon over the heads of all existing legally organized powers. Had Julius or Napoleon committed these acts they would have been pronounced *coups d'état.*"   *Political Science and Comparative Constitutional Law,* Vol. I, p. 105.

[2] Farrand, *Records,* Vol. I, p. 123.

On July 23 the resolution regarding ratification came before the Convention again for discussion,[1] when it was moved that the Constitution be referred to the state legislatures. One of the principal objections urged against this plan was the possibility of a later legislature's repealing the ratification by a preceding body of the same authority; but the chief problem was whether there was more likelihood of securing a confirmation by legislatures or by conventions. "Whose opposition will be most likely to be excited against the system?" asked Randolph. "That of the local demagogues who will be degraded by it from the importance they now hold. These will spare no efforts to impede that progress in the popular mind which will be necessary to the adoption of the plan. . . . It is of great importance, therefore, that the consideration of this subject should be transferred from the legislatures where this class of men have their full influence to a field in which their efforts can be less mischievous. It is, moreover, worthy of consideration that some of the states are averse to any change in their constitution, and will not take the requisite steps unless expressly called upon to refer the question to the people."

Mr. Gorham, of Massachusetts, was of the same opinion. He "was against referring the plan to the legislatures. 1. Men chosen by the people for the particular purpose will discuss the subject more candidly than members of the legislature who are to lose the power which is to be given up to the general government. 2. Some of the legislatures are composed of several branches. It will consequently be more difficult in these cases to get the plan through the legislatures than through a convention. 3. In the states many of the ablest men are excluded from the legislatures,

[1] *Ibid.*, Vol. II, p. 89.

but may be elected into a convention. Among these may be ranked many of the clergy who are generally friends to good government. . . . 4. The legislatures will be interrupted with a variety of little business; by artfully pressing which, designing men will find means to delay from year to year, if not to frustrate altogether, the national system. 5. If the last article of the Confederation is to be pursued the unanimous concurrence of the states will be necessary."

In the Convention, Ellsworth preferred to trust the legislatures rather than popularly elected conventions. "He thought more was to be expected from the legislatures than from the people. The prevailing wish of the people in the eastern states is to get rid of the public debt; and the idea of strengthening the national government carries with it that of strengthening the public debt." After the plan of ratification by conventions was carried in spite of Ellsworth's objections, he defended it in his appeal to the populace by saying: "It proves the honesty and patriotism of the gentlemen who composed the general Convention, that they chose to submit their system to the people rather than to the legislatures, whose decisions are often influenced by men in the higher departments of government, who have provided well for themselves and dread any change least they should be injured by its operation. I would not wish to exclude from a state convention those gentlemen who compose the higher branches of the assemblies in the several states, but choose to see them stand on an even floor with their brethren, where the artifice of a small number cannot negative a vast majority of the people. This danger was foreseen by the federal convention and they have wisely avoided it by appealing directly to the people." [1]

[1] Farrand, *Records*, Vol. III, p. 137.

A study of the opinions of the members of the Convention shows that four leading reasons led to the agreement on ratification by state conventions. It permitted the disregard of the principle of unanimous approval by the states. A firmer foundation would be laid for the Constitution if it had the sanction of special conventions rather than temporary legislatures. One of the first objects of the Constitution was to restrict the authority of state legislatures, and it could hardly be expected that they would voluntarily commit suicide. Another leading purpose of the Convention was to pay the public debt at par, and the members had learned from the repeated appeals to the state legislatures for funds to meet this national obligation that no relief was to be expected from this source. There was a better chance of getting the right kind of citizens elected to a convention than to a legislature. By separating the election of delegates to state conventions from the election of members to the state legislatures, the supporters of the Constitution were better able to concentrate their campaign of education. As for the provision of the Articles of Confederation requiring the approval of every state for any amendment in the Articles, the urgent necessities of the advocates of the new system could not permit such a mere technicality to stand in their way.

The question of their legal right to cast aside their instructions and draft a totally new instrument was more or less troublesome for those who entertained a strict regard for the observance of the outward signs of propriety. No doubt the instructions of the delegations from the several states limited them to the "revision" of the Articles of Confederation, and it is highly improbable that in the state of public temper then prevailing a Convention would have assembled at all if its revolutionary purposes had been

understood.   During the debates behind closed doors Mr.
Paterson declared that the delegates were bound by their
instructions, but Randolph replied that "he was not scru-
pulous on the point of power"; and Hamilton agreed with
this view saying, "We owed it to our country to do on this
emergency whatever we should deem essential to its happiness.   The states sent us here to provide for the exigencies
of the union.   To rely on and propose any plan not adequate to these exigencies merely because it was not clearly
within our powers would be to sacrifice the means to the
end." [1]

Outside the halls of the Convention it also became necessary to defend this revolutionary departure from their instructions.   Madison took up the cause in *The Federalist* [2]
and made out an unanswerable case for his side, frankly
pleading the justification of revolution if the legal arguments
which he advanced were deemed insufficient.

At the outset he is unwilling to admit that the Convention had broken with its instructions and performed a
revolutionary act.   He, accordingly, puts forward a legal
and moral justification first, based upon an analysis of the
instructions of the delegates.   They were bound, he shows,
to make such revisions in the Articles as would render them
adequate to the exigencies of the union; but an adequate
government, he pleads, could not be made by revising the
Articles, and the Convention was either compelled to sacrifice the greater for the less by strictly obeying its instructions or to do its whole duty by sacrificing the letter of the
law.   Then he clinches the argument: "Let them declare
whether it was of most importance to the happiness of the
people of America that the Articles of Confederation should
be disregarded and an adequate government be provided

---

[1] Farrand, *Records*, Vol. I, pp. 255 ff.; p. 283.   [2] No. 40.

and the Union preserved; or that an adequate government should be omitted and the Articles of Confederation preserved."

But Madison, after having paid his respects to Legality, hastens to add that in all great changes in government "forms ought to give way to substance." A rigid adherence to mere technicalities "would render nominal and nugatory the transcendent and precious right of the people 'to abolish or alter their governments as to them shall seem most likely to effect their safety and happiness.'" That is, the right of revolution is, at bottom, the justification for all great political changes. If it is argued that this right of revolution should not be exercised by a small group of men, such as the Convention of fifty-odd delegates at Philadelphia, Madison replies that it is impossible for the whole people to move forward in concert, and "it is therefore essential that such changes be instituted by some informal and unauthorized propositions made by some patriotic and respectable citizen or number of citizens." This was the manner in which the recent revolt against England was carried out; and in the present case the people had the right to pass upon the work of the Philadelphia assembly.

The opponents of the Constitution were able to see the significance of that clause of the Constitution which cast aside the legal system under which they were living and provided that the new instrument should go into effect when ratified by nine states — as between those states. "Cornelius," in Massachusetts, exhibited great anxiety on this point, and in his letters of December 11 and 18, 1787, he asked concerning this departure: "Will not the adoption of this constitution in the manner here prescribed be justly considered as a perfidious violation of that fundamental and solemn compact by which the United States hold an existence and claim to be a people? If a nation may so easily discharge itself from obligations to abide by its most solemn and fundamental compacts, may it not with still greater ease do the same in matters of less importance? And if nations may set the example, may not particular states, citizens, and subjects follow? What then will become of public and private faith? Where is the ground of allegiance that is due to government? Are not the bonds of civil society dissolved? Or is allegiance founded only in power? Has moral obligation no place in civil government? In mutual compacts can one party be bound while the other is free? Or, can one party disannul such compact, without the consent of the other? If so, constitutions and national compacts are, I conceive, of no avail; and oaths of allegiance must be preposterous things." [1]

On all hands the "unconstitutional" procedure of the Convention was attacked by the Anti-Federalists. "A system of consolidation," says another writer, "has been formed with the most profound secrecy and without the least authority: And has been suddenly and without any previous notice transmitted by the federal convention for ratification — Congress not disposed to give any opinion on the plan, have transmitted it to the legislatures — The legislatures have followed the example and sent it to the people. The people of this state, unassisted by Congress or their legislature, have not had time to investigate the subject, have referred to the newspapers for information, have been divided by contending writers, and under such circumstances have elected members for the state convention — and these members are to consider whether they will accept the plan of the federal convention, with all its imperfections, and bind the people by a system of government, of

[1] Harding, *The Federal Constitution in Massachusetts*, pp. 118–119.

the nature and principles of which they have not at present a clearer idea than they have of the Copernican system." [1]

Whatever was thought of the merits of the controversy over the proposed plan of ratification, it was accepted by the state legislatures which were invited by Congress to transmit the Constitution to special conventions. It remains to inquire, therefore, what methods were employed in calling these conventions and setting the seal of approval on the new and revolutionary proposals of the Philadelphia assembly.

The resolution calling the convention in New Hampshire to pass upon the federal Constitution was adopted by the legislature on December 14, 1787. The time for holding the elections was left to the selectmen of the several towns, who were instructed to warn the duly qualified voters of the event. The date for the meeting of the convention was fixed on the second Wednesday of February, 1788.[2] Four hundred copies of the Constitution were ordered to be printed for distribution.

The elections seem to have been held about mid-January, for the New Hampshire Spy, for January 25, 1788, contains a long list of delegates already chosen, and adds that "several of the towns not mentioned in the above list were to have had their meetings this week."

A majority of the members of the state convention so chosen, writes a student, who has inquired into the personnel of that body, "were undoubtedly opposed to the Constitution. . . . The talent of the convention was decidedly on the side of the Federalists and a majority of the ablest members were in favor of ratification. . . . For a time the

---

[1] The Massachusetts Centinel, January 2, 1788.
[2] Batchellor, *State Papers of New Hampshire*, Vol. XXI, pp. 151–165; *Documentary History of the Constitution*, II, p. 141.

friends of the Constitution had hopes of securing its ratification without a recess of the convention. Although the
greater number of the members from the upper part of the
state came down rather opposed to its adoption, yet on the
final question it was hoped that a majority would be found
to favor it. But these hopes proved delusive. While some
of the members who came to the convention instructed to
vote against the Constitution had been led by the discussions
to a change of opinion and now favored it, they still felt
bound by their instructions, and frankly said that if a final
vote was to be taken before they had an opportunity to
consult their constituents their vote would be adverse to
ratification."[1] Under these circumstances the Federalists
adjourned the convention and set to work to convert the
enemy. When the convention reassembled a few months
later, they were able to carry the day by the uncomfortably
small margin of 57 to 47.[2]

In Massachusetts the Federalists lost no time in moving
for a convention. As early as October 20, 1787, they
carried a favorable resolution in the senate of the state, and
secured the concurrence of the house four days later. This
resolve provided that the delegates should be chosen by
those inhabitants "qualified by law to vote in the election
of representatives," and the elections should take place
"as soon as may be" in the several towns and districts.
The date for the meeting of the delegates was fixed as the
second Wednesday in January next. On January 9, 1788,
the Convention met at Boston; and a real battle of wits
ensued.

[1] J. B. Walker, *A History of the New Hampshire Convention*, pp. 22 ff.
[2] Four members are not recorded, and "there is a pretty well authenticated
tradition that a certain prominent federalist of Concord gave a dinner party on the
last day of the session at which several members reckoned as opposed to ratification
were present and discussing the dinner when the final vote was taken." *Ibid.*, p.
43, note.

As in New Hampshire, the delegates, when they came together fresh from their constituents, appeared to be opposed to adopting the new instrument of government. A careful scholar, who has studied the period intensively, takes this view: "Had a vote been taken on the adoption of the Constitution as soon as the convention assembled, there can be no question but that it would have been overwhelmingly against the proposed plan." [1]

Even after powerful influences had been brought to bear, the margin for the Federalists was uncomfortably close — 187 to 168. Harding remarks: "The majority in favor of ratification, it will be seen was only nineteen. The nine delegates whose names were returned to the convention, but who were not present when the vote was taken, might almost have turned the scale in the other direction. Bearing in mind that it was mainly the Antifederalist towns that were unrepresented, it may be safely asserted that out of the forty-six delinquent corporations there were enough which were Antifederalist to have procured the rejection of the constitution. This calculation, however, is based on the assumption that a corresponding increase did not take place in the Federalist representation. Had all the towns entitled to send representatives done so, and had all the delegates been present to cast their votes, it is probable that the final result would not have been changed, though the Federalist majority would have been cut down to scarcely more than a bare half-dozen." [2]

After turning over the debates in the Massachusetts convention, one can scarcely escape the conclusion that the victory in eloquence, logic, and pure argumentation lay on the side of the Federalists; and it would not be worth while

[1] Harding, *The Federal Constitution in Massachusetts*, p. 67.
[2] Harding, *op. cit.*, p. 99.

to consider at all the charges that improper influence was brought to bear on the delegates, were it not for the fact that they were made at the time and have lasted in the literature on the ratification in Massachusetts. We have "the sober assertion of a reputable historical writer within the last thirty years" to the effect "that enough members of the Massachusetts convention were bought with money from New York to secure the ratification of the new system by Massachusetts."[1] Harding, after making an examination of the charges, dismissed them as "baseless"; and quite properly, for whoever would convict men of such high standing in the community as King, Gorham, and Strong of being associated with such a reprehensible transaction should produce more than mere unsubstantiated evidence.

The legislature of Connecticut, determined not to be behindhand in setting the approval of the state on the new instrument, called a convention on October 11, 1787.[2] A month was given to the electors to deliberate over the choice of delegates who were to decide the momentous issue. The election was held on November 12; the convention assembled on January 3, 1788; and after a few days' discussion gave its assent on January 9, 1788, by a vote of 128 to 40.[3]

In New York the voters were given more time than in Connecticut to consider the new Constitution before they were called upon to settle the question of ratification at the polls by choosing delegates to the state convention. It was not until February 1, 1788, that the legislature of that commonwealth issued the call for the special election to be held on the last Tuesday of the following April.[4]

---

[1] Harding, *op. cit.*, p. 101.
[2] *Documentary History of the Constitution*, Vol. II, pp. 86–87; Connecticut Courant, October 22, 1787.   [3] Bancroft, *op. cit.*, Vol. II, p. 257.
[4] *Debates and Proceedings of the New York State Convention* (1905 ed.), p. 3.

The contest in New York was hot from the start. Governor Clinton, in his message to the legislature in January, 1788, did not mention the Constitution — an omission which gave the Federalists some hope as they had feared an executive attack. The resolution calling the state convention passed the lower house by a narrow margin; and in the senate a motion to postpone the matter was almost carried, receiving nine out of nineteen votes.[1]

When, at length, the convention assembled, at least two-thirds of the sixty-four members were found to be against ratification. Such is the view of Bancroft, and the contemporary press bears out his conclusion.[2] Nevertheless, by much eloquence and no little manoeuvring, the Federalist champions were able to obtain a majority of 30 to 27. The assent of the requisite number of opponents was secured only after an agreement that a circular should be issued recommending the call of another national convention at once to revise the Constitution as adopted.

In pursuance of this agreement, the legislature at its next session, on February 5, 1789, called upon Congress to summon another convention to revise the new instrument of government at once. The address of the legislature stated that the Constitution had been ratified "in the fullest confidence of obtaining a revision of the said Constitution by a general convention, and in confidence that certain powers in and by the said Constitution granted would not be exercised until a convention should have been called and convened for proposing amendments to the said Constitution." The legislature went on to say that it complied with the unanimous sense of the state convention, "who all united in opinion that such a revision was necessary to

---

[1] Bancroft, *op. cit.*, Vol. II, p. 340.
[2] *Ibid.*, p. 340; and see below, p. 244.

recommend the said Constitution to the approbation and support of a numerous body of their constituents, and a majority of the members of which conceived several articles of the Constitution so exceptionable, that nothing but such confidence and an invincible reluctance to separate from our sister states could have prevailed upon a sufficient number to assent to it without stipulating for previous amendments." [1]

The commonwealth of New Jersey made haste to ratify the new Constitution as soon as possible after its transmission by Congress.   On November 1, 1787, the legislature issued the call for the convention, ordering the inhabitants who were "entitled to vote for representatives in General Assembly," to elect delegates on the fourth Tuesday in the following November, *i.e.*, November 27.   The date for the meeting of the convention was fixed as the second Tuesday in December, the 11th, and on the 18th day of that month, the members, "Having maturely deliberated on and considered the aforesaid proposed Constitution," unanimously agreed to its adoption.[2]

The legislature of Delaware, influenced by "the sense and desire of great numbers of the people of the state, signified in petitions to their general assembly," adopted a resolution on November 10, 1787, calling for the election of delegates within a few days — that is on November 26 — for the state convention to pass upon the Constitution.   The convention met at Dover on December 3 ; and after four days' deliberation on the matter adopted the Constitution by unanimous vote on December 6, 1787.[3]

[1] *State Papers: Miscellaneous*, Vol. I, p. 7.   For valuable side-lights on the opposition to the Constitution, see E. P. Smith's essay, "The Movement towards a Second Constitutional Convention," in Jameson, *Essays in the Constitutional History of the United States*, pp. 46 ff.

[2] *Documentary History of the Constitution*, Vol. II, pp. 46 ff.

[3] Bancroft, *History of the Constitution of the United States*, Vol. II, p. 250; *Documentary History of the Constitution*, Vol. II, p. 25; *Delaware State Council Minutes,*

In Pennsylvania the proceedings connected with the ratification were precipitous and narrowly escaped being irregular. Before it was known that Congress would even transmit the Constitution to the states for their consideration, George Clymer,[1] who had been a member of the national Convention and was then serving in the Pennsylvania legislature, "rose in his place and moved that a state convention of deputies be called, that they meet at Philadelphia, and that they be chosen in the same manner and on the same day as the members of the next general assembly."[2] In vain did the opponents urge that this was irregular, that it was not known whether Congress would act favorably, and that deliberation rather than haste should characterize such a weighty procedure. The legislature, nevertheless, resolved to call the convention, and adjourned until the afternoon, leaving the date of the convention and manner of selecting delegates to be settled later. The opposition thereupon decided to secure delay by staying away and preventing the transaction of business for want of a quorum.

Meanwhile the news reached Philadelphia that Congress had sent the Constitution to the states for their consideration. The Federalists in the legislature, now having secured the sanction of regularity, determined not to brook further delay, so they sent officers after some of the recalcitrants, who thought "filibustering" justifiable in view of the importance of securing more deliberation before acting. These officers, ably assisted by a Federalist mob "broke into their lodgings, seized them, dragged them through the streets to the State house, and thrust them into the assembly

1776–1792, pp. 1081–82 (*Delaware Historical Society Papers*); Connecticut Courant, Dec. 24, 1787.
[1] See above, p. 82.
[2] McMaster and Stone, *Pennsylvania and the Federal Constitution*, p. 3.

room, with clothes torn and faces white with rage. The quorum was now complete." [1] The legislature (September 29) fixed the election of delegates to the state convention at a date five weeks distant, November 6, 1787. Thus the people of the state were given a little over a month to deliberate on this momentous issue before selecting their agents to voice their will. Some Federalists, like Tench Coxe, expressed regret at the necessity of adopting these high-handed methods; but the stress was so great that it did not admit of delay.

After the convention assembled, the Federalists continued their irregular practices, although from the vote on the Constitution in the convention this latter manipulation seems to have been a work of supererogation. Everything was done that could be done to keep the public out of the affair. "Thomas Lloyd applied to the convention for the place of assistant clerk. Lloyd was a shorthand writer of considerable note, and when the convention refused his request, determined to report the debates and print them on his own account. His advertisement promised that the debates should be accurately taken in shorthand and published in one volume octavo at the rate of one dollar the hundred pages. These fine promises, however, were never fulfilled. Only one thin volume ever came out, and that contains merely the speeches of Wilson and a few of those of Thomas M'Kean. The reason is not far to seek. He was bought up by the Federalists, and in order to satisfy the public was suffered to publish one volume containing nothing but speeches made by the two federal leaders." [2] The Federalists appear to have suppressed other attempts at issuing the debates, and they "withdrew their subscriptions from every publica-

[1] McMaster and Stone, *op. cit.*, p. 4.
[2] *Ibid.*, p. 14.

tion that warmly supported the Antifederal cause." [1] The Constitution was ratified by a vote of 46 to 23.

Against these precipitous actions on the part of the Federalists in carrying the ratification of the Constitution, a minority of the state convention, twenty-one members, protested in an address to the people after the day had been lost. The protestants told how the federal Convention had been called by Congress, and then recited the facts as they viewed them: "So hastily and eagerly did the states comply [with the call of Congress for the Convention] that their legislatures, without the slightest authority, without ever stopping to consult the people, appointed delegates, and the conclave met at Philadelphia. To it came a few men of character, some more noted for cunning than patriotism, and some who had always been enemies to the independence of America. The doors were shut, secrecy was enjoined, and what then took place no man could tell. But it was well known that the sittings were far from harmonious. Some left the dark conclave before the instrument was framed. Some had the firmness to withhold their hands when it was framed. But it came forth in spite of them, and was not many hours old when the meaner tools of despotism were carrying petitions about for the people to sign praying the legislature to call a convention to consider it. The convention was called by a legislature made up in part of members who had been dragged to their seats and kept there against their wills, and so early a day was set for the election of delegates that many a voter did not know of it until it was passed. Others kept away from the polls because they were ignorant of the new plan; some because they disliked it, and some because they did not think the convention legally called. Of the seventy thousand freemen entitled to vote

[1] *Ibid.*, p. 15.

but thirteen thousand voted." [1] For a long time the war of
the dissenters against the Constitution went on in Pennsylvania, breaking out in occasional riots, and finally in the
Whiskey Rebellion in Washington's administration; but
they were at length beaten, outgeneralled, and outclassed in
all the arts of political management.

In November, 1787, the Maryland legislature, after hear-
ing Luther Martin's masterly indictment of the Constitution and McHenry's effective reply, "unanimously ordered
a convention of the people of the state; it copied the example set by Virginia of leaving the door open for amendments; and by a majority of one the day for the choice and
the day for the meeting of its convention were postponed
till the next April." [2] Several months were thus given
for deliberation, in marked contrast to the speedy despatch
of the business in Delaware, New Jersey, Connecticut,
Pennsylvania, and Massachusetts. The elections were duly
held on the first Monday in April, 1788; and the convention assembled on April 21. The opponents of the Constitution, Chase, Mercer, and Martin, hurled themselves against
it with all their might; but, it is related, "the friends to the
federal government 'remained inflexibly silent.'" [3] After
a week's sessions, "the malcontents having tired themselves
out," the convention ratified the Constitution by a vote of

---

[1] McMaster and Stone, *op. cit.*, p. 20. The following year [1788] when the
ratification of the Constitution was celebrated in Philadelphia, James Wilson, in
an oration on the great achievement said: "A people free and enlightened, establishing and ratifying a system of government which they have previously considered, examined, and approved! This is the spectacle which we are assembled to
celebrate; and it is the most dignified one that has yet appeared on our globe. . . .
What is the object exhibited to our contemplation? A whole people exercising
its first and greatest power — performing an act of sovereignty, original and unlimited! . . . Happy country! May thy happiness be perpetual!" *Works*
(1804 ed.), Vol. III, pp. 299 ff.

[2] Bancroft, *op. cit.*, Vol. II, p. 278; *Votes and Proceedings of the Senate of
Maryland, November Session, 1787*, pp. 5 ff.

[3] *Ibid.*, p. 283.

sixty-three against eleven on the afternoon of Saturday, April 26. The instrument was formally sealed on the 28th.

The legislature of Virginia, by a resolution passed on October 25, 1787, and a law enacted on December 12th, called a convention to be elected in March, 1788, and to assemble on June 2, 1788.[1] In no state were the forces for and against the Constitution more ably marshalled and led. In no state was there higher order of debate in the convention than took place in Virginia, the birthplace of the Constitution. It was a magnificent battle of talents that was waged during those June days, from the 2nd until the 25th. Then "the roll was called; and from the cities of Richmond and Williamsburg, from the counties near the ocean, from the northern neck, and from the counties between the Blue Ridge and the Alleghanies, eighty-nine delegates voted for the Constitution. From the other central and southern border counties of Kentucky, seventy-nine cried No." The margin of victory was small, but it was safe.

North Carolina was recalcitrant. The call for the convention was issued by the legislature on December 6, 1787;[2] the election was held on the last Friday and Saturday of March, 1788; and the convention assembled on July 21, 1788. In this body "the Antifederalists obtained a large majority. They permitted the whole subject to be debated until the 2d of August; still it had been manifested from the first that they would not allow of an unconditional ratification." On that day the convention deferred

---

[1] Bancroft, *op. cit.*, Vol. II, p. 316. The resolution provided that the "election shall be held in the month of March next on the first day of the court to be held for each county, city, or corporation respectively." The qualifications of voters were 'the same as those now established by law." Blair, *The Virginia Convention of 1788*, Vol. I, p. 56–57. Only freeholders were eligible to seats in the Convention. *Ibid.*, p. 56. Hening, *Statutes at Large*, Vol. XII, p. 462.

[2] *Laws of North Carolina* (1821), Vol. I, p. 597; *North Carolina Assembly Journals, 1785–98*, p. 22.

the ratification of the Constitution by a vote of 184 to 84,[1] and adjourned *sine die*. The new federal government was inaugurated without North Carolina; but the economic pressure which it brought to bear on that state, combined with the influence of eminent Federalists (including Washington), and the introduction of constitutional amendments in Congress, brought her into the union on November 21, 1789.[2]

South Carolina was one of the most deliberative of all the states, for it was not until January 18, 1788, that the legislature by unanimous resolution called a convention which was elected in April, and organized in Charleston, on May 13 of that year. The discussion there was evidently of a high order. Those who participated in it took first rank in the commonwealth, and the defenders of the new system put forth efforts worthy of the distinguished forensic leaders of the Charleston bar. The opponents exhausted the armory of their arguments, and seeing the tide running against them, they sought an adjournment of five months for further deliberation; but a motion to this effect was lost by a vote of 89 to 135. Finally at five o'clock on the tenth day of the sessions, May 23, the Constitution was carried by a large majority — 149 to 73.[3]

The legislature of Georgia, on October 26, 1787, called for a state convention to be chosen "in the same manner as representatives are elected," at the next General Election, held on the first Tuesday in December, *i.e.*, December 4, 1787.

---

[1] Bancroft, *op. cit.*, Vol. II, p. 349.

[2] Hugh Williamson, writing to Madison on May 21, 1789, said: "Our people near the sea-coast are in great pain on the idea of being shut out from the Union. They say that unless they can continue in the coasting trade without the alien duty, they must starve with their families or remove from the state. Can no exception be made in favor of such apparent aliens for so long a period as the first of January next?" *Madison Mss.*, Library of Congress.

[3] Bancroft, *op. cit.*, Vol. II, p. 293.

The convention was duly chosen, and met at Augusta on December 25; and after "having taken into serious consideration the said constitution" for four or five days, solemnly ratified the instrument on January 2, 1788.[1]

Rhode Island was the last of the thirteen states to accept the Constitution. She had refused to send delegates to the federal Convention; and the triumphant paper money party there would have none of the efficiency promised by the new system. It was not until May 29, 1790, that Rhode Island ratified the Constitution, and this action was brought about by the immediate prospect of coercion on the part of the government of the United States,[2] combined with the threat of the city of Providence to join with the other towns which were Federalist in opinion, in a movement to secede from the state and seek the protection of the federal government.[3] Without these material considerations pressing upon them, the agrarians of that commonwealth would have delayed ratification indefinitely; but they could not contend against a great nation and a domestic insurrection.

A survey of the facts here presented yields several important generalizations:

Two states, Rhode Island and North Carolina refused to ratify the Constitution until after the establishment of the new government which set in train powerful economic forces against them in their isolation.

In three states, New Hampshire, New York, and Massachusetts, the popular vote as measured by the election of delegates to the conventions was adverse to the Constitution; and ratification was secured by the conversion of

[1] *Documentary History of the Constitution*, Vol. II, pp. 82 ff.
[2] F. G. Bates, *Rhode Island and the Union*, pp. 192 ff.
[3] *Ibid.*, p. 197.

opponents and often the repudiation of their tacit (and in some cases express) instructions.

In Virginia the popular vote was doubtful.

In the four states which ratified the constitution with facility, Connecticut, New Jersey, Georgia, and Delaware, only four or five weeks were allowed to elapse before the legislatures acted, and four or five weeks more before the elections to the conventions were called; and about an equal period between the elections and the meeting of the conventions. This facility of action may have been due to the general sentiment in favor of the Constitution; or the rapidity of action may account for the slight development of the opposition.

In two commonwealths, Maryland and South Carolina, deliberation and delays in the election and the assembling of the conventions resulted in an undoubted majority in favor of the new instrument; but for the latter state the popular vote has never been figured out.[1]

In one of the states, Pennsylvania, the proceedings connected with the ratification of the Constitution were conducted with unseemly haste.

[1] See below, p. 248.

CHAPTER IX

THE POPULAR VOTE ON THE CONSTITUTION

In the adoption of the Constitution, says James Wilson, we have the gratifying spectacle of "a whole people exercising its first and greatest power — performing an act of sovereignty original and unlimited."[1] Without questioning the statement that for juristic purposes the Constitution may be viewed as an expression of the will of the whole people, a historical view of the matter requires an analysis of "the people" into its constituent elements. In other words, how many of "the people" favored the adoption of the Constitution, and how many opposed it?

At the very outset, it is necessary to recall that the question whether a constitutional Convention should be held was not submitted to popular vote, and that it was not specially passed upon by the electors in chosing the members of the legislatures which selected the delegates.[2]

In the second place, the Constitution was not submitted to popular ratification. The referendum was not unknown at that time, but it was not a fixed principle of American politics.[3] At all events, such a procedure does not seem to have crossed the minds of the members of the Convention, and long afterward, Marshall stated that ratification by state conventions was the only mode conceivable.[4] In

---

[1] See above, p. 234. [2] *Ibid.*, p. 72.
[3] Dodd, *The Revision and Amendment of Constitutions;* and Garner, in The American Political Science Review, February, 1907.
[4] McCulloch *v.* Maryland, 4 Wheaton, 316.

view of the fact that there was no direct popular vote taken on the Constitution, it is therefore impossible to ascertain the exact number of "the people" who favored its adoption.

The voters, who took part in the selection of delegates to the ratifying conventions in the states, may be considered as having been divided into four elements: those who were consciously in favor of the Constitution, those who were just as consciously against it, those who were willing to leave the matter to the discretion of their elected representatives, and those who voted blindly.

The proportions which these four groups bear to one another cannot be determined, but certain facts may be brought out which will throw light on the great question: How many of the people favored the adoption of the Constitution?

The first fact to be noted in this examination is that a considerable proportion of the adult white male population was debarred from participating in the elections of delegates to the ratifying state conventions by the prevailing property qualifications on the suffrage. The determination of these suffrage qualifications was left to the state legislatures; and in general they adopted the property restrictions already imposed on voters for members of the lower branch of the state legislatures.

In New Hampshire the duly qualified voters for members of the lower house were authorized to vote for members of the convention, and those Tories and sympathizers with Great Britain who were excluded by law were also admitted for this special election.[1] In Massachusetts the voters were those "qualified by law to vote in the election of representatives."[2] In Connecticut, those "qualified by law

[1] Batchellor, *State Papers of New Hampshire*, Vol. XXI, p. 165.
[2] *Debates and Proceedings in the Convention of the Commonwealth of Massachusetts in 1788* (1856), p. 23.

to vote in town meetings" were enfranchised.[1] In New Jersey, those who were "entitled to vote for representatives in general assembly;"[2] and in Delaware, those "qualified by law to vote for Representatives to the General Assembly"[3] were empowered to vote for delegates to their respective conventions. In Pennsylvania, voters for members of the assembly selected the delegates to the convention.[4] In Maryland, voters for members of the lower house;[5] in Virginia, those possessing the "qualifications now established by law;"[6] in North Carolina, those entitled to vote for members of the House of Commons;[7] in South Carolina, those voting for members of the lower house; and in Georgia, those voting for members of the legislature (one branch) were admitted to participation in the election of delegates to their respective state conventions.[8]

In New York alone was the straight principle of manhood suffrage adopted in the election of delegates to the ratifying convention. Libby seems inclined to hold that this exception was made by the landed aristocracy in the state legislature because it was opposed to the Constitution and wished to use its semi-servile tenants in the elections; but this problem has not yet been worked out, and any final conclusion as to the "politics" of this move is at present mere guesswork.[9]

It is impossible to say just what proportion of the adult

[1] Connecticut Courant, October 22, 1787.
[2] Documentary History of the Constitution, Vol. II, p. 61.
[3] Delaware State Council Minutes, 1776–1792, pp. 1080–1082.
[4] McMaster and Stone, Pennsylvania and the Federal Constitution, p. 72.
[5] Votes and Proceedings of the Senate of Maryland, November Session, 1787, pp. 5 ff.
[6] Above, p. 69. Blair, The Virginia Convention of 1788, Vol. I, pp. 56–57. Only freeholders could sit in the Convention.
[7] North Carolina Assembly Journals, 1785–1789, p. 22.
[8] Documentary History of the Constitution, Vol. II, p. 83.
[9] Libby, Geographical Distribution of the Vote on the Federal Constitution, p. 26, and note.

males twenty-one years of age was disfranchised by these qualifications. When it is remembered that only about 3 per cent of the population dwelt in towns of over 8000 inhabitants in 1790, and that freeholds were widely distributed, especially in New England, it will become apparent that nothing like the same proportion was disfranchised as would be to-day under similar qualifications. Dr. Jameson estimates that probably one-fifth of the adult males were shut out in Massachusetts,[1] and it would probably be safe to say that nowhere were more than one-third of the adult males disfranchised by the property qualifications.

Far more were disfranchised through apathy and lack of understanding of the significance of politics. It is a noteworthy fact that only a small proportion of the population entitled to vote took the trouble to go to the polls until the hot political contests of the Jeffersonian era. Where voting was *viva voce* at the town hall or the county seat, the journey to the polls and the delays at elections were very troublesome. At an election in Connecticut in 1775, only 3477 voters took part, out of a population of nearly 200,000, of whom 40,797 were males over twenty years of age. How many were disfranchised by the property qualifications and how many stayed away through indifference cannot be shown.[2]

Dr. Jameson, by most ingenious calculations, reaches the conclusion that in Massachusetts about 55,000 men in round numbers or about 16 or 17 per cent of the population were entitled to vote under the law. Assuming that 16 per cent were entitled to vote, he inquires into the number who actually exercised the franchise in the years from 1780 to 1790 in elections for governor; and his inquiry yields

---

[1] Article cited below, p. 243.
[2] McKinley, *Suffrage Franchise in the English Colonies*, p. 420.

some remarkable results. To give his conclusions in his own words: "Something like three per cent [of the population, or about one-fifth or one-sixth of those entitled to vote] took part in the first election in the autumn of 1780. During the next six years the figures remain at about two per cent only. In 1784, only 7631 votes were cast in the whole state; in the spring of 1786 only a little over eight thousand. Then came Shays' Rebellion and the political excitement of that winter brings up the votes in the spring election of '87 to a figure nearly three times as high as in '86, and amounting to something between five and six per cent of the population. The political discussions of the next two winters respecting the new federal government keep the figure up to five per cent. Then it drops to something between three and four and there it remains until 1794." [1]

For the purposes of a fine analysis of the economic forces in the ratifying process, it would be of the highest value to have the vote on delegates to the state conventions in each town and county throughout the whole country; but unfortunately no such figures are compiled and much of the original materials upon which the statistical tables could be based have doubtless disappeared. [2] Even such tables would be unsatisfactory because in several instances there were no contests and the issue of adoption or rejection of the Constitution was not squarely put before the voters.

In a few instances, however, the number of voters participating in the election of delegates to the state conventions

---

[1] Dr. J. F. Jameson, "Did the Fathers Vote," New England Magazine, January, 1890.

[2] A detailed statement of the vote in many Connecticut towns on the members of the state convention could doubtless be compiled after great labor from the local records described in the report on the public archives of Connecticut, *Report of the American Historical Association for 1906*, Vol. II.

has come down to us. In Boston, for example, where the fight was rather warm, and some 2700 men were entitled to vote, only 760 electors turned out to pass upon the momentous issue of the national Constitution — about half as many as voted in the next gubernatorial election.[1]

The treatises on the Constitution do not give any figures on the popular vote for delegates to the state convention in New York, but the following partial list taken from contemporary papers shows that in some of the counties the vote ran to almost 10 per cent of the population, while in others the percentage of the electorate participating (even under the universal manhood suffrage provision) was about that in Massachusetts, namely, 5 per cent. It will be noted also that the distribution of representation in the convention was grossly unequal and decidedly unfavorable to the Anti-Federalists. The classification into Federalist and Anti-Federalist is based upon the election returns as reported in the contemporary press, not on the vote in the state-ratifying convention.

FEDERALIST

	POPULATION 1790	HIGHEST FEDERALIST VOTE	HIGHEST ANTI-FEDERALIST VOTE	DELEGATES IN CONVENTION[4]	RATIO OF DELEGATES TO POPULATION
New York County	33,131	2735 [2]	134	9	3,681
Westchester . .	23,941	694 [3]	399	6	3,990
Queens[5] . . .	16,014			4	4,003
Kings	4,495			2	2,247
Richmond . . .	3,835			2	1,917
				23	

[1] Harding, *The Federal Constitution in Massachusetts*, p. 55, note 3. The Connecticut Courant gives the number as 763, December 17, 1787.

[2] Daily Advertiser, May 30, 1788.   [4] Elliot, *Debates*, Vol. II, p. 206.

[3] *Ibid.*, June 3.   [5] Queens vote was divided in the Convention.

ANTI-FEDERALIST

	POPULA-TION 1790	HIGHEST FEDERALIST VOTE	HIGHEST ANTI-FEDER-ALIST VOTE	DELEGATES IN CONVENTION	RATIO OF DELEGATES TO POPULATION
Albany	75,921	2627 [1]	4681	7	10,845
Ulster	29,397	68 [2]	1372	6	4,899
Dutchess . . .	45,266	892 [3]	1765	7	6,466
Orange	18,478		340 [4]	4	4,619
Columbia . . .	27,732	1498 [5]	1863	3	9,244
Montgomery . .	28,839	811 [6]	1209	6	4,806
Suffolk	16,440			5	3,288
Washington [7] . .	15,647			4	3,911
				41	

Several conclusions are obvious from this table. Measured by the popular vote, New York was overwhelmingly against the ratification of the Constitution. With the apportionment of representation against them, the Anti-Federalists elected nearly twice as many delegates as the Federalists. The popular vote in favor of ratification was largely confined to the urban centres of New York City and Albany City, thus correcting assumptions based on the convention vote alone.

But with this decided popular vote against them the Federalists were able to carry through their program by a narrow margin of thirty to twenty-seven. Why did so many Anti-Federalists whose popular mandate was clear and unmistakable, for there was a definite fight at the polls on

[1] Daily Advertiser, June 4.
[2] *Ibid.*, June 4.   [3] *Ibid.*, June 6.
[4] *Ibid.*, June 14.
[5] New York Journal, June 5, 1788.
[6] *Ibid.*, June 5.
[7] The Journal for June 5 reports the Anti-Federalist ticket carried in Washington County by a vote of two to one.

the issue, go over to their enemies? Three Anti-Federalist members, who did go over and carry the day for the Federalists, John DeWitt, John Smith, and Melancton Smith, later appeared as holders of public securities;[1] but this does not explain the event.[2]

In Pennsylvania, the vote on the election of delegates to ratify the Constitution was apparently very slight. The dissenting minority in their famous manifesto declared: "The election for members of the convention was held at so early a period and the want of information was so great that some of us did not know of it until after it was over. . . . We apprehend that no change can take place that will affect the internal government or constitution of this commonwealth unless a majority of the people should evidence a wish for such a change; but on examining the number of votes given for members of the present State convention, we find that of upwards of seventy thousand freemen who are entitled to vote in Pennsylvania, the whole convention has been elected by about thirteen thousand voters, and though two-thirds of the members of the convention have thought proper to ratify the proposed Constitution, yet those two-thirds were elected by the votes of only six thousand and eight hundred freemen."[3] Though the partisan source of these figures might lead one to question their accuracy, nevertheless it is hardly probable that they would have greatly exaggerated figures that were open to all.

Philadelphia was the scene of perhaps the hottest contest

---

[1] See below, p. 270.

[2] See a forthcoming dissertation on this subject by Wm. Feigenbaum. There was a threat of secession on the part of some New York City interests in case the Constitution was defeated. Weight was given to this threat by the news of the ratification from New Hampshire and Virginia. The possibility of retaining New York as the seat of the new Government was used by Jay, Hamilton, and Duane as an argument in favor of ratification. James Madison, *Writings*, Vol. I, p. 405.

[3] McMaster and Stone, *op. cit.*, p. 460.

over the election of delegates that occurred anywhere.
The city had at that time a population of about 28,000 inhabitants. At the election, the candidate who stood the
highest at the polls, George Latimer, received 1215 votes
while his leading opponent received only 235 votes.[1] Thus
a total of 1450 votes was cast in the election — about 5 per
cent of the population.

The total population of the state in 1790 was 434,373, and
allowing for the difficulty of journeying to the polls in the
rural districts, it seems that the estimate of the dissenters
was probably not far from correct.

It appears that in Baltimore 1347 voters participated in
the election of representatives from that city. McHenry
at the head of the poll received 962 votes and it was known
that he favored unconditional ratification of the Constitution. His leading opponent received 385 votes.[2] This
vote was taken after a considerable demonstration, for a
newspaper report says that "On the same day, the ship
builders, the tradesmen concerned in navigation, the merchants, the manufacturers and several thousand inhabitants
walked in procession through the different streets of the
town." Baltimore had at that time a population of 13,000
so that a very large proportion of the adult males took part
in the election.

Further light is thrown on the vote in Maryland by an
opponent of ratification in a long paper printed in the
Maryland Journal of May 16, 1788, signed "Republican."
The author, says Steiner, "asserts that the 'common class'
of people knew little of the Constitution. The two thousand copies of that document printed by order of the Assembly were too few to go far. The Annapolis paper is of

[1] Scharf and Wescott, *History of Philadelphia*, Vol. I, p. 447.
[2] Hartford Courant, April 28, 1788.

small circulation, and the two Baltimore ones are never seen on the Eastern Shore, while the severe weather during the past winter prevented any newspapers from being sent over thither. Of the 25,000 voters in the state, only 6000 voted at the election and 4,000 of these votes were cast in Baltimore town and seven of the counties. The rich and wealthy worked for the Constitution to prevent the loss of their debts, and in some counties the opposition had named no candidates." [1]

In South Carolina, the distribution of representation in the convention was such as to give a decided preponderance to the personalty districts along the sea-board. The convention of 1788 was composed of approximately twice the number of the house of representatives in 1794 and the apportionment was similar in character. In the latter year, R. G. Harper, under the pen-name of "Appius" pointed out the great disparity in the weight of the upper and lower districts in the legislature: "The lower country, including the three districts of Charleston, Beaufort, and Georgetown [which were strongly in favor of ratification of the Constitution], contains 28,694 white inhabitants, and it elects seventy representatives and twenty senators. Divide 149,596, the whole number in the state, by 28,694, those of the lower country, and the result will be more than five, from whence it appears, that a large majority of both branches of the legislature is elected by less than one-fifth of the people." [2] The upper district [largely Anti-Federal], on the other hand, contained 120,902 white inhabitants, and sent only fifty-four members to the house of representatives. On this basis, the seventy-three votes cast in the convention

[1] American Historical Review, Vol. V, p. 221.
[2] "Appius," To the Citizens of South Carolina (1794). Library of Congress, Duane Pamphlets, Vol. 83.

against ratification may in fact have represented a majority of the white inhabitants and voters in the state.[1]

While one hesitates to generalize about the vote cast in favor of the Constitution on the basis of the fragmentary evidence available, it seems worth while, nevertheless, to put together several related facts bearing on the matter.

In addition to the conclusion, brought out by Dr. Jameson, that about 5 per cent of the population voted in Massachusetts in the period under consideration, we have other valuable data. Dr. Paullin has shown that the electoral vote in the presidential election of 1788 in New Hampshire was 2.8 per cent of the free population; that the vote in Madison's electoral district in Virginia in the same election was 2.7 per cent of the white population; that the vote in the first congressional election in Maryland was 3.6 per cent of the white population and that the vote in the same congressional election in Massachusetts was 3 per cent.[2] Speaking of the exercise of the franchise as a whole in the period, Dr. Paullin says, "The voting was done chiefly by a small minority of interested property holders, a disproportionate share of whom in the northern states resided in the towns, and the wealthier and more talented of whom like a closed corporation controlled politics."

In view of these figures, in view of the data given above on the election of delegates (to the ratifying conventions) in the cities of Boston, Philadelphia, and Baltimore, in view of the fact that the percentage participating in the country was smaller than in the towns, and in view of the fact that only 3 per cent of the population resided in cities

[1] By a careful study of local geography and the distribution of representation this could be accurately figured out.

[2] "The First Elections under the Constitution," *Iowa Journal of History and Politics*, Vol. II, pp. 3 ff.

of over 8000, it seems a safe guess to say that not more than 5 per cent of the population in general, or in round numbers, 160,000 voters, expressed an opinion one way or another on the Constitution. In other words, it is highly probable that not more than one-fourth or one-fifth of the adult white males took part in the election of delegates to the state conventions. If anything, this estimate is high.

Now in four of the states, New Hampshire, Massachusetts, New York, and Virginia, the conventions at the time of their election were either opposed to the ratification of the Constitution or so closely divided that it was hard to tell which way the final vote would go. These four states, with Rhode Island and North Carolina,[1] which were at first against ratification, possessed about three-fifths of the population — in round numbers 1,900,000 out of 3,200,000 free persons. Of the 1,900,000 population in these states we may, with justice it seems, set off at least 900,000, that is, 45,000 voters as representing the opposition. Add to these the voters in Pennsylvania who opposed the ratification of the Constitution, approximately 6000, and we have 51,000 dissenting voters, against ratification. Adding the dissenters in Maryland, South Carolina,[2] and Connecticut, and taking the other states as unanimous, we may reasonably conjecture that of the estimated 160,000 who voted in the election of delegates, not more than 100,000 men favored the adoption of the Constitution at the time it was put into effect — about one in six of the adult males.

Admitting that these figures are rough guesses, it appears, nevertheless, that the Constitution was not "an expression of the clear and deliberate will of the whole people," nor of

---

[1] It will be recalled that the Constitution was put into effect without either North Carolina or Rhode Island.

[2] See above, p. 248.

a majority of the adult males, nor at the outside of one-fifth of them.

Indeed, it may very well be that a majority of those who voted were against the adoption of the Constitution as it then stood. Such a conjecture can be based on the frank statement of no less an authority than the great Chief Justice Marshall who took a prominent part in the movement which led to the formation and ratification of the new instrument of government.[1]

At all events, the disfranchisement of the masses through property qualifications and ignorance and apathy contributed largely to the facility with which the personalty-interest representatives carried the day. The latter were alert everywhere, for they knew, not as a matter of theory, but as a practical matter of dollars and cents, the value of the new Constitution. They were well informed. They were conscious of the identity of their interests. They were well organized. They knew for weeks in advance, even before the Constitution was sent to the states for ratification, what the real nature of the contest was. They resided for the most part in the towns, or the more thickly populated areas, and they could marshall their forces quickly and effectively. They had also the advantage of appealing to all discontented persons who exist in large numbers in every society and are ever anxious for betterment through some change in political machinery.

Talent, wealth, and professional abilities were, generally speaking, on the side of the Constitutionalists. The money to be spent in the campaign of education was on their side also; and it was spent in considerable sums for pamphleteering, organizing parades and demonstrations, and engaging the interest of the press. A small percentage of the enor-

[1] See below, p. 299.

mous gain to come through the appreciation of securities alone would have financed no mean campaign for those days.

The opposition on the other hand suffered from the difficulties connected with getting a backwoods vote out to the town and county elections. This involved sometimes long journeys in bad weather, for it will be remembered that the elections were held in the late fall and winter. There were no such immediate personal gains to be made through the defeat of the Constitution, as were to be made by the security holders on the other side. It was true the debtors knew that they would probably have to settle their accounts in full and the small farmers were aware that taxes would have to be paid to discharge the national debt if the Constitution was adopted; and the debtors everywhere waged war against the Constitution — of this there is plenty of evidence.[1] But they had no money to carry on their campaign; they were poor and uninfluential — the strongest battalions were not on their side. The wonder is that they came so near defeating the Constitution at the polls.

[1] Libby, *op. cit.*, pp. 50 ff.

CHAPTER X

As in natural science no organism is pretended to be understood as long as its merely superficial aspects are described, so in history no movement by a mass of people can be correctly comprehended until that mass is resolved into its component parts. To apply this concept to the problem before us: no mathematically exact conclusion can be reached concerning the material interests reflected in the Constitution until "the people" who favored its adoption and "the people" who opposed it are individualized and studied as economic beings dependent upon definite modes and processes of gaining a livelihood. A really fine analytical treatment of this problem would, therefore, require a study of the natural history of the (approximately) 160,000 men involved in the formation and adoption of the Constitution; but for the present we must rely on rougher generalizations, drawn from incomplete sources.

It would be fortunate if we had a description of each of the state conventions similar to that made of the Philadelphia Convention;[1] but such a description would require a study of the private economy of several hundred men, with considerable scrutiny. And the results of such a search would be on the whole less fruitful than those secured by the study of the Philadelphia Convention, because so many members of the state-ratifying bodies were obscure persons of whom biography records nothing and whose property holdings do

[1] Above, Chapter V.

not appear in any of the documents that have come down to us. In a few instances, as in the case of Pennsylvania, a portion of this work has been done in a fragmentary way — as regards economic matters; and it may be hoped that a penetrating analysis of the public security holdings and other property interests of the members of all state conventions may sometime be made — as far as the sources will allow. Nevertheless, for the purposes of this study, certain general truths concerning the conflict over the ratification of the Constitution in the several states have already been established by scholars like Libby, Harding, Ambler.

The first of these authors, Dr. Libby, has made a painstaking study of the *Geographical Distribution of the Vote on the Constitution*, in which he sets forth the economic characteristics of the areas for and against the adoption of the Constitution. These conclusions are all utilized in this chapter; but they are supplemented by reference to the later researches of Harding [1] and Ambler,[2] and by a large amount of new illustrative materials here presented for the first time. The method followed is to exhibit, in general, the conflict of economic interests in each of the several states over the adoption of the Constitution.

New Hampshire. — There were three rather sharply marked economic districts in New Hampshire which found political expression in the convention that ratified the Constitution. Two of the three were the sea-coast area and the interior or middle region. "The former," says Libby, "the coast area, represented the commercial and urban interests; here were to be found most of the professional men, leaders of thought, men of wealth and influence. The second section, the interior, was composed

[1] *Massachusetts and the Federal Constitution* (Harvard Studies).
[2] *Sectionalism in Virginia.*

of those representing the small farmers; a population cut off from the outside world by lack of good roads, and which raised little for market except to exchange for the few things that could not be produced at home. The former class, progressive and liberal and familiar with the practical details of government, as a rule voted for the Constitution. The latter, conservative by environment and having little knowledge of what went on outside the narrow bounds of the home village or township, quite as generally voted against the Constitution." [1]

The third region in New Hampshire (whose representatives favored ratification) was "the Connecticut valley or border district" whose interests were akin to those of the sea towns because it had commercial connection with the outside world through the Connecticut River. It was to this region particularly that Oliver Ellsworth must have appealed in his open letter to the citizens of New Hampshire in which he said: "New York, the trading towns on the Connecticut River, and Boston are the sources from which a great part of your foreign supplies will be obtained, and where your produce will be exposed for market. In all these places an import is collected, of which, as consumers, you pay a share without deriving any public benefit. You cannot expect any alteration in the private systems of these states unless effected by the proposed government." [2]

Several economic facts of prime significance in the ratification of the Constitution in New Hampshire are afforded by the tax returns of 1793. These show that of the £61,711 : 9 : 5 "total value of stock in trade" in the state in that year (Vermont being then cut off) no less than £42,512 : 0 : 5 or over two-thirds was in Rockingham county, the seat of the commercial town of Portsmouth, whose citizens were the lead-

[1] Libby, *op. cit.*, pp. 7–8.   [2] *Ibid.*, p. 11.

ing agitators for the new system, and whose delegates in the
state convention were overwhelmingly in favor of ratification.
Moreover, of the total amount of the "money on hand or
at interest" in the state, £35,985 : 5 : 6, about two-thirds,
£22,770 : 9 : 4 was in Rockingham county. It is of further
significance that of the £893,327 : 16 : 10 worth of real estate
and buildings in the state, less than one-half, £317,970 : 7 : 2,
was in that county.[1] Thus the stronghold of Federalism
possessed about two-thirds of all the personalty and only
about one-half of the realty values in the commonwealth.

All personalty was not equally interested in ratifying
the Constitution, as pointed out above; holders of public
paper multiplied their values from six to twenty times in
securing the establishment of the new system. Further
interesting data would be revealed, therefore, if we could
discover the proportion of public securities to other personalty and their geographic distribution.[2] The weight of
the securities in New Hampshire is shown by the fact that
the tax list for 1793 gives only £35,985 as the total
amount of money on hand or at interest (including public
securities)[3] in the state, while the accounts of the Treasury department show that $20,000 in interest on the
public debt went to the loan office of that state to discharge that annual federal obligation.[4] It is highly probable that the tax list is very low, but even at that the public
securities constituted a considerable mass of the capital of
the commonwealth. The leading supporters of the Con-

---

[1] Data given here are from *State Papers: Finance*, Vol. I, p. 442. It should be
remembered that the figures would have been relatively different in 1787 on account of the union of Vermont with New Hampshire, but they are doubtless
roughly correct.

[2] Some painstaking research in the Treasury Department would produce valuable
data toward the solution of this problem.

[3] *State Papers: Finance*, Vol. I, p. 442 (public funds included. See p. 419).

[4] See above for the table, p. 36.

stitution in New Hampshire were large holders of public paper,[1] and there is no doubt that as personalty was the dynamic element in the movement for the Constitution, so securities were the dynamic element in the personalty.

Massachusetts. — The vote in Massachusetts on the Constitution was clearly along class or group lines: those sections in which were to be found the commerce, money, securities — in a word, personalty — were in favor of the ratification of the new instrument of government; and those sections which were predominantly rural and possessed little personalty were against it. Libby classifies the sections on the basis of the vote as follows: —

Eastern section   . . . . Yeas, 73 per cent   Nays, 27 per cent
Middle section   . . . . Yeas, 14 per cent   Nays, 86 per cent
Western section   . . . . Yeas, 42 per cent   Nays, 58 per cent

Speaking of this table he says: "Such striking differences as these indicate clearly that there is something fundamental lying back of the vote.   Each of these sections is an economic and social unit, the first representing the coast region, the second the interior, and the third the Connecticut valley and border districts of the state.   In the eastern section the interests were commercial; there was the wealth, the influence, the urban population of the state. . . .   The middle section of Massachusetts represented the interior agricultural interests of the state — the small farmers.   From this section came a large part of the Shays faction in 1786. The Connecticut valley or western district may be subdivided into the northern, most interior, and predominantly Antifederal section, and the southern section, nearest the coast and predominantly Federal, with the trading towns of the Connecticut River in its southeastern part."[2]

---

[1] Ms. Treasury Department: New Hampshire Loan Office Books.
[2] Libby, *op. cit.*, p. 12.

Harding, after an independent study of the opposition
to the Constitution in Massachusetts, comes to substantially
the same conclusion. Among the weighty elements in the
struggle he places "the conflict of interest, partly real and
partly fancied, between the agricultural and the commercial
sections of the state." Underlying the whole opposition,
he continues, "was the pronounced antagonism between
the aristocratic and the democratic elements of society in
Massachusetts. . . . Massachusetts was not alone in this
experience; in most, if not all, of the states a similar contest
had arisen since the war. The men who at Philadelphia
had put their names to the new Constitution were, it seems
quite safe to affirm, at that time identified with the aristocratic interest. . . . There can be no question that this
feeling [of antagonism between democracy and aristocracy]
underlay most of the opposition in the Massachusetts convention." [1]

Of course this second element of opposition — aristocracy
versus democracy — introduced by Harding is really nothing but the first under another guise; for the aristocratic
party was the party of wealth with its professional dependents; and the democratic party was the agrarian element
which, by the nature of economic circumstances, could have
no large body of professional adherents. This economic
foundation of the class division was fully understood by
Adams and set forth with unmistakable clearness in his
Defence of the American Constitutions. Hamilton, Madison,
and all thinkers among the Federalists understood it also.
To speak of a democratic interest apart from its economic
sources is therefore a work of supererogation; and it does
not add, in fact, to an exposition of the real forces at work.
Harding himself recognizes this and explains it in a luminous
fashion in his introductory chapter.

[1] *The Federal Constitution in Massachusetts*, p. 75.

And what were the economic and social antecedents of the opponents of the Constitution in the Massachusetts convention? Harding, with his customary directness, meets the inquiry: "A half-dozen obscure men, it must be answered, whose names are utterly unknown, even to most students of this period." He continues: "William Widgery (or Wedgery) of New Gloucester, Maine, was one of these.[1] A poor, friendless, uneducated boy, he had emigrated from England before the Revolution, had served as a lieutenant on board a privateer in that contest, had then settled in Maine, had acquired some property, and by 1788 had served one term in the Massachusetts legislature. . . . Samuel Thompson, of Topsham, Maine, was another of the anti-federalist leaders. A self-made man, he had the obstinacy of opinion which such men often show. . . . He was wealthy for the times, but inclined to be niggardly. . . . Another determined opponent of the proposed Constitution was Samuel Nasson (or Nason) of Sanford, Maine. Born in New Hampshire and a saddler by trade, he became a store keeper in Maine, served awhile in the War . . . and finally settled down as a trader at Sanford. . . . In 1787 he served a term in the General Court, but declined a re-election because he felt 'the want of a proper education.' . . . From Massachusetts proper, Dr. John Taylor, of Douglas, Worcester County, was the most prominent opponent of the new Constitution. . . . But the slightest information, it seems, can now be gathered as to his history and personality. He had been one of the popular majority in the legislature of 1787 where he had taken an active part in procuring the extension of the Tender Law. . . . Another delegate from this part of the state who was prominent in the opposition was Captain Phanuel Bishop, of Rehoboth, Bristol County. In

[1] As to the opposition in Maine, see General Knox's view, below, p. 301.

him the Rhode Island virus may be seen at work. . . . He
was a native of Massachusetts and had received a public
school education. When or why he had been dubbed Captain is not now apparent. Belknap styles him 'a noted in-
surgent'; and he had evidently ridden into office on the crest
of the Shaysite wave. His first legislative experience had
been in the Senate of 1787 where he had championed the
debtor's cause." [1]

This completes the list of leaders who fought bitterly
against the Constitution to the end in Massachusetts, according to a careful student of the ratification in that state:
three self-made men from the Maine regions and two representatives of the debtor's cause. Nothing could be more
eloquent than this description of the alignment.

Neither Harding nor Libby has, however, made analysis of the facts disclosed by the tax lists of Massachusetts
or the records in the Treasury Department at Washington,
which show unquestionably that the live and persistent
economic force which organized and carried through the
ratification was the personalty interests and particularly the
public security interests. As has been pointed out, these
had the most to gain immediately from the Constitution.
Continental paper bought at two and three shillings in the
pound was bound to rise rapidly with the establishment of
the federal government. No one knew this better than the
members of the federal Convention from Massachusetts
and their immediate friends and adherents in Boston.

Of the total amount of funded 6 per cents in the state,
£113,821, more than one-half, £65,730, was concentrated
in the two counties, Essex and Suffolk, of which Boston was
the urban centre — the two counties whose delegates in
the state convention were almost unanimous in supporting

[1] *The Federal Constitution in Massachusetts*, pp. 63–66.

the Constitution. Of the total amount of 3 per cents, £73,100, more than one-half, £43,857, was in these two counties. Of the deferred stock, amounting to £59,872, more than one-half, £32,973, was in these two counties. Of the total amount of all other securities of the state or the United States in the commonwealth, £94,893, less than one-third or £30,329, was in these counties. Of the total amount of money at interest in the state, £196,698, only about one-third, £63,056, was in these two counties, which supports the above conjecture that public securities were the active element.[1]

Further confirmation for this conjecture seems to be afforded by the following tables, showing the distribution of the vote and of public securities.[2] The first group shows the votes of the delegates from Essex and Suffolk counties — the Federalist strongholds — on the ratification, and also the amount of public securities in each as revealed by the tax lists of 1792:

ESSEX

For the Constitution . . . 38 votes   Against . . . 6 votes

SUFFOLK

For the Constitution . . . 34 votes   Against . . . 5 votes

Table of public securities listed for taxation in each of these counties:

	SUFFOLK	ESSEX
Funded, sixes	£29,228	£36,502
Funded, threes	17,096	26,761
Funded, not on interest	14,854	18,119
Other securities	14,056	16,273
Money at Interest	29,941	33,115

---

[1] *State Papers: Finance*, Vol. I, pp. 451. Of course some changes in distribution may have occurred between 1789 and 1792, but this may be taken as approximately correct.

[2] *State Papers: Finance*, Vol. I, p. 443; Libby, *op. cit.*, p. 107 for the vote.

Now let us take the vote in the convention, and the property in two counties which were heavily against the Constitution.[1] The vote is as follows:

WORCESTER

For the Constitution . . . 7 votes Against . . . 43 votes

BERKSHIRE

For the Constitution . . . 7 votes Against . . . 15 votes

The tables of public securities and money in these counties follow:

	WORCESTER	BERKSHIRE
Funded, sixes	£12,924	£981
Funded, threes	8,184	665
Funded, not on interest	5,736	384
Other securities	10,903	602
Money at interest	25,594	6298

Now if we take the securities in these two counties which went heavily against the Constitution several economic facts are worthy of notice. Of the total amount of 6 per cents in the state, only £13,905, or about one-eighth is to be found in them. Of the 3 per cents, we find £8849, or about one-eighth of the total amount in the commonwealth. But if we take money at interest, we find £31,892, or about one-sixth of the total amount in the state. This is not surprising, for Worcester was the centre of the Shays rebellion in behalf of debtors, and a large portion of their creditors were presumably in the neighborhood.[2]

"The courts were burdened with suits for ordinary debts by means of which creditors sought to put in more lasting

[1] Libby, *op. cit.*, for vote, p. 107; *State Papers: Finance*, Vol. I. pp. 450 and 449 for taxes lists.

[2] The full significance of the Worcester vote and property lists would involve an analysis of the distribution of each among the towns.

form the obligations which their debtors could not at that time meet. In Worcester county alone, with a population of less than 50,000, more than 2000 actions were entered in 1784, and during the next year 1700 more were put on the list." [1]

These figures, like all other statistics, should be used with care, and it would require a far closer analysis than can be made here to work out all of their political implications. We should have a thorough examination of such details as the distribution of the public securities among towns and individual holders; and such a work is altogether worthy of a Quetelet.

Meanwhile, it may be said with safety that the communities in which personalty was relatively more powerful favored the ratification of the Constitution, and that in these communities large quantities of public securities were held. Moreover, there was undoubtedly a vital connection between the movement in support of the Constitution and public security holding, or to speak concretely, among the leading men in Massachusetts who labored to bring about the ratification was a large number of public creditors.

For example, Boston had twelve representatives in the state-ratifying convention, all of whom voted in favor of the Constitution. Of these twelve men the following were holders of public securities: [2]

Samuel Adams	John Coffin Jones
James Bowdoin, Sr.	William Phillips
Thomas Dawes, Jr.	Thomas Russell
Christopher Gore	John Winthrop

[1] *American Antiquarian Society Proceedings* (1911), p. 65.

[2] Ms. Treasury Department: *Index to the Three Per Cents (Mass.)*. Gore, Dawes, and Phillips appear on the New Hampshire Journals and other Massachusetts Records.

In other words, at least eight out of the twelve men representing the chief financial centre of the state were personally interested in the fate of the new Constitution. How deeply, it is impossible to say, for the Ledgers seem to have disappeared from the Treasury Department and only the Index to the funded debt remains. Supplementary records, however, show some of them to have been extensively engaged in dealing in paper. The four men who, apparently, were not security holders were John Hancock, Caleb Davis, Charles Jarvis, and Rev. Samuel Stillman.[1]

The towns surrounding Boston in Suffolk county also returned a number of men who were holders of securities :[2]

Fisher Ames, Dedham	Rev. Daniel Shute, Hingham
John Baxter, Medfield	Increase Sumner, Roxbury
James Bowdoin, Jr., Dorchester	Cotton Tufts, Weymouth
Richard Cranch, Braintree	Ebenezer Wales, Dorchester
J. Fisher, Franklin	Ebenezer Warren, Foxboro
William Heath, Roxbury	Rev. Anthony Wibird, Brain-
Thomas Jones, Hull	tree
Benj. Lincoln, Hingham	

In other words, twenty-two of the thirty-four men from Boston and Suffolk county who voted in favor of the ratification of the Constitution in the Massachusetts convention were holders of public securities, and all of the twenty-two except two (Wales and Warren) probably benefited from the appreciation of the funds which resulted from the ratification.[3]

---

[1] The *Index* shows several holders by the name of Davis: Jonathan, James, Aaron, Susanna, John, Nathl., Joseph, Moses, Thomas, Saml., Wendell, and John G. Whether they were relatives of Caleb is not apparent. Leonard and Nathl. Jarvis also appear on the Book. Also Mary and Belcher Hancock.

[2] All of these men except Wales and Warren appear on the *Index to the Three Per Cents (Mass.)*. Wales and Warren appear on the books as holders of old certificates (*Loan Office Certificates, 1779–1788, Mass.*) ; and it does not appear when or how they disposed of their holdings.

[3] See above, p. 75, note 3.

To recapitulate. There were thirty-nine members of the Massachusetts convention from Suffolk county, which includes Boston. Of these, thirty-four voted for the ratification of the Constitution, and of the thirty-four who so voted, two-thirds, or twenty-two to be exact, were holders of public paper.

That other supporters of the Constitution from other Massachusetts counties held paper so extensively is not to be expected, and a casual glance through the records shows that this surmise is probably true. Boston was the centre of the Federalist agitation, and it supplied the sinews of war for the campaign which finally secured the adoption of the new system of government.

Connecticut. — The vote on the Constitution in Connecticut was so largely in favor of ratification that no very clear lines of cleavage are apparent on the surface.[1] The opposition, as measured by the vote of the delegates in the Convention, was "scattered and unimportant. Its two chief centres were in New Haven county on the coast, and in five or six towns on the Connecticut river at the northern boundary, connecting with a group of opposition towns in Massachusetts."[2] It is worthy of note that the considerable towns for the time, Windsor, Norwalk, Stamford, Litchfield, Hartford, and New Haven were for the Constitution, while much of the opposition came from small inland towns like Cornwall, Norfolk, and Sharon.[3]

The map facing this page shows that the Federalist towns

---

[1] On September 3, 1787, the Connecticut Courant in a letter from Philadelphia (Aug. 24) says: "One of the first objects with the national government to be elected under the new constitution, it is said, will be to provide funds for the payment of the national debt, and thereby restore the credit of the United States, which has been so much impaired by the individual states. Every holder of a public security of any kind is, therefore, deeply interested in the cordial reception and speedy establishment of a vigorous continental government."

[2] Libby, *op. cit.*, p. 14.   [3] *Ibid.*, p. 113.

were the financial centres of the time in Connecticut. The
representatives of the " shaded " towns in the state convention voted against the Constitution; those from the partially
" shaded " towns were divided; and those from the plain
white towns voted for the Constitution.[1] Each black dot
represents a holder of one 6 per cent assumed debt bond.[2]
It is apparent at a glance that there must have been some
relation between security-holding and the " sentiments," to
use Madison's term,[3] of the respective proprietors. Hartford
alone had almost as many security holders as all of the Anti-
Federalist towns combined. It would be interesting to
have a map showing the distribution of all other forms of
wealth as well as the assumed debt.

What a more searching study would produce were we able
to carry the contest back into the town meetings that
chose the delegates cannot be conjectured. But the local
evidence — even that which was recorded — has largely
disappeared or would require years of search to unearth.
Moreover, the tax system in Connecticut at the time was
not such as to yield the data most needed for such an inquiry, for "loans to the state and the United States were
exempt from assessment." [4] Whether this grew out of a
public policy or the fact that the chief politicians of the day
were large holders of securities — evidenced by the records
in the Treasury Department at Washington — is also a
matter for conjecture. No documents, no history.

Nevertheless, as in Massachusetts, the public securities
formed a dynamic element in the movement for ratification.

----

[1] Towns not represented or not voting in the convention are counted *against* the
Constitution.

[2] The assumed debt is taken because the Ledgers of that debt are in excellent
shape and apparently complete. They do not contain, however, half of the security
holders in that state. Several of the towns that had no assumed debt-holders were
represented in the convention by holders of other paper. See table, p. 267.

[3] See above, p. 15.   [4] *State Papers: Finance*, Vol. I, p. 423.

One hundred and twenty-eight members of the Connecticut convention voted in favor of the new system. Of these men at least sixty-five held public paper in some amount (ranging from a few dollars to tens of thousands) previous to or about the time of the adoption of the Constitution. They are given here in alphabetical order with the names of the towns which they represented.

Nehemiah Beardsley, New Fairfield

Philip B. Bradley, Ridgefield

Hezekiah Brainerd, Haddam

Daniel Brinsmade, Washington

Gideon Buckingham, Milford

Thaddeus Burr, Fairfield

Charles Burrall, Canaan

Samuel Canfield, New Milford

Samuel Carver, Bolton

Jabez Chapman, East Haddam

Moses Cleaveland, Canterbury

Wheeler Coit, Preston

Seth Crocker, Willington

James Davenport, Stamford

John Davenport, Stamford

Benjamin Dow, Voluntown

Joshua Dunlop, Plainfield

Eliphalet Dyer, Windham

Pierpont Edwards, New Haven

Oliver Ellsworth, Winsor

Jabez Fitch, Greenwich

Daniel Foot, Colchester

Isaac Foot, Stafford

Mathew Griswold, Lyme (President of the Convention)

Nathan Hale, Canaan

Asaph Hall, Goshen

Jeremiah Halsey, Preston

William Hart, Saybrook

Cornelius Higgins, Haddam

Benjamin Hinman, Southbury

Caleb Holt, Willington

Jedediah Huntington, Norwich

Samuel Huntington, Norwich

Eli Hyde, Franklin

Wm. Samuel Johnson, Stratford

Richard Law, New London

Andrew Lee, Lisbon

Isaac Lee, Berlin

Elisha Mills, Stratford

Stephen Mitchel, Wethersfield

Josiah Mosely, Glastonbury

Roger Newberry, Winsor

Wm. Noyes, Lyme

Samuel H. Parsons, Middletown

Charles Phelps, Stonington

John Phelps, Stafford

Joshua Porter, Salisbury

Jeremiah Ripley, Coventry

Ephraim Root, Coventry

Jesse Root, Hartford

Lemuel Sanford, Reading

Epaphras Sheldon, Torrington

Roger Sherman, New Haven

Simeon Smith, Ashford

Jonathan Sturges, Fairfield

Dyar Throop, East Haddam

John Treadwell, Farmington
Jeremiah Wadsworth, Hartford
Ichabod Warner, Bolton
John Watson, East Winsor
Jeremiah West, Tolland

Ebenezer White, Chatham
William Williams, Lebanon
Joseph Woodbridge, Groton
Erastus Wolcott, East Winsor
Oliver Wolcott, Litchfield [1]

It must not be thought that the ramifications of economic interest ends with these names.[2]   A large number of men who do not appear on the records as holding securities personally, belonged to families having such holdings.   For example, John Chester, of Wethersfield, is apparently not on the books, but he was a colonel in the war and doubtless received the soldiers' certificates or other paper at some period.   Thomas Chester and Sarah Chester of Wethersfield appear on the records.   Whether there were family connections might be ascertained by a study of local history. It is evident what infinite pains would be required to trace out all of these genealogical data.

New York.— There can be no question about the predominance of personalty in the contest over the ratification in New York.   That state, says Libby, "presents the problem in its simplest form.   The entire mass of interior counties . . . were solidly Anti-federal, comprising the agricultural portion of the state, the last settled and the most thinly populated.   There were however in this region two Federal cities (not represented in the convention [as such]), Albany in Albany county and Hudson in Columbia county.

---

[1] The sources for the information as to these securities are in the Treasury Department: *Connecticut Loan Office, 1781–1783* (Register of Certificates); *Connecticut Loan Office, Ledger B, Assumed Debt; Ledger C, 1790–1796; Ledger A, 1790–1797; Loan Office Certificates of 1779,* etc.

[2] No doubt a study of local economic interests in Connecticut would yield highly important data.   See, for example, the early capitalist enterprises connected with the navigation of the Connecticut River.   *Proceedings of the American Antiquarian Society, 1903–1904,* p. 404.   Such local histories as E. D. Larned, *A History of Windham County,* contain veritable mines of information on the economic interests of men prominent in local politics.

. . . The Federal area centred about New York city and county: to the southwest lay Richmond county (Staten Island); to the southeast Kings county, and to the northeast Westchester county; while still further extending this area, at the northeast lay the divided county of Dutchess, with a vote in the convention of 4 to 2 in favor of the Constitution, and at the southeast were the divided counties of Queens and Suffolk. . . . These radiating strips of territory with New York city as a centre form a unit, in general favorable to the new Constitution; and it is significant of this unity that Dutchess, Queens, and Suffolk counties broke away from the anti-Federal phalanx and joined the Federalists, securing thereby the adoption of the Constitution." [1]

Unfortunately the exact distribution of personalty in New York and particularly in the wavering districts which went over to the Federalist party cannot be ascertained, for the system of taxation in vogue in New York at the period of the adoption of the Constitution did not require a state record of property.[2] The data which proved so fruitful in Massachusetts are not forthcoming, therefore, in the case of New York; but it seems hardly necessary to demonstrate the fact that New York City was the centre of personalty for the state and stood next to Philadelphia as the great centre of operations in public stock.

This somewhat obvious conclusion is reinforced by the evidence relative to the vote on the legal tender bill which the paper money party pushed through in 1786. Libby's analysis of this vote shows that "No vote was cast against the bill by members of counties north of the county of New York. In the city and county of New York and in Long

---

[1] Libby, *op. cit.*, p. 18. Libby here takes the vote in the New York convention, but that did not precisely represent the popular vote. Above, p. 244.

[2] *State Papers: Finance*, Vol. I, p. 425.

Island and Staten Island, the combined vote was 9 to 5 against the measure. Comparing this vote with the vote on the ratification in 1788, it will be seen that of the Federal counties 3 voted against paper money and 1 for it; of the divided counties 1 (Suffolk) voted against paper money and 2 (Queens and Dutchess) voted for it. Of the anti-Federal counties none had members voting against paper money. The merchants as a body were opposed to the issue of paper money and the Chamber of Commerce adopted a memorial against the issue." [1]

Public security interests were identified with the sound money party. There were thirty members of the New York constitutional convention who voted in favor of the ratification of the Constitution and of these no less than sixteen were holders of public securities: [2]

James Duane, New York (C 6)
John DeWitt, Dutchess (N.Y. 3)
Alexander Hamilton, [3] New York
Richard Harrison, New York (C 6)
Jonathan Havens, Suffolk (C 6 as Trustee for a religious society).
John Jay, New York (C 6)
Samuel Jones, Queens (C 6)
Philip Livingston, Westchester (C 6)
Robert R. Livingston, New York (N.Y. 3)
Nicholas Low, New York (C 6)
Richard Morris, [4] New York (C 6)
Isaac Roosevelt, New York (R)
Gozen Ryerss, Richmond (N.Y. 3)
John Smith, Suffolk (C 6)

---

[1] Libby, op. cit., p. 59.

[2] Those marked "C 6," Ms. Treasury Department: New York, 6% Funds, 1790; "N. Y. 3" ibid., 3% Funds; "R," New York Loan Office Receipts, Ms. Division, Library of Congress. Melancton Smith appears on the Ledgers of the Connecticut Loan Office; and N. Y. Loan Office, 1791, folio 138, for $10,000 worth of sixes and threes. [3] See above, p. 107.

[4] Not present on final vote, but see Elliot, Debates, Vol. II, p. 411.

Melancton Smith, Dutchess (Conn.)
Philip Van Cortland, Westchester (C 6)
Jesse Woodhull, Orange (C 6)

New Jersey. — New Jersey was among the states which pushed through the ratification of the Constitution without giving the agrarian party time to organize its forces; and, from the records, the vote in the state convention was unanimous. This unanimity is rather startling in view of the fact that the year before a paper money party had been able to force through an emission bill by a narrow margin. Either there was a violent reaction against inflation, or the Federalist campaign had been highly organized. What little opposition appears to have been raised in that state seems to have been by the debtor and paper money class.[1]

It must be admitted, however, that no detailed study of the ratification in New Jersey has ever been made. Libby passes it over briefly; and the older writers like Bancroft and Curtis dismiss it with their usual lightness of touch. Unfortunately for such a study, the records of the convention in that state are no more than bare minutes; and the materials in the Treasury Department from the New Jersey loan office are extremely fragmentary. Until extended search in local and state history is made on the points here raised, New Jersey must be dismissed cursorily.

There were thirteen counties in the state represented in the Convention, and each of nine counties had one or more representatives who had learned the elementary lessons in public finance through holding at least some small amounts of public securities — often certificates of only trivial value.

---

[1] Libby, *op. cit.*, pp. 60–61. Writing on October 14, 1787, Madison said "I do not learn that any opposition is likely to be made [to the ratification] in New Jersey," *Writings of James Madison*, Vol. I, p. 342.

The meagre character of the records of that state do not permit of a satisfactory statement. There were three delegates from Bergen county; of these John Fell appears on the Register of Land Office Certificates; there is no record of Peter Zabriskie either as a subscriber to original funds or as owner of securities; but a Jacob Zabriskie appears on a later Ledger. From Essex county, John Chetwood and David Crane appear among the holders; from Middlesex, John Beatty, John Neilson, and Benjamin Manning — the entire delegation; from Somerset, Fred. Frelinghuysen; from Gloucester, Andw. Hunter; from Salem, Edmund Wetherby; from Hunterdon, David Brearley and Joshua Corshon; from Morris, John Jacob Faesch; and from Sussex, Robert Ogden and Thomas Anderson, and even the Secretary, Saml. W. Stockton, was a considerable holder. Thus every county except Cumberland, Cape-of-May, Burlington, and Monmouth had its spokesmen for public creditors.[1]

Delaware. — Although there had been a strong paper money party in Delaware it does not seem to have manifested any considerable influence in the ratification of the Constitution, for that commonwealth was the first to set its seal on the new instrument, and it did so with apparent unanimity. No detailed scrutiny of the local contests over the election of delegates has ever been made; and the records of the loan office of that state preserved in the Treasury Department are defective. The records for taxation are

---

[1] These records are drawn principally from incomplete lists of early certificates issued, or from some later funding books in the Treasury Department. The real weight of securities in the New Jersey convention must remain problematical, at least, for the present. The amounts set down to the names above recorded are for the most part insignificant — a few hundred or thousand dollars at the most, and often smaller. The point, it may be repeated, is not the amount but the practical information derived from holding even one certificate of the nominal value of $10.

also of little help. The absence of any contest of course contributes to obscuring the economic forces which may have been at work.[1]

Pennsylvania. — In strong contrast to the uniformity in Delaware is the sharp division which existed in Pennsylvania. There, says Libby, "the opposition to the Constitution came from those counties belonging to the great interior highland of the state, extending from the head waters of the Schuylkill to the Alleghany and Monongahela rivers, with only Huntingdon county (one vote — Federal) interrupting the continuity from east to west. . . . The Federal area contained . . . York, Lancaster, Chester, Montgomery, Philadelphia, Bucks, Luzerne, and Northampton, and the largest population, most of the men of wealth and influence and the commercial classes of the state. Pittsburg with 400 inhabitants was Federal in an Anti-Federal county." [1]

Each of the eastern counties of Pennsylvania was represented in the state convention by one or more members who held public securities.[3] From Philadelphia city and county, five of the ten members, all of whom favored ratifica-

---

[1] Dr. Jameson says of the records of the Delaware convention : "Neither Journal nor debates, has, I believe, ever been published," *American Historical Association Report* (1902), Vol. I, p. 165.

[2] Libby, *op. cit.*, pp. 26 ff.

[3] The Massachusetts Gazette, on October 19, 1787, prints a letter from Philadelphia (dated October 5) in which the activities of speculators in public securities are fully set forth: "Since the grand federal convention has opened the budget and published their scheme of government, all goes well here. Continental loan office certificates and all such securities have risen twenty-five per cent. Even the old emission which has long lain dormant begins to show its head. Last week many thousand pounds' worth of it were bought up. Moneyed men have their agents employed to buy up all the continental securities they can — foreseeing the rapid rise of our funds. Such men as have the cash to spare will certainly make large fortunes. . . . We send our factors to the distant towns who know nothing of the rise and buy them cheap ; for there is no buying them on reasonable terms in Philadelphia, as the wealthy men are purchasing them to lay up. Thus we go on — pray how is it with you?"

tion, were interested in stocks, George Latimer, James Wilson, Thomas M'Kean, Samuel Ashmead, and Enoch Edwards. From Bucks came John Barclay, a large dealer, to whose credit $17,056.56 is set down in one entry. Two of the six members from Chester, John Hannum and Thomas Bull, were security holders. James Morris, of Montgomery county, John Black and David Grier, from York, Timothy Pickering, from Luzerne, Stephen Balliet, David Deshler, and Joseph Horsfield of Northampton (three of the four from that county) were interested. From Lancaster came Jasper Yeates, a large holder (one entry $11,986.65), Robert Coleman, Sebastian Graff, and John Hubley (four of the six delegates), who had a first-hand knowledge of the relation of a new and stable government to public paper.

In other words at least nineteen out of the forty-six men who voted for the Constitution in the Pennsylvania convention were interested in public paper at or about the time of the adoption of the Constitution. Their names follow with the references to each,[1] but it is not to be supposed that this list is complete, for the records of Pennsylvania are not full, and a great many of the transactions in that state were not with the local loan office, but directly with the Treasury, a part of whose early records were probably burned in one of the fires at the Treasury Building:

Samuel Ashmead (I)	Robert Coleman (R)
Stephen Balliet (LT)	David Deshler (M)
John Barclay (JA)	Enoch Edwards (JA)
John Black (M)	Sebastian Graff (I)
Thomas Bull (I)	David Grier (I)

[1] Ms. Treasury Department: "I," *Index to Funded 6 C*; "JA," *Journal A, 1790–1791* (sixes and threes); "JB," *Journal B*; "R," *Register Loan Office Certificates, 1788*; "77," *Register Certificates of 1777*; "3 C," *Ledger C, 3% Stock*; "LT," *Treasury Ledger*; "M," Miscellaneous.

John Hannum (3 C)
Joseph Horsfield (M)
John Hubley (77)
George Latimer (JB)
Jasper Yeates (JA)

Thomas M'Kean (M)
James Morris (I)
Timothy Pickering (I)
James Wilson (I)

Fortunately, also other data are easily available for the study of the economic interests of the members of the Pennsylvania convention. McMaster and Stone[1] have appended to their work on the ratification of the Constitution in that state brief biographical sketches of the members of the convention, in which many clues are given to their respective economic interests. The following table is prepared from these biographies, and every effort is made to state in the language of the authors the exact occupation and interests of the delegates. These details are given so that the student may draw his conclusions independently.

MEMBERS WHO VOTED IN FAVOR OF RATIFICATION

John Allison "received a thorough English and classical education;" laid out the town of Greencastle in 1781; in the War, rank of Colonel.

John Arndt. Father a mill owner on the Bushkill; for a time a commissary of supplies during the War; "advanced large sums of money to the government, most of which was refunded to him;" devoted the latter years of his life to "mercantile pursuits."

Samuel Ashmead. "Little is known of his early history, save that he received a good education and was brought up to mercantile pursuits." [Securities.]

Hilary Baker "received a good classical education, entered mercantile life, became an iron merchant, which business he carried on for some years."

Stephen Balliet, "acquired a very limited education and was brought up to mercantile life under his father;" an agent for

---

[1] *Pennsylvania and the Federal Constitution.* It will be noted that there were at least seven members of the Order of Cincinnati in the convention, all of whom were in favor of the Constitution.

forfeited estates in Northampton county. Held many offices. Colonel in War. [Securities.]

John Barclay "was a son of Alexander Barclay, an officer of the Crown under the proprietary government, and received a classical education." Captain in the War and member of the Cincinnati. Sometime president of the Bank of the Northern Liberties. [Securities.]

John Black was a graduate of Nassau Hall. Was an eminent Presbyterian clergyman in his time. [Securities.]

John Boyd. Little known of early life and education. In the War. Member of the Cincinnati. After the War "entered into merchandising at the town of Northumberland" and was interested in a mill.

Thomas Bull. "Meagre education" and "learned the trade of a stone-mason. Prior to the Revolution he was the manager of Warwick Furnace." Resumed this place after service in the War. [Securities.]

Thomas Campbell "was a farmer by occupation." Captain in the War and member of the Cincinnati.

Stephen Chambers. A lawyer. Captain in the War and member of the Cincinnati.

Thomas Cheyney, "An intelligent and progressive farmer." Grandfather bequeathed to his father half of a large tract of land in Thornbury.

Robert Coleman. "By his energy and indomitable perseverance became the most enterprising and successful iron-master in Pennsylvania." [Securities.]

David Deshler was a shop-keeper and afterwards operated grist and saw mills. He "advanced money out of his private means at a time when not only the United States treasury but also that of Pennsylvania was empty." [Securities.]

Richard Downing operated "a fulling, grist, and saw mill."

Enoch Edwards "received a classical education, studied medicine, and was in practice when he went into the War serving as a surgeon. [Securities.]

Benjamin Elliott "settled in the town of Huntingdon prior to the Revolution." Held many local offices. Regular occupation, if any, not given.

William Gibbons resided for a time in Philadelphia and later moved to "a fine farm left him by his parents." Later held local offices. Lieutenant Colonel.

Sebastian Graff. Son of a Lancaster "shopkeeper," and was in "active business when the War broke out." [Securities.]

George Gray. "The fifth of that name in the line of descent from George Gray, a wealthy member of the Society of Friends." Office-holder; in the War; apparently a gentleman of means.

David Grier. Classical education. Lawyer. Served in the War, rank of Colonel. [Securities.]

John Hannum. Settled on a large farm. Local office-holder. In the War, rank of Colonel. [Securities.]

Thomas Hartley. Classical education. Lawyer. In the War, rank of Colonel; member of the Cincinnati. Purchased a tract of one thousand acres of land during the Revolution.

Joseph Horsfield. Man of good education. Local postmaster under Washington. [Securities.]

John Hubley was a lawyer by profession. [Securities.]

John Hunn was a captain in the merchant marine service at the outbreak of the War. Engaged in privateering during the war and saw service in the field also.

George Latimer was a merchant, bank director, and wealthy capitalist. [Securities.]

Thomas M'Kean received a classical education. Was a lawyer. Extensive office-holder. In the War, and a member of the Cincinnati. Capitalist of some quality. [Securities.]

William MacPherson was the son of a noted "privateersman in the French and Spanish wars." Educated at the College of New Jersey. Officer in the British Army; but joined the American cause. Major and member of the Cincinnati. Man of some means.

James Morris possessed "a house and gristmill and ninety-four acres of land" which his father had given him. [Securities.]

F. A. Muhlenberg. Studied at the University of Halle. Clergyman, but entered into the politics of the Revolutionary War. Extensive office-holder.

John Neville. Soldier and large landholder. Office-holder and member of the Cincinnati.

Benjamin Pedan. Farmer and office-holder.

Timothy Pickering. Harvard graduate. In the War, rank of Adjutant-general; member of the Cincinnati. Lawyer and office-holder and land speculator. [Securities.]

John Richards owned a fine estate. He was "a progressive farmer, a store-keeper, and iron-master."

Jonathan Roberts was brought up as a farmer. Office-holder.

Benjamin Rush, graduate of the College of New Jersey and distinguished physician in Philadelphia.

Thomas Scott settled in Western Pennsylvania as a farmer. Became local office-holder and later (1791) entered the practice of law.

Henry Slagle was a provincial magistrate. Joined the Revolutionary cause and held a number of political offices and was connected with the loan office.

Abraham Stout seems to have been "an influential farmer."

Anthony Wayne was the son of a farmer and surveyor. Soldier, and a member of the Cincinnati.

James Wilson. Lawyer. Member of the constitutional Convention of 1787. Wealthy land speculator. [Securities.]

William Wilson. Officer in the War. Office-holder. In mercantile business and millowner.

Henry Wynkoop. Collegiate education. Major in the War and office-holder.

Thomas Yardley, farmer owning a large tract of land.

Jasper Yeates, educated at the College of Philadelphia, lawyer, judge, and man of large means for his time. [Securities.]

OPPONENTS OF RATIFICATION

John Baird "took up land" and "appears to have been a man of mark west of the Alleghanies." Held local offices.

Richard Bard was a farmer and proprietor of a mill.

John Bishop "was brought up as a farmer, an occupation he was engaged in all his life. . . . He had extensive business connections, and became an iron-master. He was a large landholder." Advanced large sums of money to the Revolutionary cause.

Nathaniel Breading received a classical education, taught school, was in the War, and held local offices. "In deference to his constituents he did not sign the ratification."

William Brown descendant of a farmer; was a frontiersman; in the War.

James Edgar was born on a farm and died on a farm.

William Findley received a fair English education and "towards the close of the war he removed with his family to Western Pennsylvania and took up a tract of land . . . on which he resided until his death."

John Andre Hanna received a good classical education; admitted to the bar and was a successful lawyer at Harrisburg.

John Harris was a farmer and laid out Mifflintown.

Joseph Hiester acquired the rudiments of a good education, and "until near age he worked upon his father's farm when he went to Reading and learned merchandising." Was in the War.

Jonathan Hoge. Nothing known.

Abraham Lincoln was brought up on a farm and died on a farm. Local office-holder.

John Ludwig was a substantial farmer. Was in the War. Local office-holder.

Nicholas Lotz was a millwright by occupation and established a mill near Reading. Was in the War.

James Marshel "moved to the western country some three years prior to the Revolution, and settled in what is now Cross Creek Township." Frontiersman and local officer.

James Martin was born in the Cumberland valley and resided in what was then (1772) Colerain township. Was in the War.

Adam Orth was "brought up amid the dangers and struggles of Pennsylvania pioneer life. He received the limited education of the 'back settlements.' . . . He was one of the pioneers in the manufacture of iron in Lebanon county."

John Reynolds.

Joseph Powell.

John Smilie. His father settled in Lancaster county and evidently was a farmer. In 1781 John Smilie "removed with his family to then Westmoreland county," which meant that he went to the frontier. Office-holder.

William Todd went to Western Pennsylvania about 1765 and later "removed to Westmoreland county where he settled upon land subsequently warranted to him."

John Whitehill, "son of an Irish immigrant who settled on Pequea Creek in 1723." Received a good education. Local office-holder. At his death he left "a large landed estate."

Robert Whitehill, brother of the above Whitehill. "In the spring of 1771 he removed to Cumberland county, locating on a farm two miles west of Harrisburg." Extensive public career. "Died at his residence in Cumberland county two miles west of the Susquehanna." Evidently dependent largely upon agriculture, but farmer of some means.

Obviously such a table is more or less superficial so far as economic aspects are concerned, for the forms of wealth possessed by each member and the numerical proportions of the several forms at the time of the Pennsylvania state convention are not apparent. More than the ordinary margin must therefore be allowed for error on both sides. Evidently also it is difficult to classify these men from the meagre data given; but the following table may be taken to be roughly correct as to the men about whom we have some economic facts.

	FOR THE CONSTITUTION	AGAINST
Merchants	4	1
Lawyers	8	1
Doctors	2	
Clergymen	2	
Farmers	10	13
Capitalists	12	3
Total classifiable	38	18

Of the thirty-eight in favor of the Constitution, who may be reasonably classified, ten, or one-fourth, represented agricultural interests primarily. Of the eighteen, opposed to the Constitution, who may be satisfactorily classified, thirteen or more than two-thirds were primarily identified with agricultural interests. Of the forty-six favorable, twenty were capitalists and lawyers; of the twenty-three opposed, four were in these categories. When all allowance for error is made, the result is highly significant and bears out the general conclusion that the Constitution was a reflex of personalty rather than realty interests.

Maryland. — In Maryland the mercantile interests of the towns were all on the side of the Constitution; and as the urban centres were the seats of operations in public securities these too must be thrown into the balance. The opposition came from the rural districts and particularly from the paper money constituencies. Libby discovered there, "a correspondence between the friends of paper money and debt laws and the Anti-Federal party of 1788, both as to leaders and to the rank and file of the respective parties." [1]

But it should be noted that we are now leaving the regions of small farms and of estates tilled by free labor and are coming into the districts where slavery and the plantation system dominate rural economy. Indeed, the slave-holding plantations were so extensive and the small farming class so restricted that the paper money party would have been seriously weakened had it not been for the fact that their ranks were recruited from other sources. A contemporary, speaking of the election of delegates to the convention, says: "Baltimore and Hartford counties alone are clearly anti-Federal, in which are many powerful and popular men who have speculated deeply in British confiscated property and for that reason are alarmed at shutting the door against state paper money. The same men, their relations and particular friends are more violently anti-Federal because they paid considerable sums into the treasury in depreciated continental currency and are scared at the sweeping clause . . . which

[1] Libby, *op. cit.*, p. 66.

may bring about a due execution of the treaty between Great Britain and America to their loss.[1]

Virginia. — Fortunately, for Virginia we have a somewhat detailed study of the economic forces in the politics of that commonwealth by Dr. Charles H. Ambler. By way of preparation he examines the geographical distribution of economic characteristics, and takes up first the Tidewater region. Of this portion of the state, he says, "The industrial, social and political life of the Tidewater centered in the large estate. . . . The society which developed in the Tidewater . . . resembled that of the mother country. It consisted of several strata separated by no clearly marked lines. Along the large rivers there were the great landowners who lived in a style of luxury and extravagance beyond the means of other inhabitants. Immediately below them were the half-breeds, persons descended from the younger sons and daughters of the landed proprietors. They had all the pride and social tastes of the upper class but not its wealth. Then came the 'pretenders,' men of industry and enterprise but not of established families. . . . Below these classes were the 'yeomen,' most of whom were very poor. The system of entail and primogeniture operated to preserve these strata intact."[2] The Tidewater region was almost solid in favor of ratifying the Constitution.

The second geographical division of Virginia, according to Dr. Ambler, was the Piedmont region, which resembled in many respects the Tidewater but had some decided characteristics of its own. "Although one and two-thirds times as large as the Tidewater, the Piedmont, in 1790 contained a much smaller negro slave population. Immigrants from the northern colonies, who, as will be shown, had pushed

---

[1] Letter, quoted in Libby, *op. cit.*, p. 65.
[2] *Sectionalism in Virginia*, pp. 6–9; p. 58.

into the Valley, came into the Piedmont from the rear. For the most part they were conscientiously opposed to slave-holding and consequently did not become tobacco-growers. On the other hand the poorer whites of the Tidewater had been pushed by the gradual advance of the plantation into the less desirable lands of the Piedmont. Lack of ability and the presence of conscientious scruples prevented them from becoming large planters. These elements constituted a large and influential democratic and non-slaveholding population in the Piedmont." [1] This region was largely against ratifying the Constitution.

Beyond the Piedmont lay the Valley which was largely settled by Scotch-Irish and Germans, and the economic basis was the small farm with all that it implies. Here the political theories, says Ambler "differed widely from those entertained in the east. The Germans and the Scotch-Irish brought to the Valley the sacred traditions of the years of religious wars which taught hatred to an established church, antipathy to a government by the privileged, and a love for civic and personal liberty. To the Scotch-Irish, the political leaders, civil liberty meant freedom of person, the right of fee-simple possession, and an open door to civic honors." [2] The markets for this region were at Baltimore and Philadelphia. This fact, coupled with several peculiar social characteristics may partially account for the heavy vote for the Constitution; but the sentiment in favor of the new government in this region has not yet been traced to economic reasons.

To the far West lay the Kentucky region whose frontier economic characteristics need no description. There the sentiment was almost solid against the ratification of the Constitution.

---

[1] Ambler, *op. cit.*, pp. 8, 59.   [2] *Ibid.*, pp. 15–16.

At the time of the movement for the adoption of a new
national Constitution, the self-sufficient western regions of
Virginia were practically indifferent; and the eastern section
was the part of the state in which there was a conscious determination to bring about a change. At this time, says
Ambler, "The towns of the Tidewater chafed under the
British restrictions upon trade and desired better commercial
relations between the states. Of the numerous petitions to
the assembly on these subjects, that from Norfolk was, perhaps, the most significant. It claimed that the restrictions
on the West India trade and the foreign commercial monopolies were producing injury to Virginia, and asked for restriction on British trade and better commercial relations
between the states. . . . Petitions of a similar tone came
from Fredericksburg, Falmouth, Alexandria, and Port
Royal." [1]

Against the indifference and opposition of the western
districts, the east prevailed in the contest over the proposition to send delegates to the federal Convention; and
Washington, Madison, Mason, Henry, Randolph, Wythe,
and Blair were named — "all residents of the Tidewater,
except Henry and Madison." [2] This result was partly
due to the fact that the Tidewater region was over-repre-
sented in the state legislature according to population, and
partly to the superior cohesion of the interests affected.[3]

The same economic antagonism that was manifested in
the selection of delegates to the federal Convention was
again manifested in the state convention called to ratify
the Constitution. "The democratic leaders of the interior,
says Ambler, "declared that it [the Constitution] sacrificed

---

[1] Ambler, *op. cit.*, pp. 48–52.

[2] Henry not only refused to attend but opposed the adoption of the Constitution
with all his might.

[3] *Ibid.*, p. 36.

the state's sovereignty. Accordingly they made a desperate fight to secure the election of delegates pledged to vote against ratification. When the canvass was ended it was not known which side would be successful, so evenly were the friends and enemies of the new plan of federal government matched. From the Tidewater came a strong delegation favorable to ratification. It numbered among its members the most prominent characters of the Virginia bar, former sympathizers with Great Britain, and representatives of interests essentially commercial. The other delegates favorable to ratification came from the Valley and the northwestern part of the state. Most of them had seen service in the Revolutionary armies and were largely under the influence of Washington. The Kentucky country and the Piedmont sent delegates opposed to ratification. . . . The vote on the ratification was: ayes 89, nays 79 . . . practically all the lower Tidewater [being] in favor of ratification. Only two delegates from Shenandoah valley and that part of the Trans-Alleghany north of the Great Kanawha voted nay. The democratic Piedmont and the Kentucky country was almost unanimous in opposition to the Constitution." [1]

These conclusions reached by Ambler closely support Libby's survey. In speaking of the distribution of the vote on the Constitution in Virginia, he says: "Four well-marked sections are to be noted. . . . The first, the eastern, comprised all the counties in tidewater Virginia. Its vote on the Constitution stood 80 per cent for and 20 per cent against ratification. This was the region of the large towns, and where commercial interests were predominant. The middle district, lying farther west to the Blue Ridge mountains, represented the interior farming interests of the

---

[1] Ambler, *op. cit.*, pp. 53 ff.

state ; the class of small farmers made up the principal part
of its population. Its vote on the Constitution stood 26
per cent for and 74 per cent against adoption. The third, the
West Virginia district is really double, composed of the
Shenandoah Valley, in which lay the bulk of the population
and the sparsely settled Trans-Alleghany region. This,
also, was an agricultural section with a population chiefly
Scotch-Irish and Germans from Pennsylvania. Its vote
stood 97 per cent for and 3 per cent against the Constitution.[1] . . . The fourth, or Kentucky district comprised
all that territory west of the great Kanawha to the Cumberland River. Its vote stood 10 per cent for and 90 per cent
against. . . . The question of the opening of the Mississippi
river was the decisive one in determining the vote of this
section." [2]

That public securities also carried some weight in the
Virginia counties which were strongly favorable to the
Constitution is shown by the following table of the delegates
(all, except Thomas Read, favorable to the Constitution)
to the state convention from the towns and the seaboard
or tidewater regions. Those italicised were holders of paper
to some amount and appear on the *Index to Virginia Funds*
in the Mss. of the Treasury Department. Those not italicised were not discovered on the books.

Fairfax County — *David Stuart* and *Charles Simms.*
King George — Burdet Ashton and William Thornton.
Westmoreland — *Henry Lee* and *Bushrod Washington.*
Northumberland — Walter Jones and Thomas Gaskins.
Richmond County — *Walker Tomlin* (as Executor) and *William*
Peachy (as Executor).
Lancaster — James Gordon and Henry Towles.
Gloucester — *Warner Lewis* and Thomas Smith.

[1] For an explanation of the Federalist complexion of this region see Ambler's
explanation, *Sectionalism in Virginia*, p. 16.
[2] Libby, *op. cit.*, pp. 34–35.

York — *John Blair* and *George Wyeth.*
Princess Anne — Anthony Walke and Thomas Walke.
Norfolk — James Webb and *James Taylor.* (Portsmouth.)
Henrico — (Richmond City) — *Edmund Randolph* and *John Marshall.*
James City — *Nathl. Burwell* and *Robert Andrews.*
Elizabeth City — Miles King and Worlich Westwood.
Charlotte — *Paul Carrington* and Thomas Read.[1]

North Carolina. — North Carolina was at first overwhelmingly Anti-Federal. It had peculiar economic characteristics. Though in the south, it had a large body of small farmers; and the great slave-tilled plantation was not such a marked feature of its economy as it was of South Carolina. It had small mercantile interests as compared with Massachusetts, New York, Maryland, Pennsylvania, and South Carolina, with their considerable seaport towns. And perhaps most significant of all was the fact that a very large proportion of the public securities in that state were bought up by speculators from northern cities[2] and therefore not held by native inhabitants in the centres of influence. This must have had a very deadening effect on the spirit of the movement for ratification.

Owing to these peculiarities, it is impossible to lay out North Carolina into such sharply differentiated economic regions as some of the other commonwealths. Nevertheless, certain lines are marked out by Libby in his survey of the vote in 1789 when the Constitution was finally ratified. "The counties around Albemarle and Pamlico Sounds constituted the bulk of the federal area. . . . This region was the earliest settled, the most densely populated, and represented most of the mercantile and commercial interests of the state." With this region went some additional inland

---

[1] Voted against ratification.
[2] This is evident from the records in the Treasury Department.

districts when the swing to the Federalists carried the state for ratification. The second region was in the centre of the state where the "interests were wholly agricultural;" this region was strongly Anti-Federal. To it was added the Tennessee region, also Anti-Federal, for the same reasons that carried western Virginia against the Constitution.[1]

South Carolina. — South Carolina presents the economic elements in the ratification with the utmost simplicity. There we find two rather sharply marked districts in antagonism over the Constitution. "The rival sections," says Libby, "were the coast or lower district and the upper, or more properly, the middle and upper country. The coast region was the first settled and contained a larger portion of the wealth of the state; its mercantile and commercial interests were important; its church was the Episcopal, supported by the state." This region, it is scarcely necessary to remark, was overwhelmingly in favor of the Constitution. The upper area, against the Constitution, "was a frontier section, the last to receive settlement; its lands were fertile and its mixed population were largely small farmers. . . . There was no established church, each community supported its own church and there was a great variety in the district."[2]

A contemporary writer, R. G. Harper, calls attention to the fact that the lower country, Charleston, Beaufort, and Georgetown, which had 28,694 white inhabitants, and about seven-twelfths of the representation in the state convention, paid £28,081 : 5 : 10 taxes in 1794, while the upper country, with 120,902 inhabitants, and five-twelfths of the representation in the convention, paid only £8390 : 13 : 3 taxes.[3] The lower districts in favor of the Constitution therefore

[1] Libby, *op. cit.*, pp. 38 ff.   [2] *Ibid.*, p. 42–43.
[3] "Appius," *To the Citizens of South Carolina* (1794), Library of Congress, Duane Pamphlets, Vol. 83.

possessed the wealth of the state and a disproportionate share in the convention — on the basis of the popular distribution of representation.[1]

These divisions of economic interest are indicated by the abstracts of the tax returns for the state in 1794 which show that of £127,337 worth of stock in trade, faculties, etc. listed for taxation in the state, £109,800 worth was in Charleston, city and county — the stronghold of Federalism. Of the valuation of lots in towns and villages to the amount of £656,272 in the state, £549,909 was located in that city and county.[2]

The records of the South Carolina loan office preserved in the Treasury Department at Washington show that the public securities of that state were more largely in the hands of inhabitants than was the case in North Carolina. They also show a heavy concentration in the Charleston district.

At least fourteen of the thirty-one members of the state-ratifying convention from the parishes of St. Philip and Saint Michael, Charleston (all of whom favored ratification) held over $75,000 worth of public securities, which amount was distributed unevenly among the following men:

John Blake	Isaac Motte
Danl. Cannon	C. C. Pinckney
Edw. Darrell	John Pringle
John F. Grimke	David Ramsay
Wm. Johnson	Nathaniel Russel
Thomas Jones	Josiah Smith
Lewis Morris	Danl. de Soussure [3]

[1] See above, p. 248.

[2] *State Papers: Finance*, Vol. I, p. 462. In 1783 an attempt to establish a bank with $100,000 capital was made in Charleston, S.C., but it failed. "Soon after the adoption of the funding system, three banks were established in Charleston whose capitals in the whole amounted to twenty times the sum proposed in 1783." D. Ramsay, *History of South Carolina* (1858 ed.), Vol. II, p. 106.

[3] Ms. Treasury Department: *South Carolina Loan Office Ledger*, consult Index. No general search was made for other names.

Georgia. — Georgia was one of the states that gave a speedy and unanimous consent to the adoption of the Constitution. If there was any considerable contest there, no record of it appears on the surface; and no thorough research has ever been made into the local unprinted records.[1] Libby dismisses the state with the suggestion that the pressing dangers from the Indians on the frontiers, which were formidable and threatening in the summer and autumn of 1787, were largely responsible for the swift and favorable action of the state in ratifying the new instrument of government that promised protection under national arms.[2]

Three conclusions seem warranted by the data presented in this chapter:

Inasmuch as the movement for the ratification of the Constitution centred particularly in the regions in which mercantile, manufacturing, security, and personalty interests generally had their greatest strength, it is impossible to escape the conclusion that holders of personalty saw in the new government a strength and defence to their advantage.

Inasmuch as so many leaders in the movement for ratification were large security holders, and inasmuch as securities constituted such a large proportion of personalty, this economic interest must have formed a very considerable dynamic element, if not the preponderating element, in bringing about the adoption of the new system.

The state conventions do not seem to have been more

---

[1] On the subject of ratification in Georgia, Dr. Jameson says: "Nothing of either journal or debates is known to have been printed, unless in some contemporary newspaper outside the state; the Georgia newspapers seem to have nothing of the sort." *American Historical Association Report* (1902), Vol. I, p. 167.

[2] This danger may have had some influence in the concessions made by the Georgia delegates in the Convention for they were kept informed of the Indian troubles in the summer of 1787. Force Transcripts, *Georgia Records, 1782–1789:* Library of Congress.

"disinterested" than the Philadelphia convention; but in fact the leading champions of the new government appear to have been, for the most part, men of the same practical type, with actual economic advantages at stake.

The opposition to the Constitution almost uniformly came from the agricultural regions, and from the areas in which debtors had been formulating paper money and other depreciatory schemes.[1]

---

[1] Some holders of public securities are found among the opponents of the Constitution, but they are not numerous.

CHAPTER XI

HAVING discovered the nature of the social conflict connected with the formation and adoption of the Constitution, and having shown the probable proportion of the people who participated in the conflict and the several group-interests into which they fell, it is interesting, though not fundamentally important, to inquire whether the leading thinkers of the time observed the nature of the antagonisms present in the process. A full statement of the results of such an inquiry would require far more space than is at command in this volume; and consequently only a few illustrative and representative opinions can be given.

No one can pore for weeks over the letters, newspapers, and pamphlets of the years 1787–1789 without coming to the conclusion that there was a deep-seated conflict between a popular party based on paper money and agrarian interests, and a conservative party centred in the towns and resting on financial, mercantile, and personal property interests generally. It is true that much of the fulmination in pamphlets was concerned with controversies over various features of the Constitution; but those writers who went to the bottom of matters, such as the authors of *The Federalist*, and the more serious Anti-Federalists, gave careful attention to the basic elements in the struggle as well as to the incidental controversial details.

The superficiality of many of the ostensible reasons put forth by the opponents of the Constitution was penetrated by Madison. Writing to Jefferson, in October, 1788, he says: "The little pamphlet herewith inclosed will give you a collective view of the alterations which have been proposed by the State Conventions for the new Constitution. Various and numerous as they appear, they certainly omit many of the true grounds of opposition. The articles relating to Treaties, to paper money, and to contracts, created more enemies than all the errors in the system, positive and negative, put together." [1]

Naturally the more circumspect of the pamphleteers who lent their support to the new system were careful about a too precise alignment of forces, for their strength often lay in the conciliation of opponents rather than in exciting a more deep-seated antagonism. But even in such conciliatory publications the material advantages to be expected from the adoption of the Constitution are constantly put forward.

Take, for example, this extract from a mollifying "Address to the Freemen of America" issued while the Convention was in the midst of its deliberations: "Let the public creditor, who lent his money to his country, and the soldier and citizen who yielded their services, come forward next and contribute their aid to establish an effective federal government. It is from the united power and resources of America only that they can expect permanent and substantial justice. . . . Let the citizens of America who inhabit the western counties of our states fly to a federal power for protection [against the Indians]. . . . Let the farmer who groans beneath the weight of direct taxation seek relief from a government whose extensive jurisdiction will enable

[1] *Writings*, Vol. I, p. 423.

it to extract the resources of our country by means of imposts and customs. Let the merchant, who complains of the restrictions and exclusions imposed upon his vessels by foreign nations, unite his influence in establishing a power that shall retaliate those injuries and insure him success in his honest pursuits by a general system of commercial regulations. Let the manufacturer and mechanic, who are everywhere languishing for want of employment, direct their eyes to an assembly of the states. It will be in their power only to encourage such arts and manufactures as are essential to the prosperity of our country." [1]

It is in the literature of the contest in the states where the battle over ratification was hottest that we find the most frank recognition of the fact that one class of property interests was in conflict with another. This recognition appears not so much in attacks on opponents as in appeals to the groups which have the most at stake in the outcome of the struggle, although virulent abuse of debtors and paper money advocates is quite common. Merchants, money lenders, public creditors are constantly urged to support the Constitution on the ground that their economic security depends upon the establishment of the new national government.

Perhaps the spirit of the battle over ratification is best reflected in the creed ironically attributed to each of the contending parties by its opponents. The recipe for an Anti-Federalist essay which indicates in a very concise way the class-bias that actuated the opponents of the Constitution, ran in this manner: "Wellborn, nine times — Aristocracy, eighteen times — Liberty of the Press, thirteen times repeated — Liberty of Conscience, once — Negro

[1] Address to the Freemen of America," *The American Museum* for June, 1787, Vol. I, p. 404.

slavery, once mentioned — Trial by jury, seven times — Great Men, six times repeated — Mr. Wilson, forty times. . . . — put them altogether and dish them up at pleasure." [1]

To this sarcastic statement of their doctrines, the Anti-Federalists replied by formulating the "Political Creed of Every Federalist" as follows: "I believe in the infallibility, all-sufficient wisdom, and infinite goodness of the late convention; or in other words, I believe that some men are of so perfect a nature that it is absolutely impossible for them to commit errors or design villainy. I believe that the great body of the people are incapable of judging in their nearest concerns, and that, therefore, they ought to be guided by the opinions of their superiors. . . . I believe that aristocracy is the best form of government. . . . I believe that trial by jury and the freedom of the press ought to be exploded from every wise government. . . . I believe that the new constitution will prove the bulwark of liberty — the balm of misery — the essence of justice — and the astonishment of all mankind. In short, I believe that it is the best form of government which has ever been offered to the world. I believe that to speak, write, read, think, or hear any thing against the proposed government is damnable heresy, execrable rebellion, and high treason against the sovereign majesty of the convention — And lastly I believe that every person who differs from me in belief is an infernal villain. AMEN." [2]

MARSHALL'S ANALYSIS OF THE CONFLICT

It must not be thought that this antagonism of economic interests which, in the language of controversy, frequently took on the form of a war between "aristocracy" and

---

[1] New Hampshire Spy, November 30, 1787.
[2] American Museum, July, 1788, Vol. IV, p. 85.

"democracy" was observed only by partisans whose views were distorted by the heat of battle. On the contrary, it was understood by the keenest thinkers—in fact, one may say that the more profound the wisdom of the observer, the clearer was his comprehension of the issues at stake. Next to Madison, whose concept of the Constitution-making process has already been fully discussed,[1] John Marshall probably understood best the nature of the new instrument, the social forces which produced it, and the great objects it was designed to accomplish. In speaking from the bench, as Chief Justice, he used, of course, the language of jurisprudence and spoke of the Constitution as a creation of the whole people.[2] But as a historian of great acumen, in which capacity he was not hampered by the traditional language of the bench and bar, Marshall sketched with unerring hand the economic conflict which led to the adoption of the Constitution, and impressed itself upon the nature of that instrument. In his masterly *Life of Washington*, he sets forth this conflict in unmistakable terms:

1. In the first place, the mercantile interest was sorely tried under the Articles of Confederation. There "was a general discontent with the course of trade. It had commenced with the native merchants of the north who found themselves incapable of contending in their own ports with foreigners; and was soon communicated to others. The gazettes of Boston contained some very animated and angry addresses which produced resolutions for the government of the citizens of that town, applications to their state legislature, a petition to congress, and a circular letter to the merchants of the several sea ports throughout the United States. . . . The merchants of the city of Philadelphia

---

[1] Above, p. 156.
[2] McCulloch *v.* Maryland, 4 Wheaton, 316; below, p. 299.

presented a memorial to the legislature of that state, in which, after lamenting it as a fundamental defect in the constitution that full and entire power over the commerce of the United States had not been originally vested in Congress . . . they prayed that the legislature would endeavour to procure from Congress a recommendation to the several states to vest in that body the necessary powers over the commerce of the United States." [1]

2. The public creditors had lost faith in the old government. "That the debt of the United States should have greatly depreciated will excite no surprise when it is recollected that the government of the Union possessed no funds, and without the assent of jealous and independent sovereigns could acquire none to pay the accruing interest; but the depreciation of the debt due from those states, which made an annual and adequate provision for the interest, can be ascribed only to a want of confidence in the governments which were controlled by no fixed principles; and it is therefore not entirely unworthy of attention. In many of those states which had repelled every attempt to introduce into circulation a depreciated medium of commerce or to defeat the annual provision of funds for the payment of the interest, the debt sunk in value to ten, five, and even less than four shillings in the pound. However unexceptionable might be the conduct of the existing legislature, the hazard from those which were to follow was too great to be encountered without an immense premium."

3. A profound division ensued throughout the United States based on different views of the rights of property. "At length," continues Marshall, "two great parties were formed in every state which were distinctly marked and which pursued distinct objects with systematic arrange-

[1] Vol. II (1850 ed.), p. 99 ff.

ment. The one struggled with unabated zeal for the exact observance of public and private engagements. By those belonging to it, the faith of a nation or of a private man was deemed a sacred pledge, the violation of which was equally forbidden by the principles of moral justice and of sound policy. The distresses of individuals were, they thought, to be alleviated only by industry and frugality, not by a relaxation of the laws or by a sacrifice of the rights of others. They were consequently the uniform friends of a regular administration of justice, and of a vigorous course of taxation which would enable the state to comply with its engagements. By a natural association of ideas, they were also, with very few exceptions, in favor of enlarging the powers of the federal government. . . .

"The other party marked out for themselves a more indulgent course. Viewing with extreme tenderness the case of the debtor, their efforts were unceasingly directed to his relief. To exact a faithful compliance with contracts was, in their opinion, a harsh measure which the people would not bear. They were uniformly in favor of relaxing the administration of justice, of affording facilities for the payment of debts, or of suspending their collection, and of remitting taxes. The same course of opinion led them to resist every attempt to transfer from their own hands into those of congress powers which by others were deemed essential to the preservation of the union. In many of these states, the party last mentioned constituted a decided majority of the people, and in all of them it was very powerful. The emission of paper money, the delay of legal proceedings, and the suspension of the collection of taxes were the fruits of their rule wherever they were completely predominant. . . . Throughout the union, a contest between these parties was periodically revived; and the public mind was perpetually agitated with hopes and fears on subjects which essentially affected the fortunes of a considerable proportion of society."

4. Finally, so sharp was this division into two parties on the lines of divergent views of property rights, that the Constitution, far from proceeding from "the whole people," barely escaped defeat altogether. So positive is this statement by the great Chief Justice and so decidedly does it contradict his juristic theory of the nature of the supreme law that the two should be studied together. For this reason, the two views enunciated by Marshall are printed in parallel columns:

"So balanced were the parties in some of them [the states] that even after the subject had been discussed for a considerable time, the fate of the constitution could scarcely be conjectured; and so small in many instances, was the majority in its favor, as to afford strong ground for the opinion that, had the influence of character been removed, the intrinsic merits of the instrument would not have secured its adoption. Indeed it is scarcely to be doubted that in some of the adopting states a majority of the people were in the opposition. In all of them, the numerous amendments which were proposed demonstrate the reluctance with which the new government was accepted; and that a dread of dismemberment, not an approbation of the particular system under consideration, had induced an acquiescence in it. . . . North Carolina and Rhode Island did not at first accept the constitution, and New York was apparently dragged into it by a repugnance to being excluded from the confederacy." Marshall, in his *Life of Washington*, written in 1804-07.

"The government [of the United States] proceeds directly from the people; it is 'ordained and established' in the name of the people; and it is declared to be ordained 'in order to form a more perfect union, establish justice, insure domestic tranquillity, and secure the blessings of liberty' to themselves and to their posterity. . . . The government of the Union then (whatever may be the influence of this fact on the case) is, emphatically and truly, a government of the people. In form and substance it emanates from them. Its powers are granted by them and are to be exercised directly on them and for their benefit. . . . It is the government of all; its powers are delegated by all; it represents all, and acts for all." Marshall, in McCulloch *vs.* Maryland (4 Wheaton, 316), in 1819.

THE CONFLICT IN THE STATES

Turning aside from these more general observations on the nature of the conflict over the ratification of the Constitution, let us now take up the struggle in the several states and examine the views entertained by some of the representative participants in it.

New Hampshire. — That New Hampshire was rather sharply divided into an "aristocratic" and a "country" party at the period of the adoption of the Constitution was remarked by an observing Frenchman;[1] and the New Hampshire Spy, published at Portsmouth, in the issue of October 27, 1787, aligns the mercantile and mechanical interest on the side of the new Constitution, adding that the "honest farmer" can have no objections, either. "The *honest man*," runs the plea, "can have no objection to a federal government, for while it obliges him to pay a sacred regard to past contracts, it will eventually secure him in his person and his property. The *mercantile interest* have suffered enough *to induce* them to wish for, and espouse a federal reform. . . . The *mechanical interest* can have no aversion to it, when they are informed that an efficient government will protect and encourage commerce, which is the very soul of mechanism. . . . Nor can the *honest farmer* have any objection; the increase of commerce will naturally increase the demand for such articles as he may have for sale; he will be enabled to pay his taxes and, if economy shakes hands with industry, increase his farm and live independent of troublesome creditors. Since then no one respectable order of citizens can have any just reason to reject the new Constitution, we may

[1] Farrand, *Records*, Vol. III, p. 232. Speaking of New Hampshire, Madison says, "The opposition [to the Constitution], I understand, is composed precisely of the same description of characters with that of Massachusetts and stands contrasted to all the wealth, abilities, and respectability of the State." *Writings*, Vol. I, p. 383.

venture to conclude that none but *fools, blockheads,* and *mad men* will dare oppose it."

Massachusetts. — The contest over the Constitution in Massachusetts was a sharp conflict between the personalty interests on the one hand and the small farmers and debtors on the other, and this fact seems to have been recognized by every thoughtful leader on both sides. This view of the social struggle was set forth on so many occasions and by so many eminent observers that it is difficult to select from the mass of material the most typical statement of the situation. Perhaps that by General Knox is not excelled for its clarity and conciseness. Writing to Washington, January 14, 1788, a few days after the state convention had begun its labors, he describes the alignment over ratification as follows:

"There are three parties existing in that state [Massachusetts] at present, differing in their numbers and greatly differing in their wealth and talents.

"The 1st. is the commercial part of the state to which are added all the men of considerable property, the clergy, the lawyers — including all the judges of all the courts, and all the officers of the late army, and also the neighborhood of all the great towns — its numbers may include 3/7ths of the state. This party are for vigorous government, perhaps many of them would have been still more pleased with the new Constitution had it been more analogous to the British Constitution.

"The 2d party are the eastern part of the state lying beyond New Hampshire formerly the province of Main — This party are chiefly looking towards the erection of a new state and the majority of them will adopt or reject the new Constitution as it may facilitate or retard their designs — this party 2/7ths.

"The 3d party are the Insurgents or their favorers, the great majority of whom are for an annihilation of debts, public and private, and therefore they will not approve the new Constitution — this party 2/7ths."[1]

Several months before Knox had formulated this view of the conflict, indeed, early in the struggle over ratification, the Federalist agitators were busy with appeals to practical economic interests. The Massachusetts Gazette of October 26, 1787, for example, contains a letter signed by "Marcus" in which the groups likely to be affected advantageously by the new Constitution are enumerated and an argument directed to each of them: "It is the interest of the merchants to encourage the new constitution, because commerce may then be a national object, and nations will form treaties with us. It is the interest of the mechanicks to join the mercantile interest, because it is not their interest to quarrel with their bread and butter. It is the interest of the farmer because the prosperity of commerce gives vent to his produce, raises the value of his lands, and commercial duties will alleviate the burden of his taxes. It is the interest of the landholder, because thousands in Europe, with moderate fortunes will migrate to this country if an efficient government gives them a prospect of tranquillity. It is the interest of all gentlemen and men of property, because they will see many low demagogues reduced to their tools, whose upstart dominion insults their feelings, and whose passions for popularity will dictate laws, which ruin the minority of creditors and please the majority of debtors. It is the interest of the American soldier as the military profession will then be respectable and Florida may be conquered in a campaign. The spoils of the West-Indies and South America may enrich the next generation of Cincinnati.

---

[1] *Documentary History of the Constitution*, Vol. IV, p. 442.

It is the interest of the lawyers who have ability and genius, because the dignities in the Supreme Court will interest professional ambition and create emulation which is not now felt. . . . It is the interest of the clergy, as civil tumults excite every passion — the soul is neglected and the clergy starve. It is the interest of all men whose education has been liberal and extensive because there will be a theatre for the display of talents."

In fact, from the very beginning of the movement, the most eminent advocates of a new system were aware of the real nature of the struggle which lay before them. They knew that there was a deep-seated antagonism between the "natural aristocracy" and the "turbulent democracy" which was giving the government of Massachusetts trouble. Such an analysis of the difficulty is set forth by Stephen Higginson, a leading Federalist of Boston, in March, 1787: "The people of the interior parts of these states [New England] have by far too much political knowledge and too strong a relish for unrestrained freedom, to be governed by our feeble system, and too little acquaintance with real sound policy or rational freedom and too little virtue to govern themselves. They have become too well acquainted with their own weight in the political scale under such governments as ours and have too high a taste for luxury and dissipation to sit down contented in their proper line, when they see others possessed of much more property than themselves. With these feelings and sentiments they will not be quiet while such distinctions exist as to rank and property; and sensible of their own force, they will not rest easy till they possess the reins of Government and have divided property with their betters, or they shall be compelled by force to submit to their proper stations and mode of living." [1]

---

[1] *Report of the Manuscripts Commission of the American Historical Association,* December 20, 1896, p. 754. A writer in the Chronicle of Freedom (reprinted in the

Discerning opponents of the Constitution, as well as its advocates, were aware of the alignment of forces in the battle. Rufus King explained to Madison in January, 1788, that the opposition was grounded on antagonism to property rather than to the outward aspects of the new system. "Apprehension that the liberties of the people are in danger," he said, "and a distrust of men of property or education have a more powerful effect upon the minds of our opponents than any specific objections against the Constitution. . . . The opposition complains that the lawyers, judges, clergymen, merchants, and men of education are all in favor of the Constitution — and for that reason they appear to be able to make the worse appear the better cause." [1]

The correctness of King's observation is sustained by a vigorous writer in the Boston Gazette and Country Journal of November 26, 1787, who charges the supporters of the Constitution with attempting to obscure the real nature of the instrument, and enumerates the interests advocating its adoption. "At length," says the writer, "the luminary of intelligence begins to beam its effulgent rays upon this important production; the deceptive mists cast before the eyes of the people by the delusive machinations of its INTERESTED advocates begins to dissipate, as darkness flies before the burning taper. . . . Those furious zealots who are for cramming it down the throats of the people without allowing

---

Massachusetts Centinel, October, 27, 1787) complains of the dangers to the freedom of the press from the new Constitution and continues: "One thing, however, is calculated to alarm our fears on this head; — I mean the fashionable language which now prevails so much and is so frequent in the mouths of some who formerly held very different opinions; — That common people have no business to trouble themselves about government." The Massachusetts Centinel (November 24, 1787) declares it to be "a notorious fact that three of the principle enemies of the proposed constitution were heart and hand with the insurgents last winter."

[1] *Life and Letters*, Vol. I, pp. 314 ff.

them either time or opportunity to scan or weigh it in the balance of their intelligences, bear the same marks in their features as those who have been long wishing to erect an aristocracy in THIS COMMONWEALTH — their menacing cry is for a RIGID government, it matters little to them of what kind, provided it answers THAT description. . . . They incessantly declare that none can discover any defect in the system but bankrupts who wish no government and officers of the present government who fear to lose a part of their power. . . . It may not be improper to scan the characters of its most strenuous advocates : it will first be allowed that many undesigning citizens may wish its adoption from the best motives, but these are modest and silent, when compared to the greater number, who endeavor to suppress all attempts for investigations; these violent partizans are for having the people gulp down the gilded pill blindfolded, whole, and without any qualification whatever, these consist generally, of the NOBLE order of C—s, holders of public securities, men of great wealth and expectations of public office, B—k—s and L—y—s : these with their train of dependents from [form] the aristocratick combination."

Probably the most reasoned statement of the antagonism of realty and personalty in its relation to the adoption of the Constitution in Massachusetts was made in the letters of "Cornelius" on December 11 and 18, 1787 : "I wish," he said, "there never might be any competition between the landed and the mercantile interests, nor between any different classes of men whatever. Such competition will, however, exist, so long as occasion and opportunity for it is given, and while human nature remains the same that it has ever been. The citizens in the seaport towns are numerous; they live compact; their interests are one; there is a constant connection and intercourse between them; they can, on any occasion, centre their votes where they please. This is not the case with those who are in the landed interest; they are scattered far and wide; they have but little intercourse and connection with each other. . . . I conceive a foundation is laid for throwing the whole power of the federal government into the hands of those who are in the mercantile interest; and for the landed, which is the great interest of this country, to lie unrepresented, forlorn, and without hope. It grieves me to suggest an idea of this kind: But I believe it to be important and not the mere phantom of imagination, or the result of an uneasy and restless disposition." [1]

Connecticut. — There was no such spirited battle of wits over ratification in Connecticut as occurred in Massachusetts. Nevertheless, Ellsworth, in that state, produced a remarkable series of essays in support of the new Constitution which were widely circulated and read. In these papers there is revealed a positive antagonism between agrarianism and personalty, but an attempt is made at conciliation by subtly blending the two interests. Ellsworth opens: "The writer of the following passed the first part of his life in mercantile employments, and by industry and economy acquired a sufficient sum on retiring from trade to purchase and stock a decent plantation, on which he now lives in the state of a farmer. By his present employment he is interested in the prosperity of agriculture and those who derive a support from cultivating the earth. An acquaintance with business has freed him from many prejudices and jealousies which he sees in his neighbors who have not intermingled with mankind nor learned by experience the method of managing an extensive circulating property. Conscious of an honest intention he wishes to address his brethren on

---

[1] Harding, *The Federal Constitution in Massachusetts*, pp. 123–124.

some political subjects which now engage the public attention and will in the sequel greatly influence the value of landed property." [1]

The fact that the essential implications of this statement about his primary economic interests being those of a farmer are untrue does not affect the point here raised : Ellsworth recognised that the opposition was agrarian in character, and he simulated the guise of a farmer to conciliate it. Later on Ellsworth classifies the opposition. In the first rank he puts the Tories as leading in resisting the adoption of the Constitution because it would embarrass Great Britain. In the second class, Ellsworth puts those who owe money. "Debtors in desperate circumstances," he says, "who have not resolution to be either honest or industrious will be the next men to take alarm. They have long been upheld by the property of their creditors and the mercy of the public, and daily destroy a thousand honest men who are unsuspicious. Paper money and tender acts is the only atmosphere in which they can breathe and live. This is now so generally known that by being a friend to such measures, a man effectually advertises himself as a bankrupt. . . . There is another kind of people who will be found in the opposition : Men of much self-importance and supposed skill in politics who are not of sufficient consequence to obtain public employment, but can spread jealousies in the little districts of country where they are placed. These are always jealous of men in place and of public measures, and aim at making themselves consequential by distrusting everyone in the higher offices of society. . . . But in the present case men who have lucrative and influential state offices, if they act from principles of self interest will be tempted to oppose an alteration which would doubtless be beneficial to the

---

[1] Ford, *Essays on the Constitution*, p. 139.

people. To sink from a controulment of finance or any other great departments of the state, thro' want of ability or opportunity to act a part in the federal system must be a terrifying consideration." [1]

Leaving aside the Tories and office-holders, it is apparent that the element which Ellsworth considers the most weighty in the opposition is the agrarian party. The correctness of his analysis is supported by collateral pieces of evidence. Sharon, one of the leading paper money towns which opposed the ratification of the Constitution in Connecticut had voted to assist Shays and had repeatedly attempted to secure paper emission legislation.[2] In a few letters and speeches against the Constitution the plaintive note of the agrarian is discernible.

The opponents of the Constitution in Connecticut found no skilled champions such as led the fight in Pennsylvania and Massachusetts; and no such spirited discussion took place. The debates in the state ratifying convention were not recorded (save for a few fragments); but the contest in the legislature over the proposition to send delegates to the Philadelphia Convention showed that the resistance came from the smaller agrarian interests similar to those in Rhode Island and Massachusetts which had stood against the whole movement.

Mr. Granger from Suffield was opposed to the proposition to send delegates to Philadelphia because "he conceived it would be disagreeable to his constituents; he thought the liberties of the people would be endangered by it; . . . and concluded by saying that he imagined these things would have a tendency to produce a regal government in this country." Mr. Humphrey from the inland town of Norfolk

---

[1] Ford, *Essays on the Constitution*, pp. 144 ff.
[2] Libby, *op. cit.*, p. 58.

sided with Mr. Granger and "concluded by saying that he approved the wisdom and policy of Rhode Island in refusing to send delegates to the convention and that the conduct of that state in this particular, was worthy of imitation." Mr. Perkins of Enfield "was opposed to the measure and said that the state would send men that had been delicately bred and who were in affluent circumstances, that could not feel for the people in this day of distress." [1]

New York. — When it is remembered that the greatest piece of argumentation produced by the contest over ratification, *The Federalist*, was directed particularly to the electorate in New York, although widely circulated elsewhere, it will appear a work of supererogation to inquire whether the leaders in that commonwealth understood the precise nature of the social conflict which was being waged.[2] Nevertheless, it may be worth while to present Hamilton's analysis of it. On the side of the Constitution, he placed the "very great weight of influence of the persons who framed it, particularly in the universal popularity of General Washington — the good will of the commercial interest throughout the states which will give all its efforts to the establishment of a government capable of regulating, protecting, and extending the commerce of the Union — the good will of most men of property in the several states who wish a government of the Union able to protect them against domestic violence and the depredations which the democratic spirit is apt to make on property . . . — a strong belief in the people at large of the insufficiency of the present confederation to preserve the existence of the Union."

Over against these forces in favor of the Constitution, Hamilton places the antagonism of some inconsiderable

---

[1] Connecticut Courant, May 21, 1787.
[2] See above, p. 156.

men in office under state governments, the influence of some considerable men playing the part of the demagogue for their own aggrandizement; — "and add to these causes the democratical jealousy of the people which may be alarmed at the appearance of institutions that may seem calculated to place the power of the community in a few hands and raise a few individuals to stations of great pre-eminence." [1]

New Jersey and *Delaware.*—The speedy ratification of the Constitution in these states gave no time for the development of a sharp antagonism, even had there been an economic basis for it. In the absence of this actual conflict over the Constitution we can hardly expect to find any consideration of the subject by contemporary writers of note.[2]

Pennsylvania. — The opposition between town and country, between personalty and realty in other words, was so marked in this commonwealth during the struggle over the ratification of the Constitution that it was patent to all observers and was the subject of frequent and extensive comment by leaders on both sides. On September 28, 1787, Tench Coxe wrote to Madison describing the disturbance over the resolution in the state legislature calling the ratifying convention, and after reciting the events of the day he added, "It appears from these facts that the Western people [*i.e.* the agrarians] have a good deal of jealousy about the new Constitution and it is very clear that the men who have been

---

[1] *Documentary History of the Constitution*, Vol. IV, p. 288. On the antagonism in New York see some clues afforded in an article in The Magazine of American History, April, 1893, pp. 326 ff.

[2] Dickinson's Fabius letters were printed after the ratification by Delaware and were directed to the "general public" rather than fellow-citizens in that common-wealth. Among the opponents to the Constitution, he put "men without principles or fortunes who think they may have a chance to mend their circumstances with impunity under a weak government." Ford, *Pamphlets on the Constitution*, p. 165.

used to lead the Constitutional [or radical party][1] are against it decidedly."[2] A month later Coxe again writes to Madison: "The opposition here has become more open. It is by those leaders of the constitutional [local radical] interest who have acted in concert with the Western interest. The people of the party in the city are chiefly federal, tho' not so I fear in the Counties."[3]

Writing about the same time from Philadelphia to Washington, Gouverneur Morris, said: "With respect to this state, I am far from being decided in my opinion that they will consent. It is true that the City and its Neighborhood was enthusiastic in the cause; but I dread the cold and sower temper of the back counties and still more the wicked industry of those who have long habituated themselves to live on the public, and cannot bear the idea of being removed from power and profit of state government which has been and still is the means of supporting themselves, their families, and their dependents."[4] Such comments on the nature of the alignment of forces might be multiplied from the writings of other Federalist leaders in Pennsylvania, but it appears to be unnecessary to say more.

The leaders on the other side were constantly discanting upon the opposition between town and country. The recalcitrant members of the legislature in their protest to the people against the hasty calling of the state convention declared, "We lamented at the time [of the selection of delegates to the national Convention] that a majority of our legislature appointed men to represent this state who were all citizens of Philadelphia, none of them calculated to represent the landed interests of Pennsylvania, and almost

[1] See Harding, "Party struggles over the First Pennsylvania Constitution," *American Historical Association Report* (1894).
[2] *Documentary History of the Constitution*, Vol. IV, p. 305.
[3] *Ibid.*, Vol. IV, p. 339.   [4] *Ibid.*, Vol. IV, p. 358.

all of them of one political party, men who have been uniformly opposed to that [state] constitution for which you have on every occasion manifested your attachment." [1]

The author of the famous "Centinel" letters saw in the movement favorable to the new Constitution a design of "the wealthy and ambitious who in every community think they have a right to lord it over their fellow creatures." [2] In fact the most philosophic argument against the adoption of the new system on account of its intrinsic nature was made by the author of these letters.

At the opening of his series, Centinel inveighs against the precipitancy which characterized the movements of the Federalists, and then attacks the Constitution as the work of an active minority. "The late revolution," he says, "having effaced in a great measure all former habits and the present institutions are so recent that there exists not that great reluctance to innovation, so remarkable in old communities and which accords with reason, for the most comprehensive mind cannot foresee the full operation of material changes on civil polity. . . . The wealthy and ambitious, who in every community think they have a right to lord it over their fellow creatures have availed themselves very successfully of this favorable disposition; for the people thus unsettled in their sentiments have been prepared to accede to any extreme of government. All the distresses and difficulties they experience, proceeding from various causes, have been ascribed to the impotency of the present confederation, and thence they have been led to expect full relief from the adoption of the proposed system of government; and in the other event immediately ruin and annihilation as a nation." [3]

[1] McMaster and Stone, *op. cit.*, p. 73.
[2] *Ibid.*, p. 567.   [3] *Ibid.*, p. 367.

After warning his countrymen against being lulled into false security by the use of the great names of Washington and Franklin in support of the Constitution, Centinel takes up the fundamental element in the new system : the balance of powers as expounded in Adams' *Defence of the Constitutions*; and shows the inherent antagonism between "democracy" and the Federalist concept of government in a manner that would do honor to the warmest advocate of the initiative and referendum in our time. "Mr. Adams' *sine qua non* of good government is three balancing powers ; whose repelling qualities are to produce an equilibrium of interests and thereby promote the happiness of the whole community. He asserts that the administrators of every government will ever be actuated by views of private interest and ambition to the prejudice of the public good; that therefore the only effectual method to secure the rights of the people and promote their welfare is to create an opposition of interests between the members of two distinct bodies in the exercise of the powers of government, and balanced by those of a third. This hypothesis supposes human wisdom competent to the task of instituting three co-equal orders in government and a corresponding weight in the community to enable them respectively to exercise their several parts and whose views and interests should be so distinct as to prevent a coalition of any two of them for the destruction of the third. Mr. Adams, although he has traced the constitution of every form of government that ever existed, as far as history affords materials, has not been able to adduce a single instance of such a government; he indeed says the British constitution is such in theory, but this is rather a confirmation that his principles are chimerical and not to be reduced to practice. If such an organization of power were practicable how long would it continue ? Not a day—for there is so great a disparity in the talents, wisdom, and industry of mankind, that the scale would presently preponderate to one or the other body, and with every accession of power the means of further increase would be greatly extended. The state of society in England is much more favorable to such a scheme of government than that of America. There they have a powerful hereditary nobility, and real distinctions of rank and interests; but even there, for want of that perfect equality of power and distinction of interests in the three orders of government, they exist but in name; the only operative and efficient check upon the conduct of administration is the sense of the people at large. . . . If the administrators of every government are actuated by views of private interest and ambition, how is the welfare and happiness of the community to be the result of such jarring adverse interests?" [1]

In opposition to the Adams-Madison theory of balanced economic interests and innocuous legislatures, which was the essence of the Federalist doctrine, Centinel expounded his reasons for believing that distinct property groups should not be set against one another in the government, and that trust in the political capacity of the broad undifferentiated mass of the community should be the basis of the Constitution; but it should be noted that his undifferentiated mass was composed largely of property holders. "I believe," he says "that it will be found that the form of government which holds those entrusted with power in the greatest responsibility to their constituents, the best calculated for freemen. A republican or free government can only exist where the body of the people are virtuous and *where property is pretty equally divided*. In such a government the people are sovereign and their sense or opinion is the criterion

[1] McMaster and Stone, *op. cit.*, pp. 568-569.

of every public measure; for when this ceases to be the case, the nature of the government is changed and an aristocracy, monarchy, or despotism will rise on its ruins. The highest responsibility is to be attained in a simple structure of government, for the great body of the people never steadily attend to the operations of government, and for the want of due information are liable to be imposed upon. If you complicate the plan by various orders, the people will be perplexed and divided in their sentiment about the sources of abuses or misconduct; some will impute it to the senate, others to the house of representatives, and so on, that the interposition of the people may be rendered imperfect or perhaps wholly abortive. But if imitating the constitution of Pennsylvania, you vest all the legislative power in one body of men (separating the executive and the judicial), elected for a short period, and necessarily excluded by rotation from permanency and guarded from precipitancy and surprise by delays imposed on its proceedings, you will create the most perfect responsibility; for then, whenever the people feel a grievance, they cannot mistake the authors and will apply the remedy with certainty and effect, discarding them at the next election." [1]

It is evident that a considerable number of the voters in Pennsylvania clearly understood the significance of the division of powers created by the Constitution. In a petition circulated and extensively signed by Philadelphia citizens immediately after the completion of the labors of the Convention and directed to the state ratifying convention, the memorialists expressed their approval of the Constitution, and added: "The division of the power of the United States into three branches gives the sincerest satisfaction to a great majority of our citizens, who have long

[1] *Ibid.*, pp. 569–570.

suffered many inconveniences from being governed by a single legislature. All single governments are tyrannies — whether they be lodged in one man — a few men — or a large body of the people." [1]

Maryland. — The contest in Maryland over the ratification was keen and spirited and every side of the question was threshed out in newspaper articles and pamphlets.[2] Through all the controversy ran the recognition of the fact that it was a struggle between debtors and creditors, between people of substance and the agrarians. Alexander Hanson in his considerable tract in favor of the ratification, dedicated to Washington, treats the charge that the Constitution was an instrument of property as worthy of a dignified answer. "You have been told," he says, "that the proposed plan was calculated peculiarly for the rich. In all governments, not merely despotic, the wealthy must, in most things, find an advantage from the possession of that which is too much the end and aim of mankind. In the proposed plan there is nothing like a discrimination in their favor. . . . Is it a just cause of reproach that the Constitution effectually secures property? Or would the objectors introduce a general scramble?" [3]

Recognizing the importance of the interests at stake, another Federalist writer, "Civis," in the Maryland Journal of February 1, 1788, appeals to the voters for delegates to the coming state convention to be circumspect in order to procure the ratification of the Constitution. He laments that "men of property, character, and abilities have too much retired from public employment since the conclusion of the war," but expresses the hope "that, in this all-im-

---

[1] Connecticut Courant, Oct. 1, 1787.
[2] See the valuable articles on "Maryland's Adoption of the Constitution," by Dr. Steiner in the American Historical Review, Vol. V.
[3] Ford, *Pamphlets on the Constitution*, p. 254.

portant crisis, they will again step forth, with a true patriotic ardour, and snatch their dear country from the dreadful and devouring jaws of anarchy and ruin." He cautions the citizens against voting for undesirable persons: "The characters whom I would especially point out as your particular aversion, in the present critical conjuncture, are all those in desperate or embarrassed circumstances, who may have been advocates for paper money, the truck-bill, or insolvent act; and who may expect to escape in the general ruin of the country."

On the other hand many opponents of the Constitution in Maryland definitely declared the contest to be one between property and the people of little substance. Such was practically the view of Luther Martin [1] in basing his resistance on the ground that the new system prevented the states from interfering with property rights. The spirit of this opposition was also well reflected in a reply to the letter of "Civis," mentioned above, which took the form of an ironical appeal to the voters to support only men of property and standing for the coming state convention. "Choose no man in debt," it runs, "because being in debt proves that he wanted understanding to take care of his own affairs. . . . A man in debt can scarcely be honest. . . . Vote for no man who was in favor of paper money, for no *honest* man was for that measure. None but *debtors* and desperate wretches advocated the diabolical scheme. . . . Elect no man who supported the law allowing insolvent debtors to discharge their persons from perpetual imprisonment, by *honestly* delivering up *all* their property to the use of their creditors. The legislature *have* no right to interfere with *private* contracts, and debtors might safely trust to the humanity and clemency of their

[1] See above, p. 205.

creditors who will not keep them in gaol all their lives, unless they deserve it. . . . Men of great property are deeply interested in the welfare of the state; and they are the most competent judges of the form of government, best calculated to preserve their property, and such liberties as it is proper for the common and inferior class of people to enjoy. Men of wealth possess natural and acquired understanding, as they manifest by amassing riches, or by keeping and increasing those they derive from their ancestors, and they are best acquainted with the wants, the wishes, and desires of the people, and they are always ready to relieve them in their private and public stations." [1]

Virginia. — Madison remarked that he found in his state "men of intelligence, patriotism, property, and independent circumstances" [2] divided over the ratification of the Constitution although in some other commonwealths men of this stamp were "zealously attached" to the new government. This general reflection is not borne out however by some of his contemporaries. Marshall, as we have noted above, [3] regarded the conflict as being between two rather sharply divided parties, those who favored maintaining public and private rights in their full integrity and those who proposed to attack them through legislation. [4] In fact, Madison himself at a later date declared that "the superiority of abilities" was on the side of the Constitution. [5] Charles Lee claimed that "except a few characters, the members [of the Virginia convention] with the most knowl-

---

[1] *Maryland Journal*, March 21, 1788.

[2] *Documentary History of the Constitution*, Vol. IV, p. 398. For the economics of this, see above, p. 30.

[3] P. 295.

[4] "It is currently reported, "says the New Hampshire Spy, on December 7, 1787, "that there are only two men in Virginia who are not in debt, to be found among the enemies to the federal constitution. Debtors, speculators in papers, and states demagogues act consistently in opposing it."

[5] *Documentary History of the Constitution*, Vol. IV, p. 584.

edge and abilities and personal influence are also in favor of the Constitution." [1]

In the opposition Patrick Henry put the whole mass of small farmers. "I believe it to be a fact," he declared in the Virginia convention, "that the great body of yeomanry are in decided opposition to it. I may say with confidence that, for nineteen counties adjacent to each other, nine-tenths of the people are conscientiously opposed to it. I may be mistaken but I give you it as my opinion; and my opinion is founded on personal knowledge in some measure, and other good authority. . . . You have not solid reality — the hearts and hands of the men who are to be governed." [2]

North Carolina. — It would have been strange if the leaders for and against the Constitution in this common-wealth had not taken cognizance of the nature of the con-flict they were waging. The popular paper money and debtor party had been powerful and active and had aroused the solicitude of all men of substance; and the represen-tatives of the latter, as practical men, knew what they were doing in supporting an overthrow of the old system. "It is essential to the interests of agriculture and commerce," ex-claimed Davie, in the state ratifying convention, "that the hands of the states should be bound from making paper money, instalment laws, and pine-barren acts. By such iniquitous laws the merchant or farmer may be defrauded of a considerable part of his just claims. But in the federal court, real money will be recovered with that speed which is necessary to accommodate the circumstances of individ-uals." [3] Speaking on the same theme, paper money, Gover-

---

[1] *Ibid.*, p. 577.

[2] Elliot, *Debates*, Vol. III, p. 592. See W. C. Ford, "The Federal Constitution in Virginia," in the *Proceedings of the Massachusetts Historical Society* for October, 1903.

[3] Elliot, *Debates*, Vol. IV, p. 159.

nor Johnston said : "Every man of property — every man of considerable transactions, whether a merchant, planter, mechanic, or of any other condition — must have felt the baneful influence of that currency." [1]

The recognition of the nature of the clash of interests is manifest in scattered correspondence, as well as in speeches. For example, in a letter to Iredell, January 15, 1788, Maclaine says : "In New Hanover county the people if left to themselves are in favor of the change. Some demagogues, a few persons who are in debt, and every public officer, except the clerk of the county court, are decidedly against any change ; at least against any that will answer the purpose. Our friend Huske is the loudest man in Wilmington against the new constitution. Whether ambition, or avarice, or a compound of both actuates him I leave you to judge. . . . I expect in a few weeks *The Federalist* in a volume. He is certainly a judicious and ingenious writer, though not well calculated for the common people. . . . Your old friend Huske and Col. Read have joined all the low scoundrels in the County [*i.e.* the country party] and by every underhand means are prejudicing the common people against the new constitution. The former is a candidate for the county." [2]

This conflict between the town and country is explained by Iredell's biographer : "Soon after the [Revolutionary] War commenced a feud between the town of Wilmington and the county of New Hanover. The leading men ' upon 'Change' were either Tories or those whose lukewarmness had provoked suspicion : the agrestic population could but illy brook their prosperity. From that day to the present [1857] the politics of the burgess have been antagonistical to those of the former. The merchants have ever

[1] Elliot, *Debates*, Vol. IV, p. 90.
[2] McRee, *Life and Correspondence of James Iredell*, Vol. II, pp. 216, 219.

been the predominant class in the borough: daily inter-course has enabled them with facility to form combinations that have given them the control of the moneyed institutions while their patronage has added a potent influence with the press." [1]

South Carolina. — The materials bearing on the ratification of the Constitution in South Carolina which are available to the northern student are relatively scanty.[2] Nevertheless, in view of the marked conflict between the agrarian back-country and the commercial seaboard, it may easily be imagined that it was not unobserved by the leaders in the contest over ratification who championed the respective regions. This antagonism came out in a pamphlet war over the amendment of the state constitution which was being waged about the time of the adoption of the new federal system. In this war, "Appius," the spokesman for the reform party is reported to have declared that "wealth ought not to be represented; that a rich citizen ought to have fewer votes than his poor neighbor; that wealth should be stripped of as many advantages as possible and it will then have more than enough; and finally, that in giving property the power of protecting itself, government becomes an aristocracy." [3]

"Appius," after this general statement of his theory, then explains wherein the distribution of economic interests engendered antagonism in politics in that state. "The upper and lower countries, have opposite habits and views in almost every particular. One is accustomed to expence, the other to frugality. One will be inclined to numerous offices, large salaries, and an expensive government; the

---

[1] McRee, *op. cit.*, Vol. II, p. 164 note.

[2] See W. A. Schaper, "Sectionalism in South Carolina," *American Historical Association Report* (1900), Vol. I.

[3] Summary by T. Ford, *The Constitutionalist* (1794), p. 21.

other, from the moderate fortunes of the inhabitants, and their simple way of life will prefer low taxes, small salaries, and a very frugal civil establishment. One imports almost every article of consumption and pays for it in produce; the other is far removed from navigation, has very little to export, and must therefore supply its own wants. Consequently one will favor commerce, the other manufactures; one wishes slaves, the other will be better without them." [1] In view of this opposition of interests, "Appius" holds that there should be a redistribution of representatives which will give the back-country its proper proportion and enable the majority to rule.

To this argument Ford replies in the language of Federalism. The rights of property are anterior to constitutions; the state constitution recognizes and guarantees these rights; the substantial interests of the minority must be forever immune from attacks by majorities. Otherwise "the weaker party in society," he declares, "would literally have no right whatever: neither life, liberty, or property would be guaranteed to them by the social compact, seeing the majority are not bound by it, but might destroy the whole and by the same rule any part of it at pleasure. . . . Virtue and vice would lose their distinction; the most vicious views would be sanctified if pursued by the greater number, and the most virtuous resistance punishable in the less. If the principles of justice are derived from a higher source than human institutions (and who will deny it?) I contend that the majority have no right to infringe them." [2] Hence, any change in the system which deprives the seaboard minority of their preponderance in the state government cannot be too severely reprobated.

It can hardly be supposed that an economic antagonism

[1] Ford, *op. cit.*, pp. 21–22.   [2] *Op. cit.*, p. 13.

in the state that was so clearly recognized by publicists in 1794, and that manifested itself in the vote on the ratification of the Federal Constitution six years before, was overlooked in the earlier contest.

Indeed, evidence that it was not appears in a pamphlet written in defence of the Constitution by Dr. David Ramsay, who was afterward a member of the ratifying convention in South Carolina. He particularly warns his fellowcitizens against the debtor element. "Be on your guard," he says, "against the misrepresentations of men who are involved in debt; such may wish to see the Constitution rejected because of the following clause, 'no state shall emit bills of credit, make anything but gold and silver coin a tender in payment of debts, pass any ex post facto law, or law impairing the obligation of contracts.' This will doubtless bear hard on debtors who wish to defraud their creditors, but it will be real service to the honest part of the community. Examine well the characters and circumstances of men who are averse to the new constitution. Perhaps you will find that the above clause is the real ground of the opposition of some of them, though they may artfully cover it with a splendid profession of zeal for state privileges and general liberty." [1]

Georgia. — The speedy and unanimous ratification of the Constitution in Georgia seems to have prevented any very vigorous pamphleteering on the question. Indeed, the energies of the state were being strained to the limit in preparing for defence against the Indians, and there was little

---

[1] Ford, *Pamphlets on the Constitution*, p. 379. On May 24, 1788, after the Constitution had been approved in South Carolina, General Pinckney wrote to Rufus King, saying, "The Anti-Federalists had been most mischievously industrious in prejudicing the minds of our citizens against the Constitution. Pamphlets, speeches, & Protests from the disaffected in Pennsylvania were circulated throughout the state, particularly in the back country." King, *Life and Correspondence*," Vol. I, p. 329.

time for theorizing. Foreign invasion generally silences domestic discord.

Conclusions

At the close of this long and arid survey — partaking of the nature of catalogue — it seems worth while to bring together the important conclusions for political science which the data presented appear to warrant.

The movement for the Constitution of the United States was originated and carried through principally by four groups of personalty interests which had been adversely affected under the Articles of Confederation: money, public securities, manufactures, and trade and shipping.

The first firm steps toward the formation of the Constitution were taken by a small and active group of men immediately interested through their personal possessions in the outcome of their labors.

No popular vote was taken directly or indirectly on the proposition to call the Convention which drafted the Constitution.

A large propertyless mass was, under the prevailing suffrage qualifications, excluded at the outset from participation (through representatives) in the work of framing the Constitution.

The members of the Philadelphia Convention which drafted the Constitution were, with a few exceptions, immediately, directly, and personally interested in, and derived economic advantages from, the establishment of the new system.

The Constitution was essentially an economic document based upon the concept that the fundamental private rights of property are anterior to government and morally beyond the reach of popular majorities.

The major portion of the members of the Convention are on record as recognizing the claim of property to a special and defensive position in the Constitution.

In the ratification of the Constitution, about three-fourths of the adult males failed to vote on the question, having abstained from the elections at which delegates to the state conventions were chosen, either on account of their indifference or their disfranchisement by property qualifications.

The Constitution was ratified by a vote of probably not more than one-sixth of the adult males.

It is questionable whether a majority of the voters participating in the elections for the state conventions in New York, Massachusetts, New Hampshire, Virginia, and South Carolina, actually approved the ratification of the Constitution.

The leaders who supported the Constitution in the ratifying conventions represented the same economic groups as the members of the Philadelphia Convention; and in a large number of instances they were also directly and personally interested in the outcome of their efforts.

In the ratification, it became manifest that the line of cleavage for and against the Constitution was between substantial personalty interests on the one hand and the small farming and debtor interests on the other.

The Constitution was not created by "the whole people" as the jurists have said; neither was it created by "the states" as Southern nullifiers long contended; but it was the work of a consolidated group whose interests knew no state boundaries and were truly national in their scope.

INDEX

Adams, John, theories attacked, 313.
Annapolis convention, 62.
Army, place in government, 171 ff.
Articles of Confederation, conditions under, 47, 58; system of government, 52.

Baldwin, Abraham, economic interests of, 74; political philosophy of, 190.
Baltimore, petitions for protection, 42; popular vote in, 247.
Bancroft, interpretation of history, 1.
Bassett, Richard, economic interests of, 75.
Bedford, Gunning, economic interests of, 76; political philosophy of, 191.
Blair, John, economic interests of, 77.
Blount, William, economic interests of, 78.
Boston, petitions for protection, 44; property interests in, 261 ff.; vote in, 244.
Bowdoin, Governor, demands stronger union, 55.
Brearley, David, economic interests of, 79.
Broom, Jacob, economic interests of, 80; political philosophy of, 191.
Burgess, Professor, cited, 62.
Butler, Pierce, economic interests of, 81; political philosophy of, 192.

Capital, attacks on, 31 ff.; invested in lands, 49; see Money and Securities.
Carroll, Daniel, economic interests of, 82.
"Centinel," essays of, 312.
Checks and balances, 159 ff.
Cincinnati, Society of the, 38 ff.
Cities, populace feared, 215.
Clymer, George, 41; economic interests of, 82; political philosophy of, 193.
Commerce, demands for protection of, 40 ff.; influence in politics, 172, 183 ff.
Congress, under the Articles of Confederation, 52; calls the Convention at Philadelphia, 63.

Connecticut tax returns, in, 31; suffrage qualifications, 66; elections to state convention, 228; vote on the Constitution, 228; voters for members of convention, 240; economic interests and ratification of the Constitution, 265 ff.; public securities in, 265; conflict over ratification, 306 ff.
Constitution, U. S., juristic theory of, 10 ff., 299; economic forces in creation and adoption, 16 ff.; movement for, 52 ff.; nature of, 152 ff.
Constitutional law, interpretation of, 13 ff.
Contracts, provision for safeguarding, 179 ff.
Convention, at Philadelphia, called, 63; movement for, 52 ff.; method of electing delegates, 64; 73 ff.
Creditors, consolidation of, 32.
Currency, depreciation of, 31.

Davie, William R., economic interests of, 84; political philosophy of, 193.
Dayton, Jonathan, economic interests of, 85.
Debt, Public, see Securities.
Debtors, political schemes, 28; war on creditors, 31 ff.; in revolt in New England, 59.
Delaware, suffrage qualification, 68; elections to state convention, 230; vote on the Constitution, 230; voters for members of convention, 241; ratification of the Constitution, 272.
Depreciation, of securities, 32.
Dickinson, John, economic interests of, 87; political philosophy of, 194.
Disfranchised, the, 24 ff.

Economic interests, appealed to, in behalf of the Constitution, 53.
Economic interpretation of history, 5 ff.; of law, 7 ff.; of constitutional law, 13; Madison's, 14 ff.; 156 ff.
Elections, popular, feared, 214; annual, 216; popular vote on the Constitu-

327